CLIVE BARKER'S

HELLRAISER

THE DARK WATCH

BOOM! STUDIOS

ROSS RICHIE CEO & Founder • MARK SMYLIE Founder of Archaia • MATT GAGNON Editor-in-Chief • FILIP SABLIK VP of Publishing & Marketing • STEPHEN CHRISTY VP of Development
LANCE KREITER VP of Licensing & Merchandising • PHIL BARBARO VP of Finance • BRYCE CARLSON Managing Editor • MEL CAYLO Marketing Manager • SCOTT NEWMAN Production Design Manager
IRENE BRADISH Operations Manager • CHRISTINE DINH Brand Communications Manager • DAFNA PLEBAN Editor • SHANNON WATTERS Editor • ERIC HARBURN Editor • REBECCA TAYLOR Editor
IAN BRILL Editor • CHRIS ROSA Assistant Editor • ALEX GALER Assistant Editor • WHITNEY LEOPARD Assistant Editor • JASMINE AMIRI Assistant Editor • CAMERON CHITTOCK Assistant Editor
KELSEY DIETERICH Production Designer • EMI YONEMURA BROWN Production Designer • DEVIN FUNCHES E-Commerce & Inventory Coordinator • ANDY LIEGL Event Coordinator • BRIANNA HART Executive Assistant
AARON FERRARA Operations Assistant • JOSÉ MEZA Sales Assistant • MICHELLE ANKLEY Sales Assistant • ELIZABETH LOUGHRIDGE Accounting Assistant • STEPHANIE HOCUTT PR Assistant

BOOM! Studios, 5670 Wilshire Boulevard, Suite 450, Los Angeles, CA 90036-5679. Printed in China. First Printing.
ISBN: 978-1-60886-398-3, eISBN: 978-1-61398-252-5

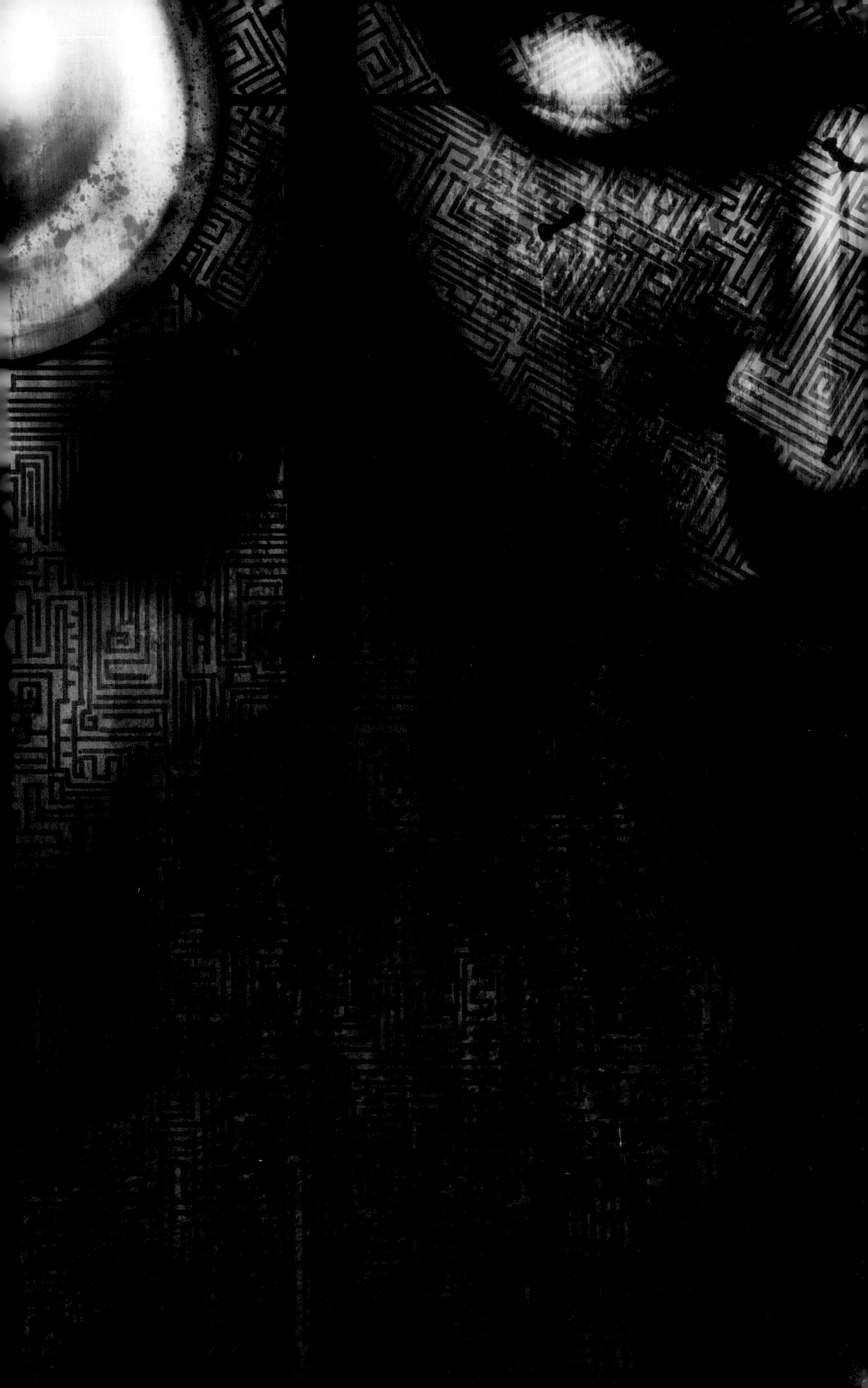

GOOD INTENTIONS

WRITTEN BY
BRANDON SEIFERT

ART BY
JESÚS HERVÁS

SOMETHING TO KEEP US APART

WRITTEN BY
CLIVE BARKER
& BEN MEARES

ART BY
JANUSZ ORDON

THE DARK WATCH: CHAPTERS 9-12

WRITTEN BY
CLIVE BARKER
& BRANDON SEIFERT

ART BY
TOM GARCIA

COLORS BY
VLADIMIR POPOV

LETTERS BY
TRAVIS LANHAM

COVER BY
NICK PERCIVAL

DESIGNER
EMI YONEMURA BROWN

ASSISTANT EDITOR
CHRIS ROSA

EDITOR
IAN BRILL

SPECIAL THANKS TO MARK MILLER

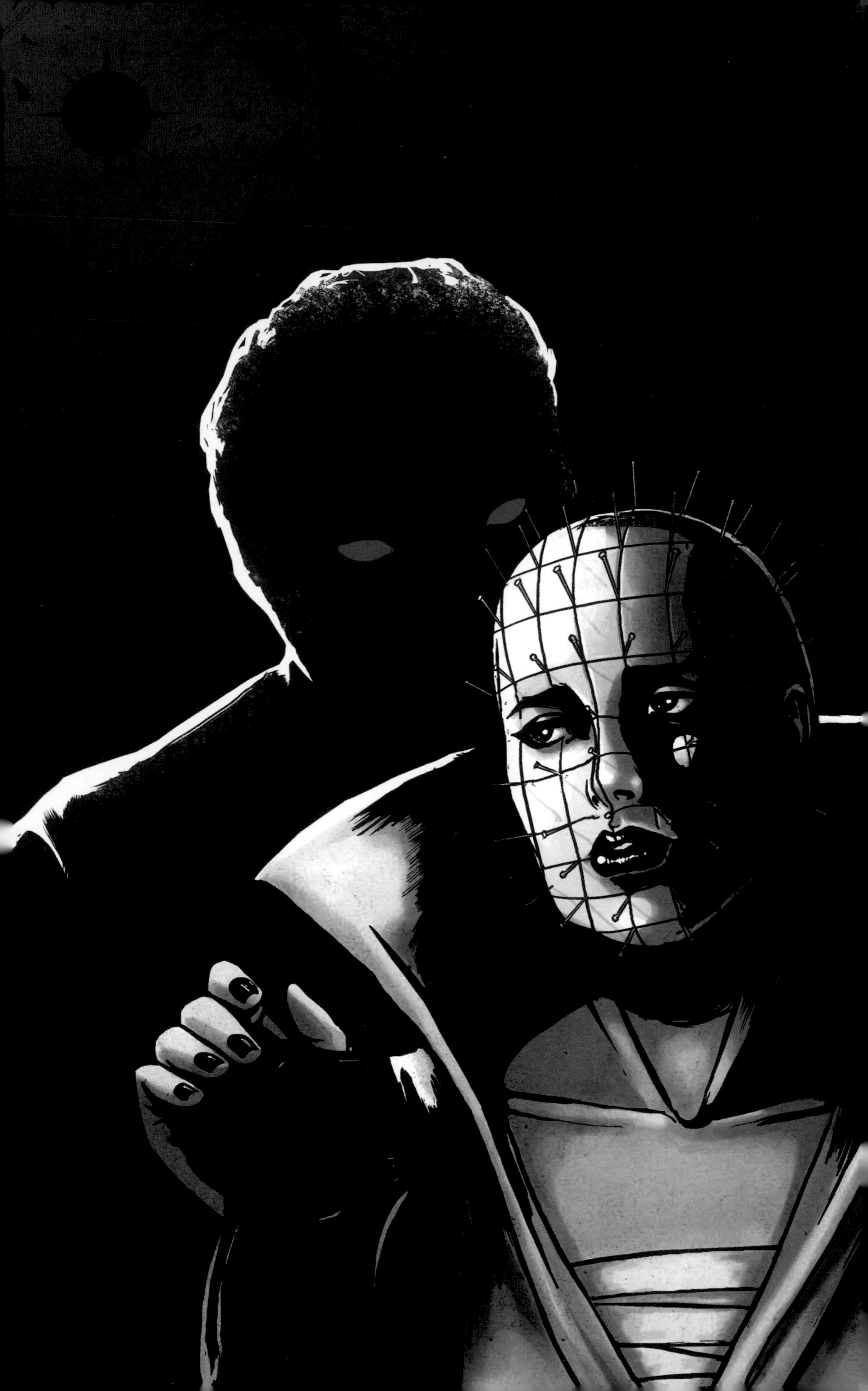

GOOD INTENTIONS &

SOMETHING TO KEEP US APART

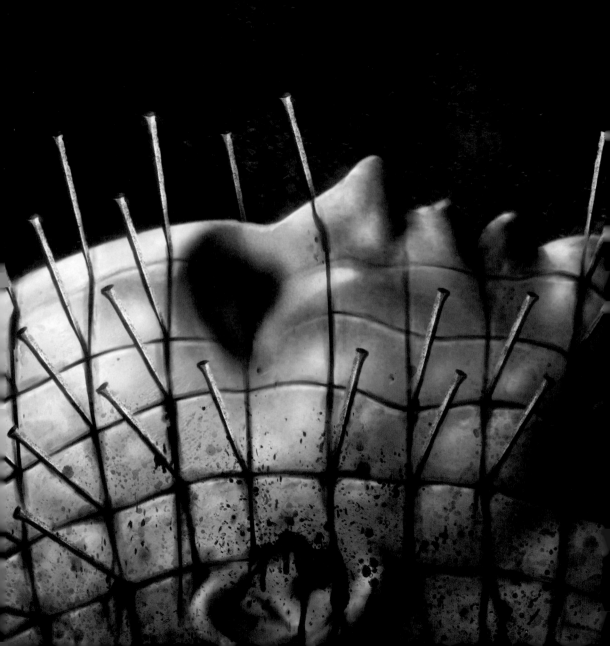

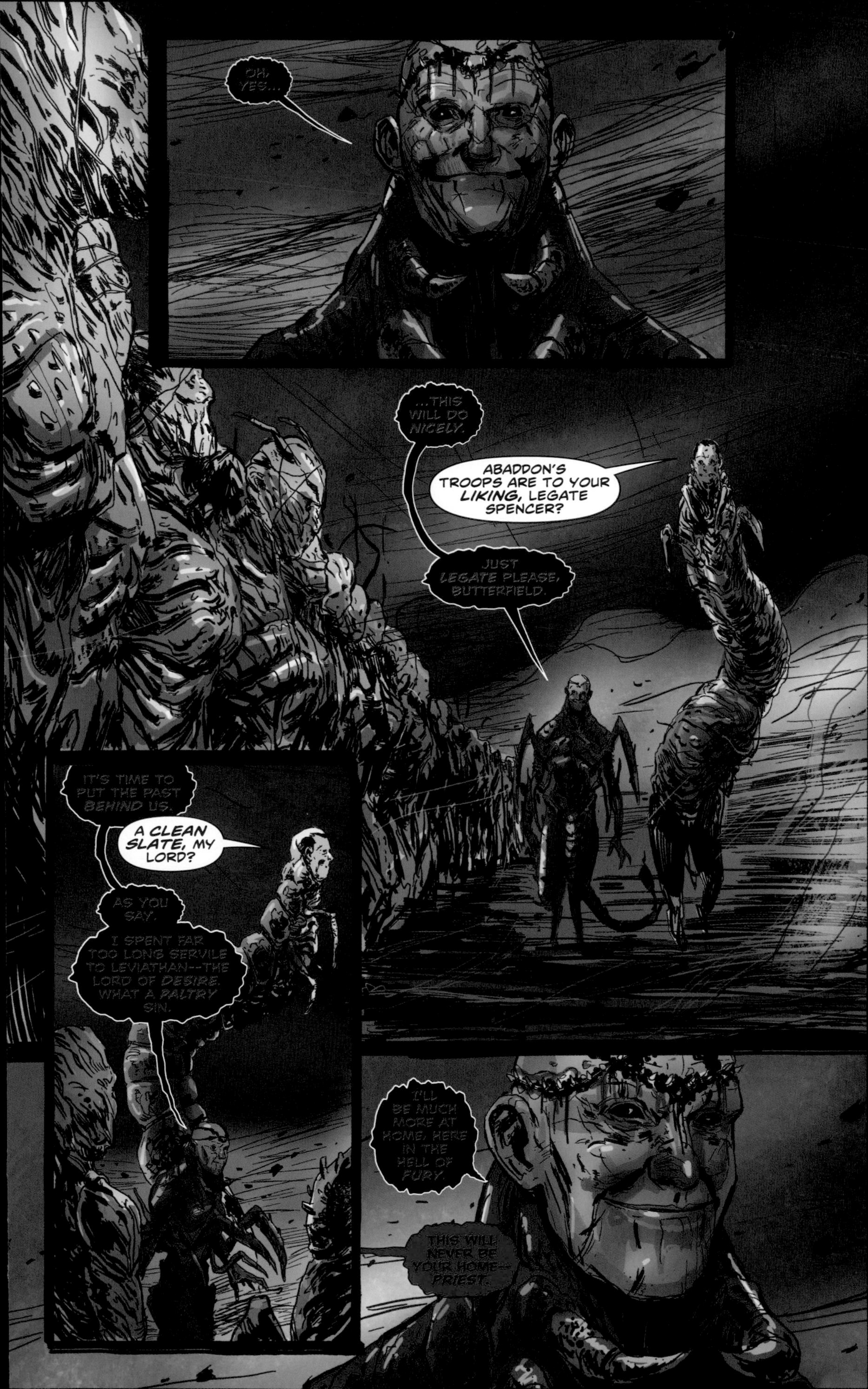
OH, YES...
...THIS WILL DO NICELY.
ABADDON'S TROOPS ARE TO YOUR LIKING, LEGATE SPENCER?
JUST LEGATE PLEASE, BUTTERFIELD.
IT'S TIME TO PUT THE PAST BEHIND US.
A CLEAN SLATE, MY LORD?
AS YOU SAY.
I SPENT FAR TOO LONG SERVILE TO LEVIATHAN--THE LORD OF DESIRE. WHAT A PALTRY SIN.
I'LL BE MUCH MORE AT HOME, HERE IN THE HELL OF FURY.
THIS WILL NEVER BE YOUR HOME--PRIEST.

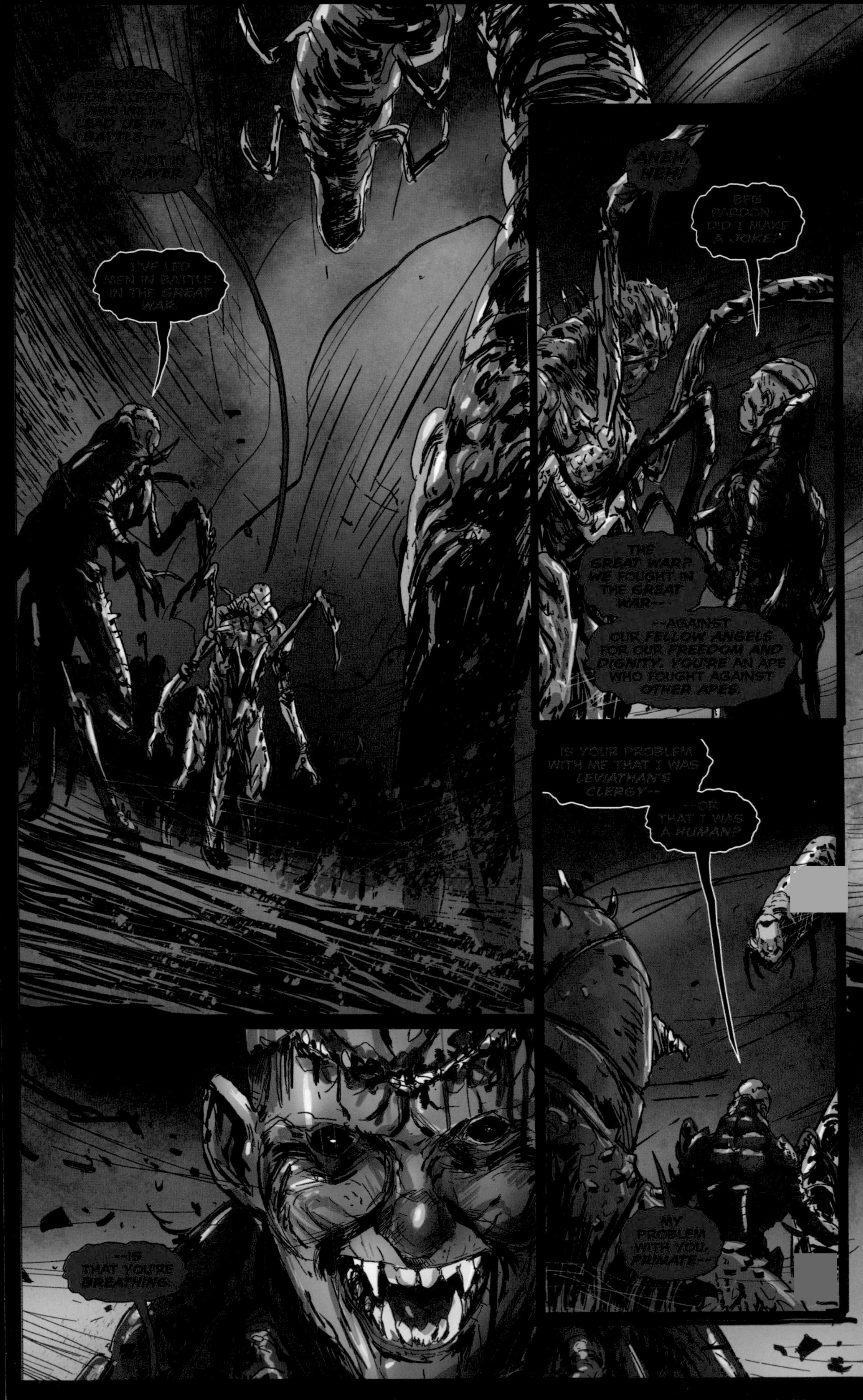
WHO WILL LEAD US IN BATTLE--
--NOT IN PRAYER.
I'VE LED MEN IN BATTLE. IN THE GREAT WAR.
AHEH, HEH!
BEG PARDON-- DID I MAKE A JOKE?
THE GREAT WAR? WE FOUGHT IN THE GREAT WAR--
--AGAINST OUR FELLOW ANGELS FOR OUR FREEDOM AND DIGNITY. YOU'RE AN APE WHO FOUGHT AGAINST OTHER APES.
IS YOUR PROBLEM WITH ME THAT I WAS LEVIATHAN'S CLERGY--
--OR THAT I WAS A HUMAN?
MY PROBLEM WITH YOU, PRIMATE--
--IS THAT YOU'RE BREATHING.

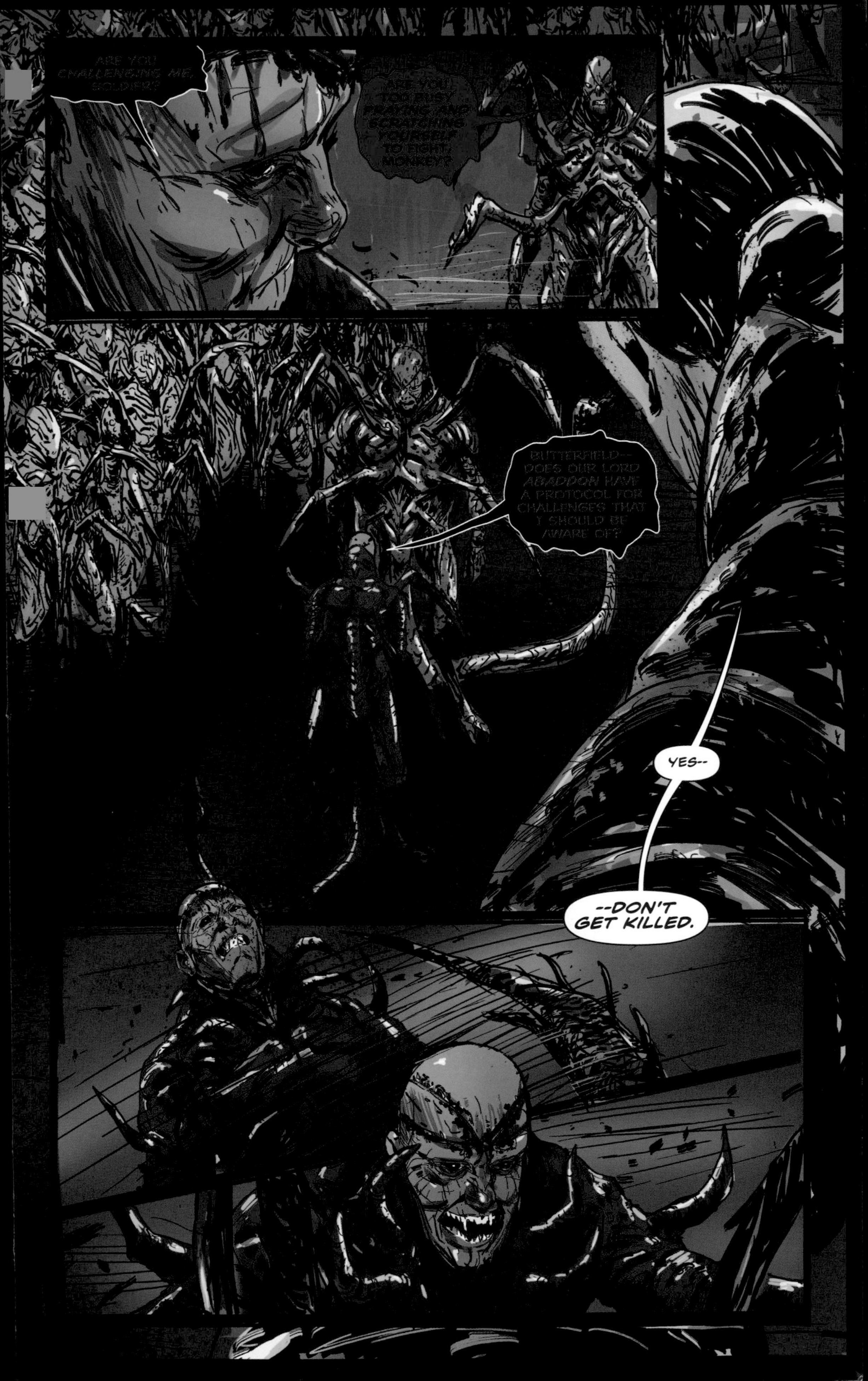
ARE YOU CHALLENGING ME, SOLDIER?
ARE YOU TOO BUSY PRAYING AND SCRATCHING YOURSELF TO FIGHT, MONKEY?
BUTTERFIELD-- DOES OUR LORD *ABADDON* HAVE A PROTOCOL FOR CHALLENGES THAT I SHOULD BE AWARE OF?
YES--
--DON'T GET KILLED.

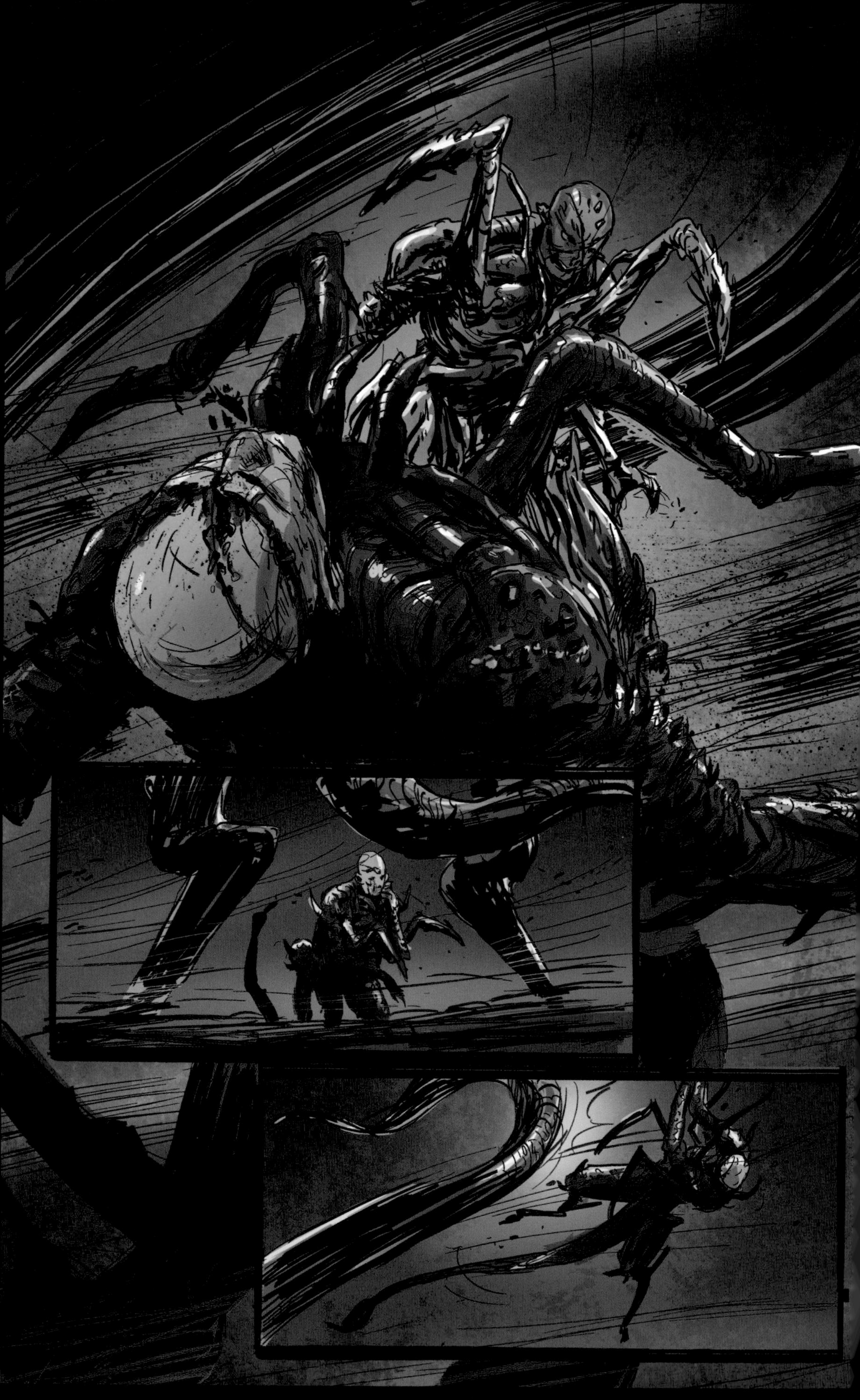

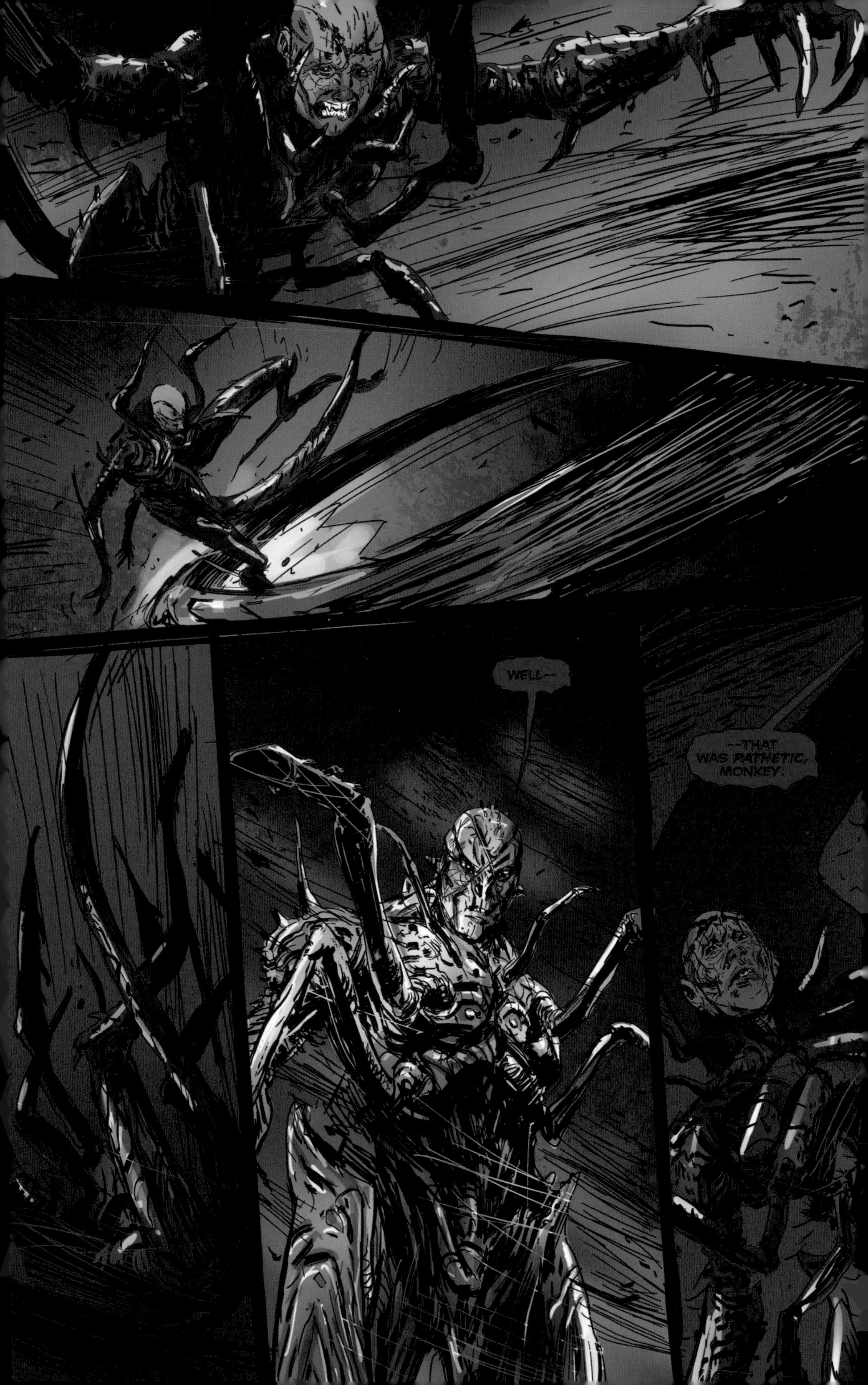
WELL--
--THAT WAS PATHETIC, MONKEY.

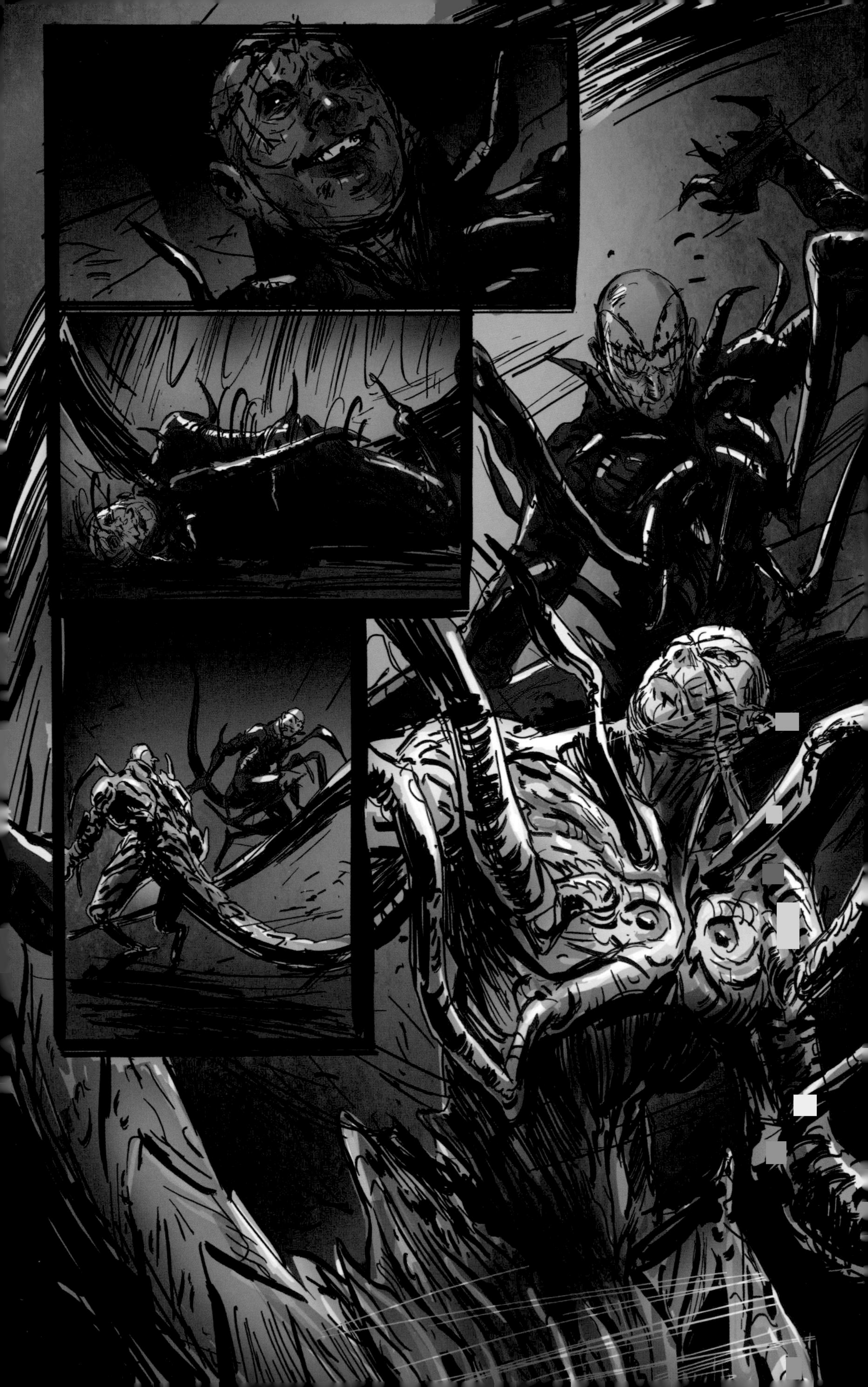

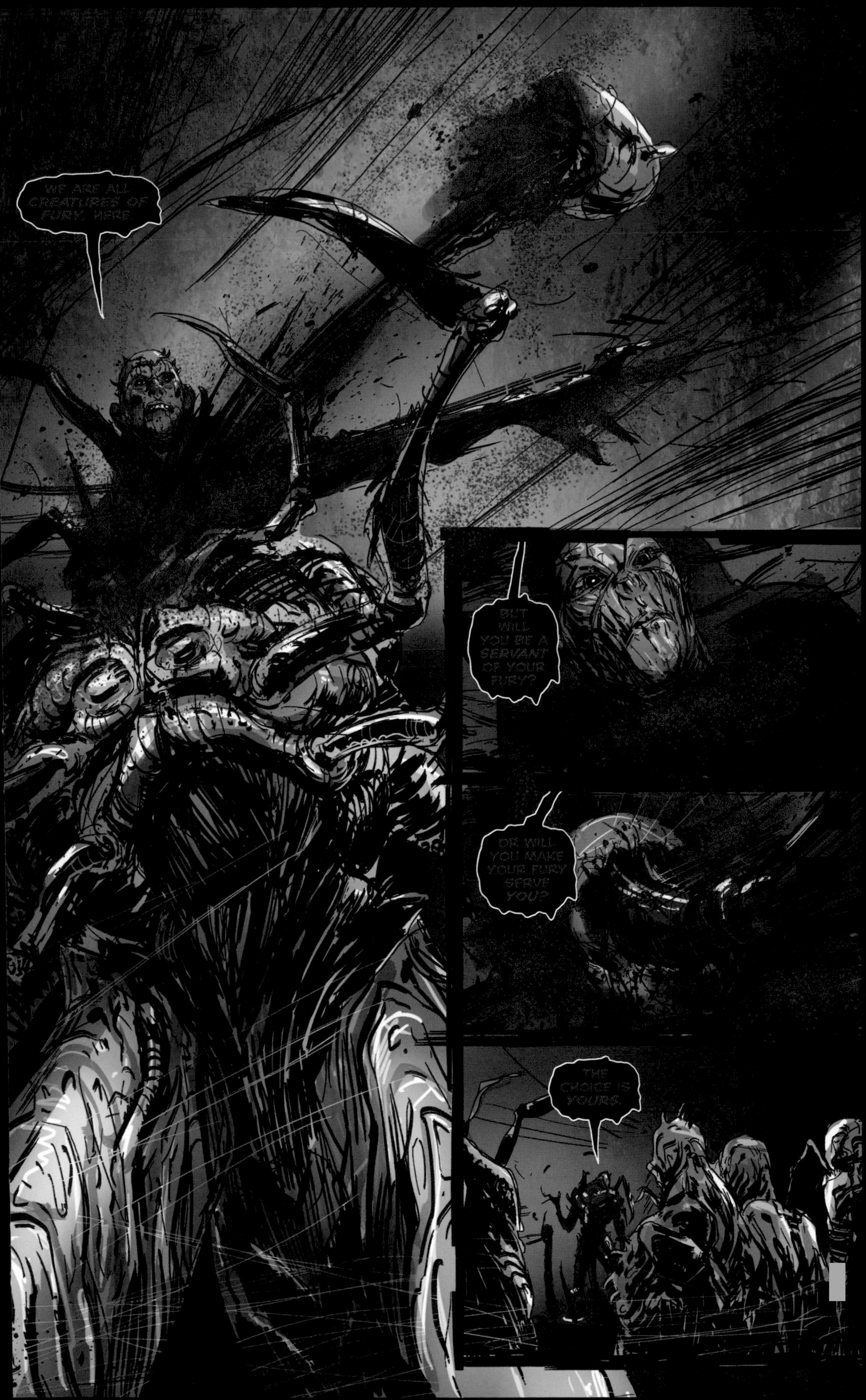
WE ARE ALL CREATURES OF FURY, HERE.
BUT WILL YOU BE A SERVANT OF YOUR FURY?
OR WILL YOU MAKE YOUR FURY SERVE YOU?
THE CHOICE IS YOURS.

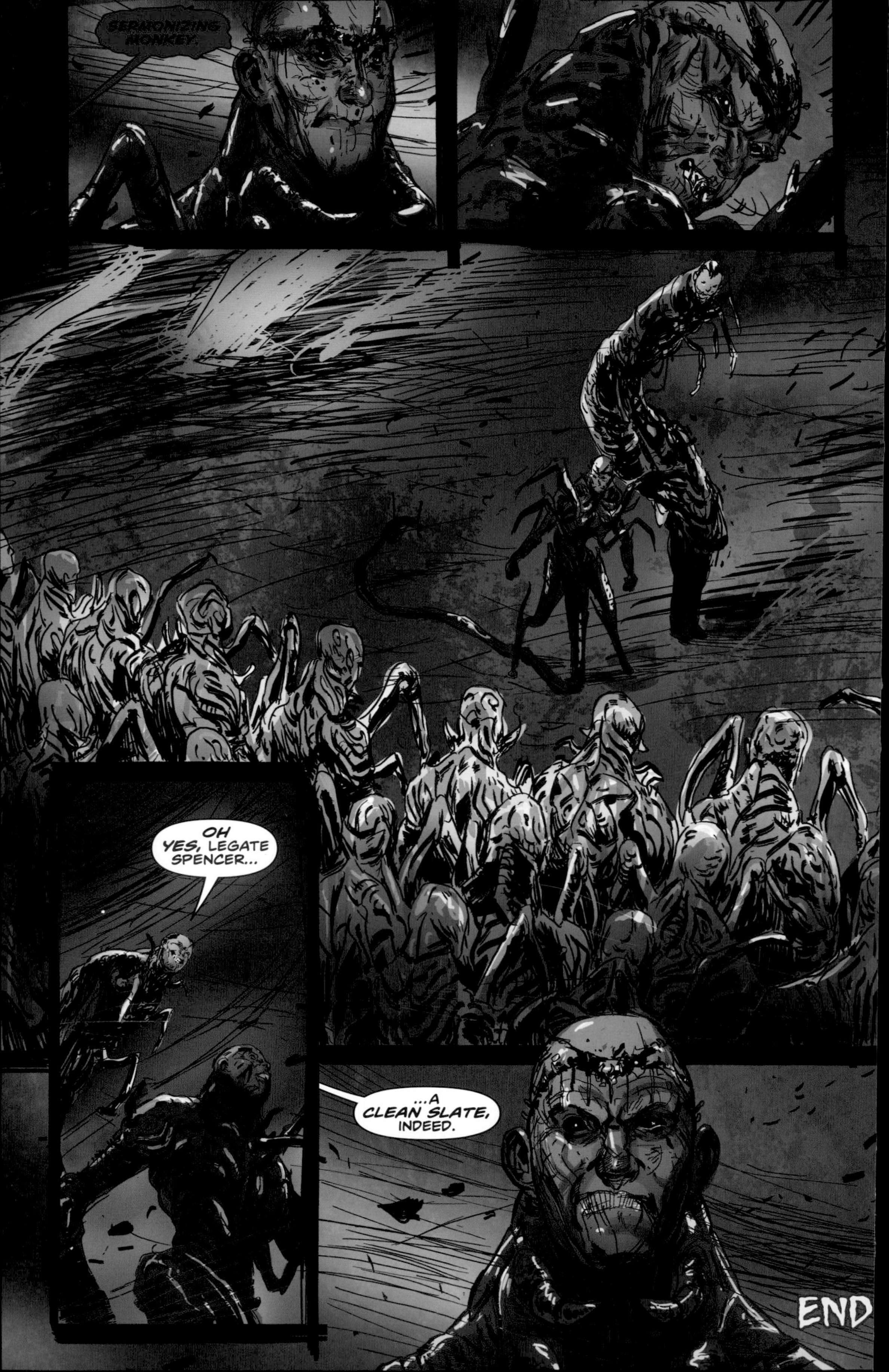
SERMONIZING MONKEY.
OH YES, LEGATE SPENCER...
...A CLEAN SLATE, INDEED.
END

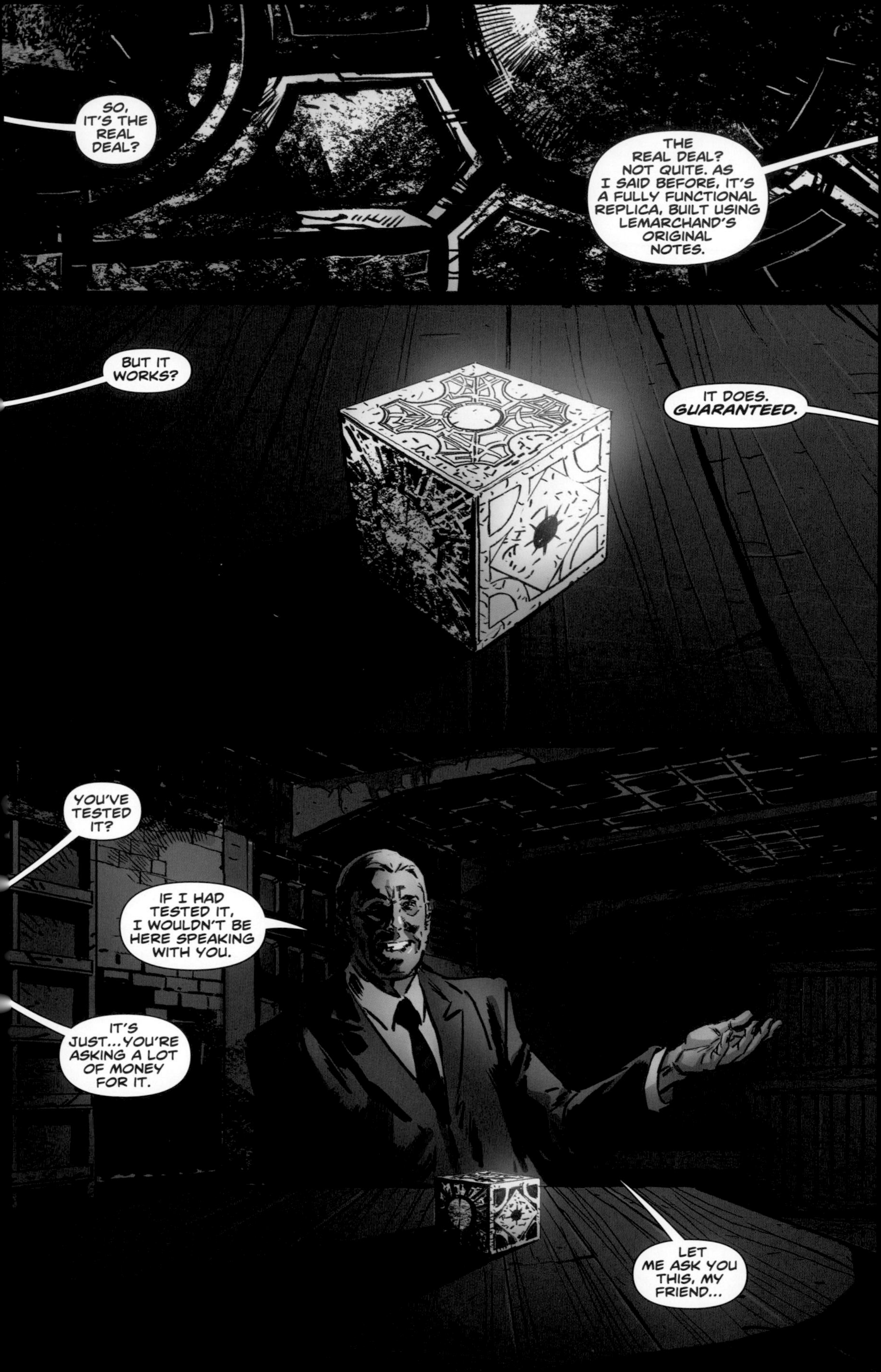
SO, IT'S THE REAL DEAL?
THE REAL DEAL? NOT QUITE. AS I SAID BEFORE, IT'S A FULLY FUNCTIONAL REPLICA, BUILT USING LEMARCHAND'S ORIGINAL NOTES.
BUT IT WORKS?
IT DOES. *GUARANTEED.*
YOU'VE TESTED IT?
IF I HAD TESTED IT, I WOULDN'T BE HERE SPEAKING WITH YOU.
IT'S JUST...YOU'RE ASKING A LOT OF MONEY FOR IT.
LET ME ASK YOU THIS, MY FRIEND...

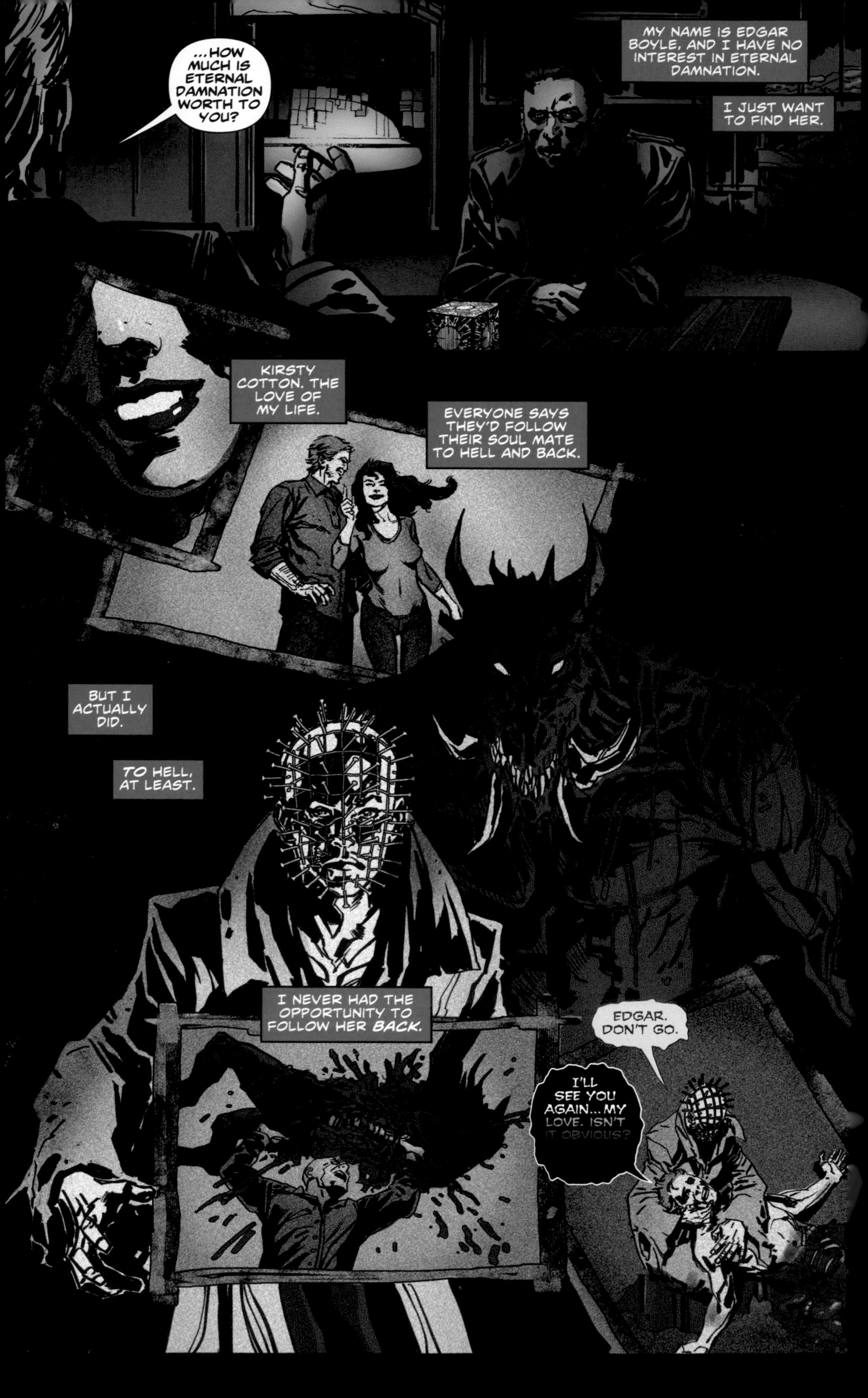
...HOW MUCH IS ETERNAL DAMNATION WORTH TO YOU?
MY NAME IS EDGAR BOYLE, AND I HAVE NO INTEREST IN ETERNAL DAMNATION.
I JUST WANT TO FIND HER.
KIRSTY COTTON. THE LOVE OF MY LIFE.
EVERYONE SAYS THEY'D FOLLOW THEIR SOUL MATE TO HELL AND BACK.
BUT I ACTUALLY DID.
TO HELL, AT LEAST.
I NEVER HAD THE OPPORTUNITY TO FOLLOW HER BACK.
EDGAR. DON'T GO.
I'LL SEE YOU AGAIN... MY LOVE. ISN'T IT OBVIOUS?

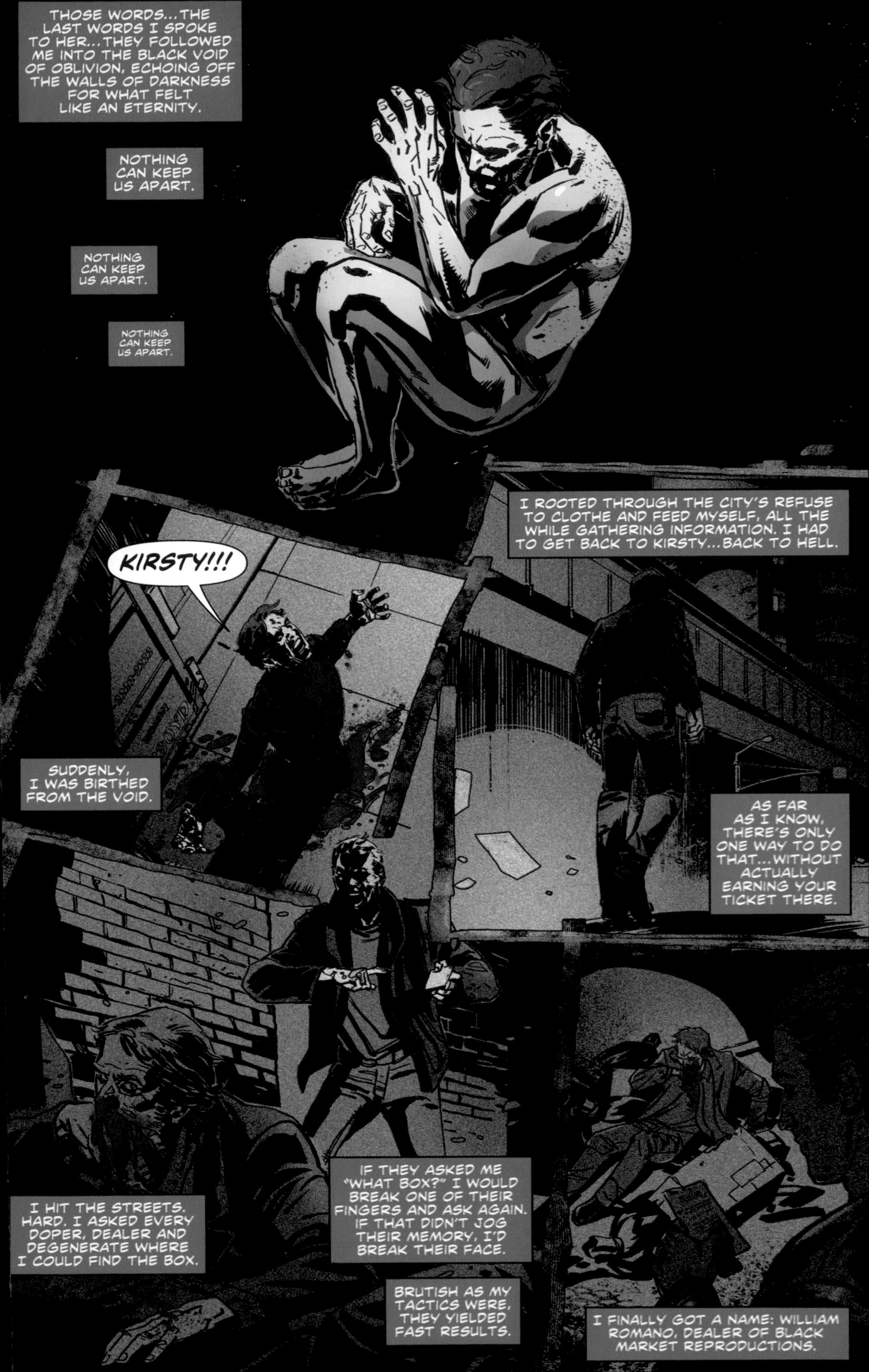
THOSE WORDS...THE LAST WORDS I SPOKE TO HER...THEY FOLLOWED ME INTO THE BLACK VOID OF OBLIVION, ECHOING OFF THE WALLS OF DARKNESS FOR WHAT FELT LIKE AN ETERNITY.
NOTHING CAN KEEP US APART.
NOTHING CAN KEEP US APART.
NOTHING CAN KEEP US APART.
KIRSTY!!!
SUDDENLY, I WAS BIRTHED FROM THE VOID.
I ROOTED THROUGH THE CITY'S REFUSE TO CLOTHE AND FEED MYSELF, ALL THE WHILE GATHERING INFORMATION. I HAD TO GET BACK TO KIRSTY...BACK TO HELL.
AS FAR AS I KNOW, THERE'S ONLY ONE WAY TO DO THAT...WITHOUT ACTUALLY EARNING YOUR TICKET THERE.
I HIT THE STREETS. HARD. I ASKED EVERY DOPER, DEALER AND DEGENERATE WHERE I COULD FIND THE BOX.
IF THEY ASKED ME "WHAT BOX?" I WOULD BREAK ONE OF THEIR FINGERS AND ASK AGAIN. IF THAT DIDN'T JOG THEIR MEMORY, I'D BREAK THEIR FACE.
BRUTISH AS MY TACTICS WERE, THEY YIELDED FAST RESULTS.
I FINALLY GOT A NAME: WILLIAM ROMANO, DEALER OF BLACK MARKET REPRODUCTIONS.

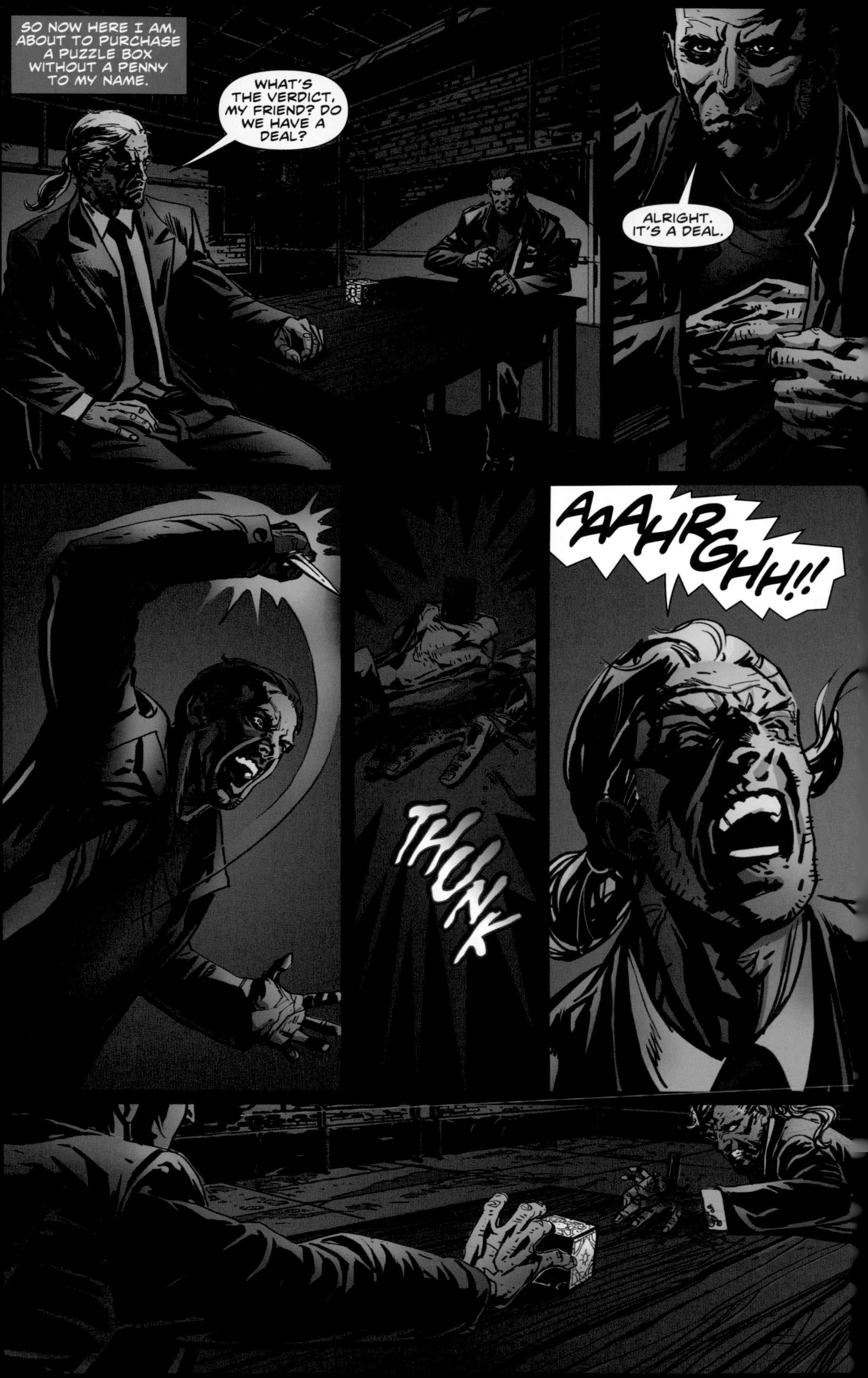
SO NOW HERE I AM, ABOUT TO PURCHASE A PUZZLE BOX WITHOUT A PENNY TO MY NAME.
WHAT'S THE VERDICT, MY FRIEND? DO WE HAVE A DEAL?
ALRIGHT. IT'S A DEAL.
THUNK
AAAHRGHH!!

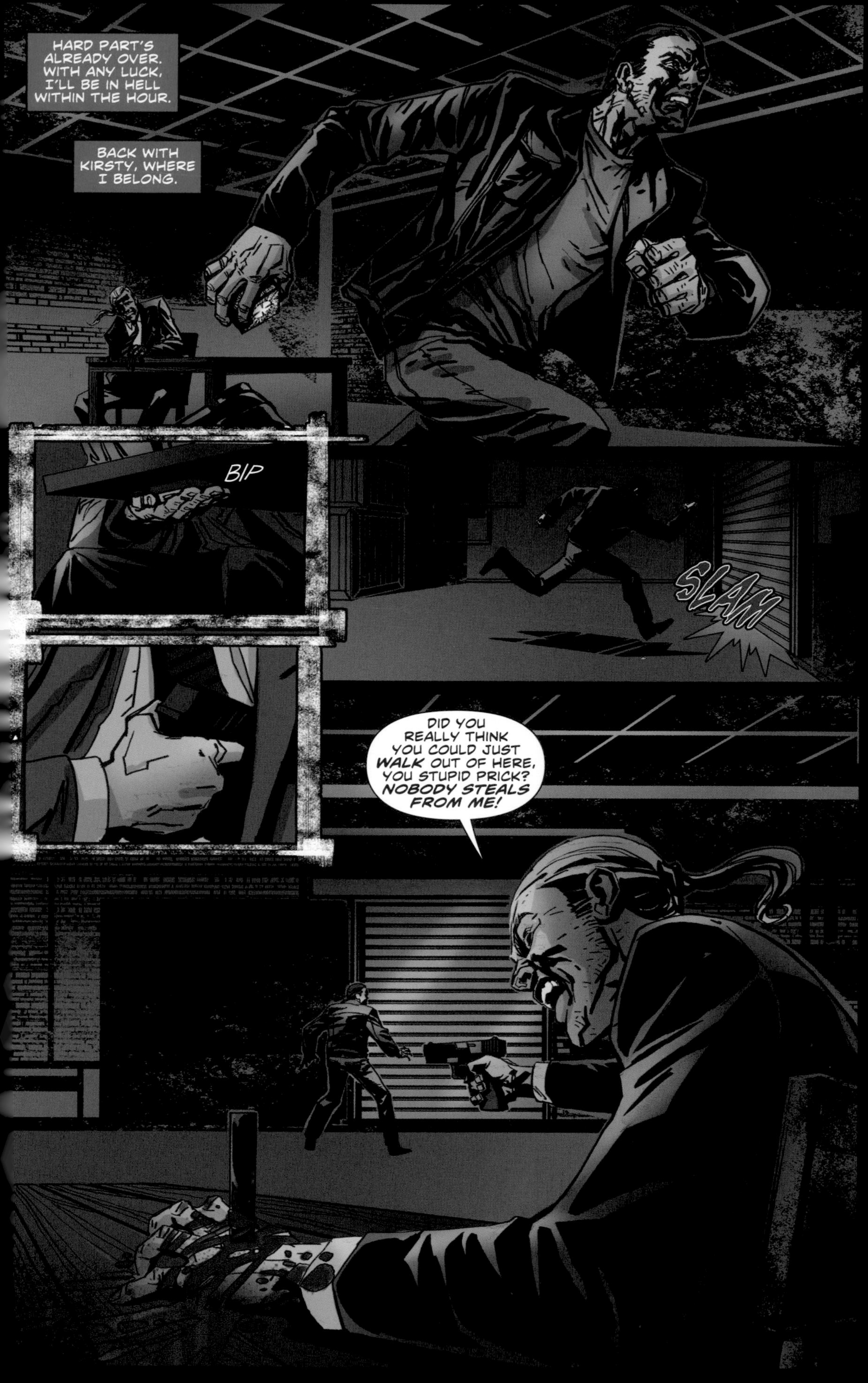

HARD PART'S ALREADY OVER. WITH ANY LUCK, I'LL BE IN HELL WITHIN THE HOUR.
BACK WITH KIRSTY, WHERE I BELONG.
BIP
SLAM
DID YOU REALLY THINK YOU COULD JUST WALK OUT OF HERE, YOU STUPID PRICK? NOBODY STEALS FROM ME!

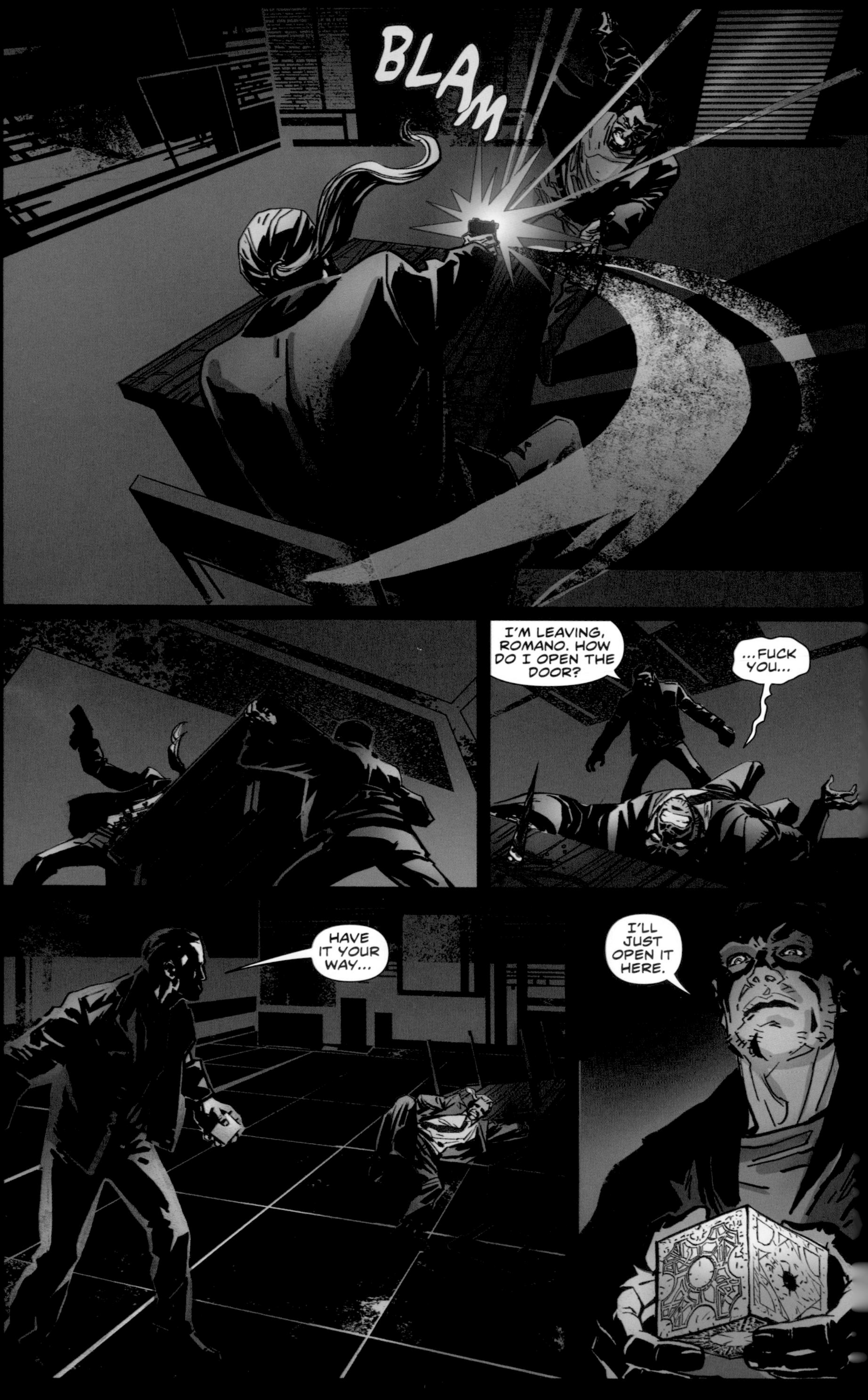
BLAM
I'M LEAVING, ROMANO. HOW DO I OPEN THE DOOR?
...FUCK YOU...
HAVE IT YOUR WAY...
I'LL JUST OPEN IT HERE.

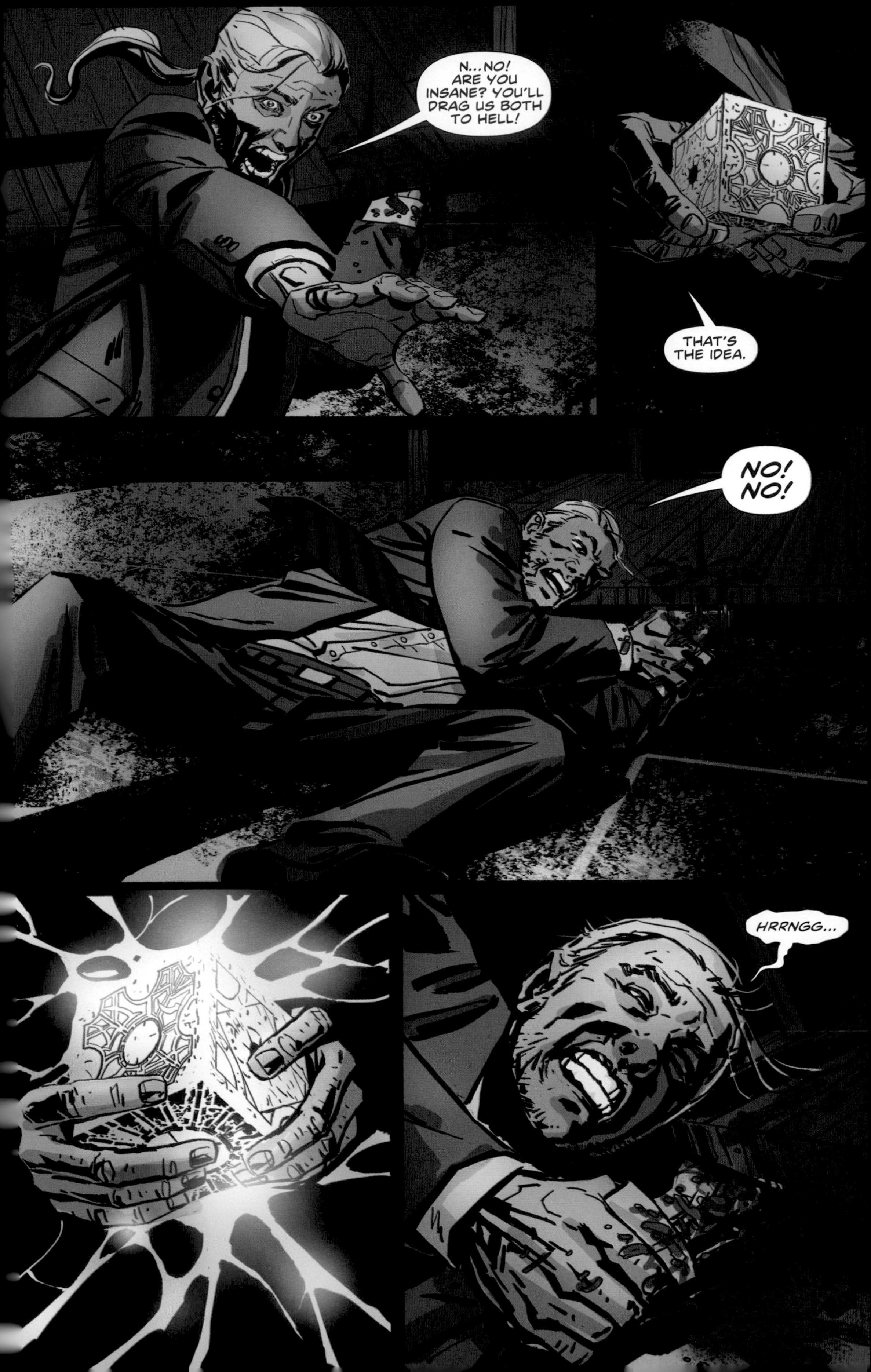
N...NO! ARE YOU INSANE? YOU'LL DRAG US BOTH TO HELL!
THAT'S THE IDEA.
NO! NO!
HRRNGG...

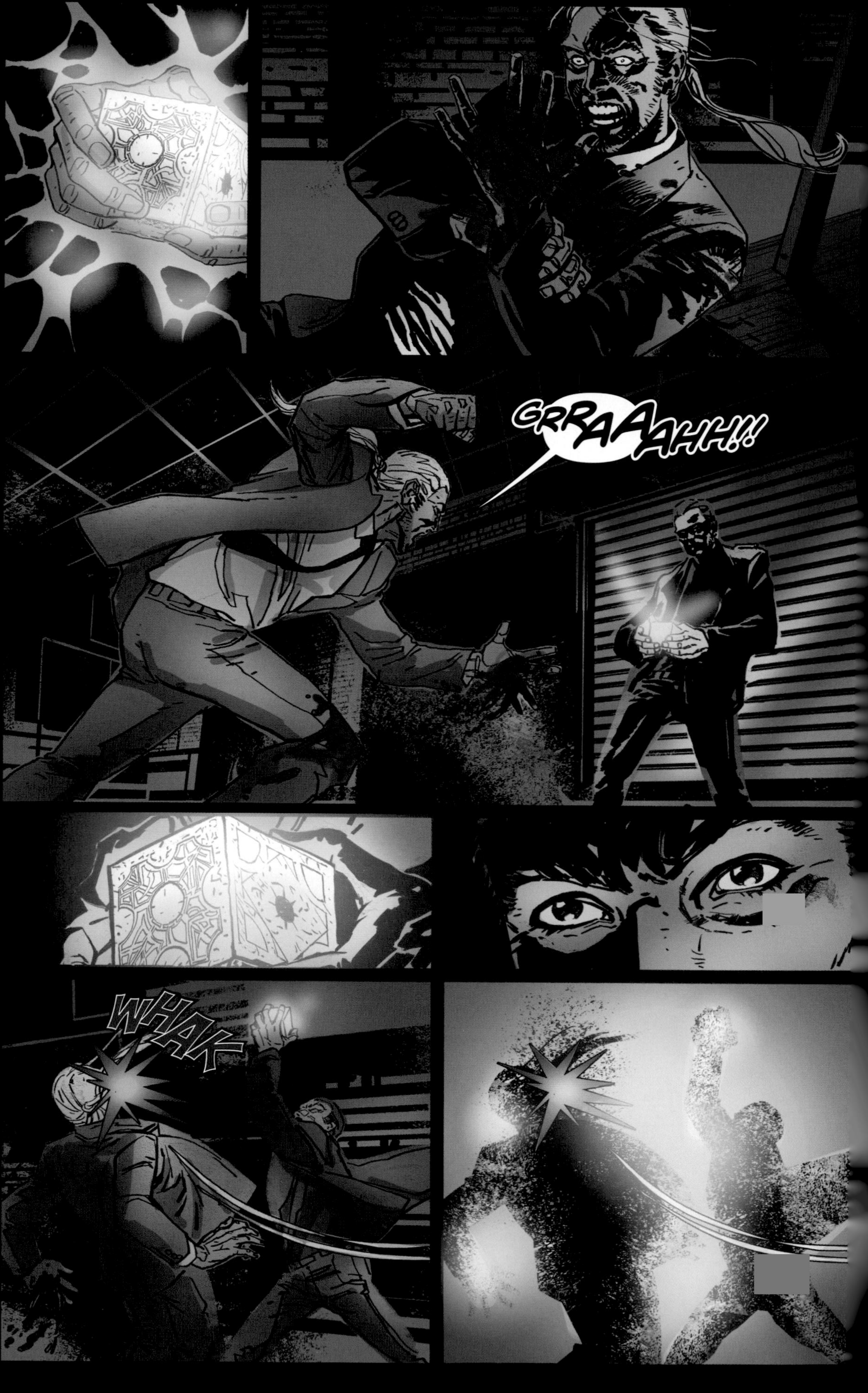
GRRAAAHH!!
WHAK

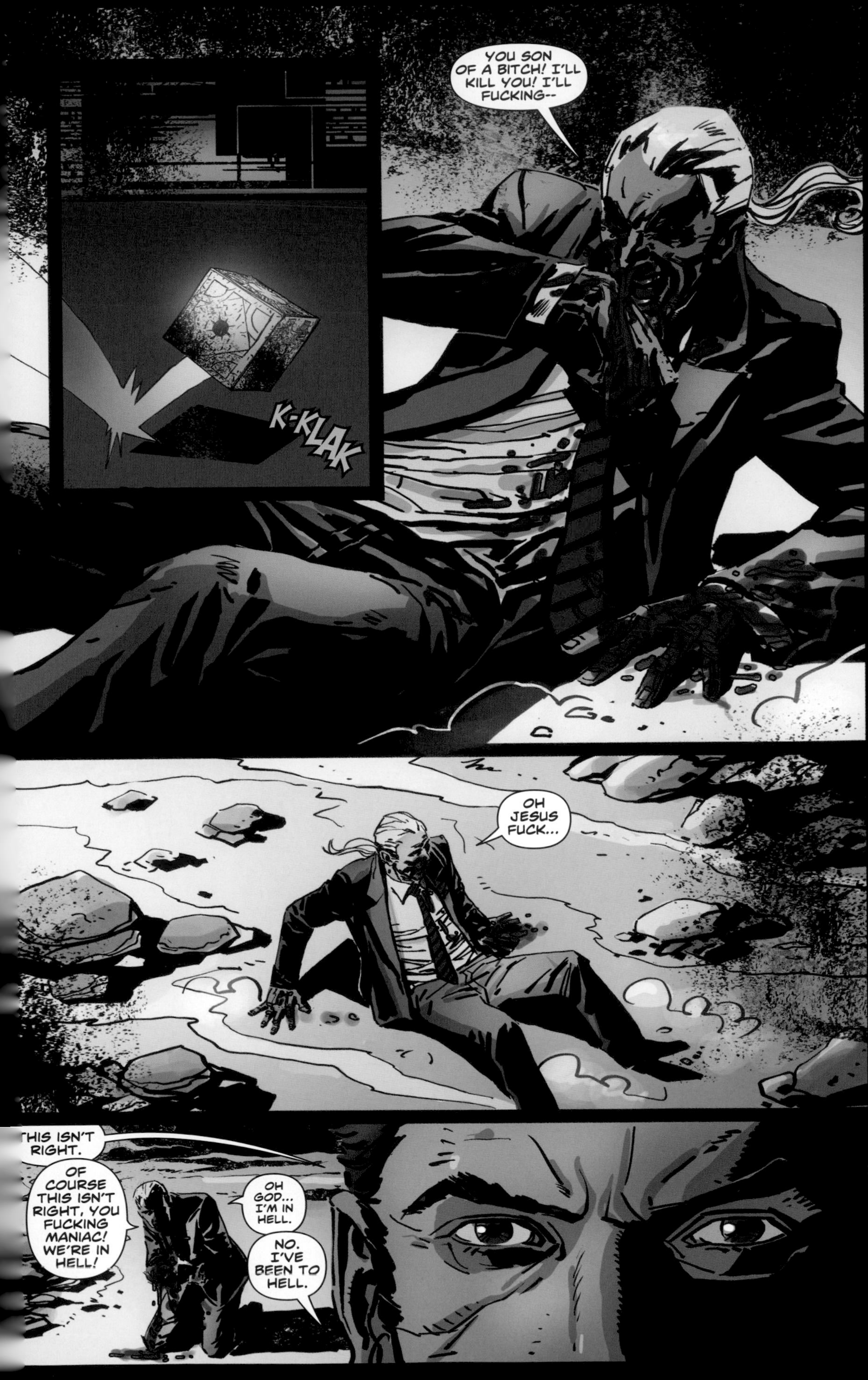
K-KLAK
YOU SON OF A BITCH! I'LL KILL YOU! I'LL FUCKING--
OH JESUS FUCK...
THIS ISN'T RIGHT.
OF COURSE THIS ISN'T RIGHT, YOU FUCKING MANIAC! WE'RE IN HELL!
OH GOD... I'M IN HELL.
NO. I'VE BEEN TO HELL.

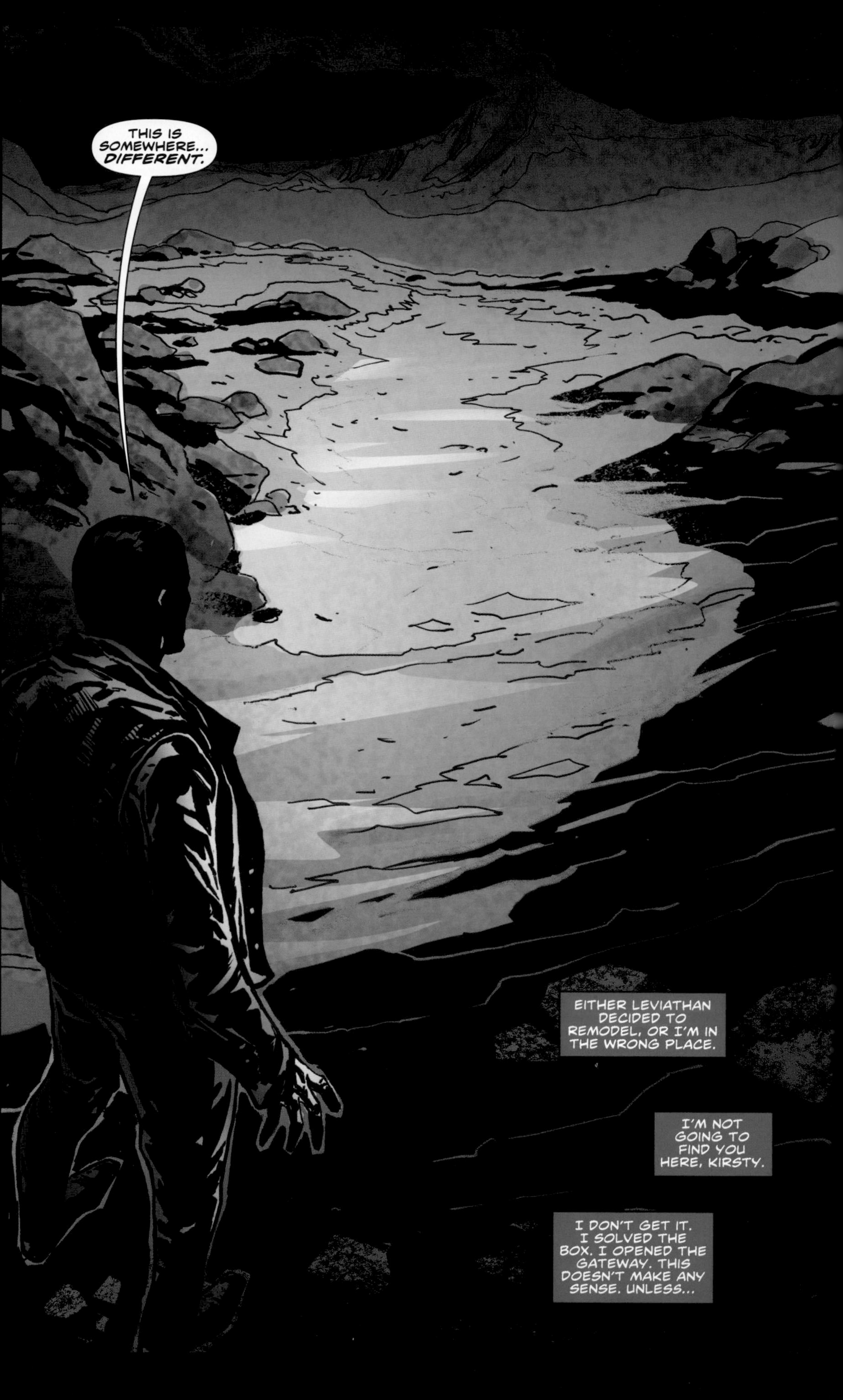
THIS IS SOMEWHERE... DIFFERENT.
EITHER LEVIATHAN DECIDED TO REMODEL, OR I'M IN THE WRONG PLACE.
I'M NOT GOING TO FIND YOU HERE, KIRSTY.
I DON'T GET IT. I SOLVED THE BOX. I OPENED THE GATEWAY. THIS DOESN'T MAKE ANY SENSE. UNLESS...

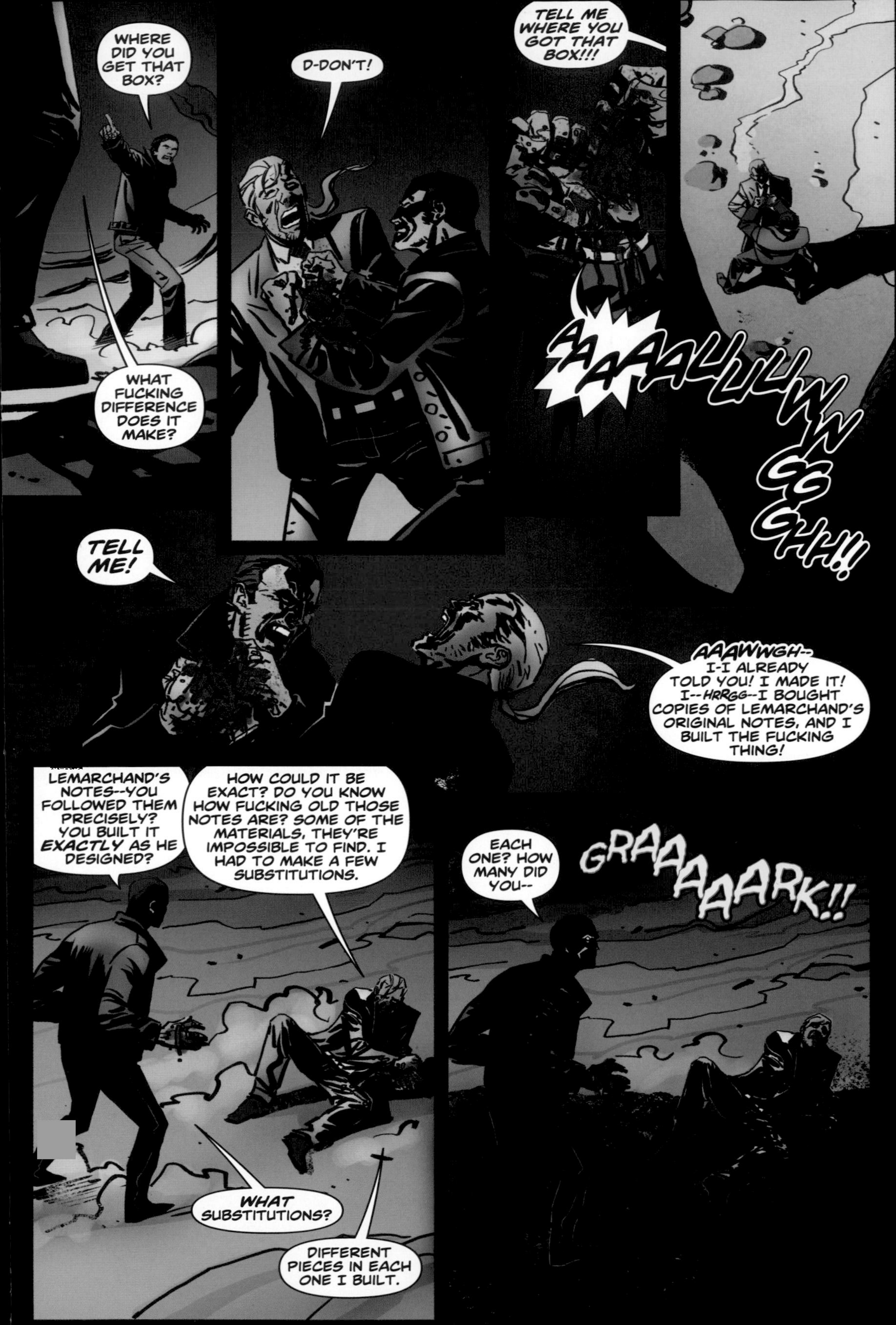
WHERE DID YOU GET THAT BOX?
WHAT FUCKING DIFFERENCE DOES IT MAKE?
D-DON'T!
TELL ME WHERE YOU GOT THAT BOX!!!
AAAAALLLLWWNGGGHH!!
TELL ME!
AAAWWGH-- I-I ALREADY TOLD YOU! I MADE IT! I--HRRGG--I BOUGHT COPIES OF LEMARCHAND'S ORIGINAL NOTES, AND I BUILT THE FUCKING THING!
LEMARCHAND'S NOTES--YOU FOLLOWED THEM PRECISELY? YOU BUILT IT EXACTLY AS HE DESIGNED?
HOW COULD IT BE EXACT? DO YOU KNOW HOW FUCKING OLD THOSE NOTES ARE? SOME OF THE MATERIALS, THEY'RE IMPOSSIBLE TO FIND. I HAD TO MAKE A FEW SUBSTITUTIONS.
WHAT SUBSTITUTIONS?
DIFFERENT PIECES IN EACH ONE I BUILT.
EACH ONE? HOW MANY DID YOU--
GRAAAAAARK!!

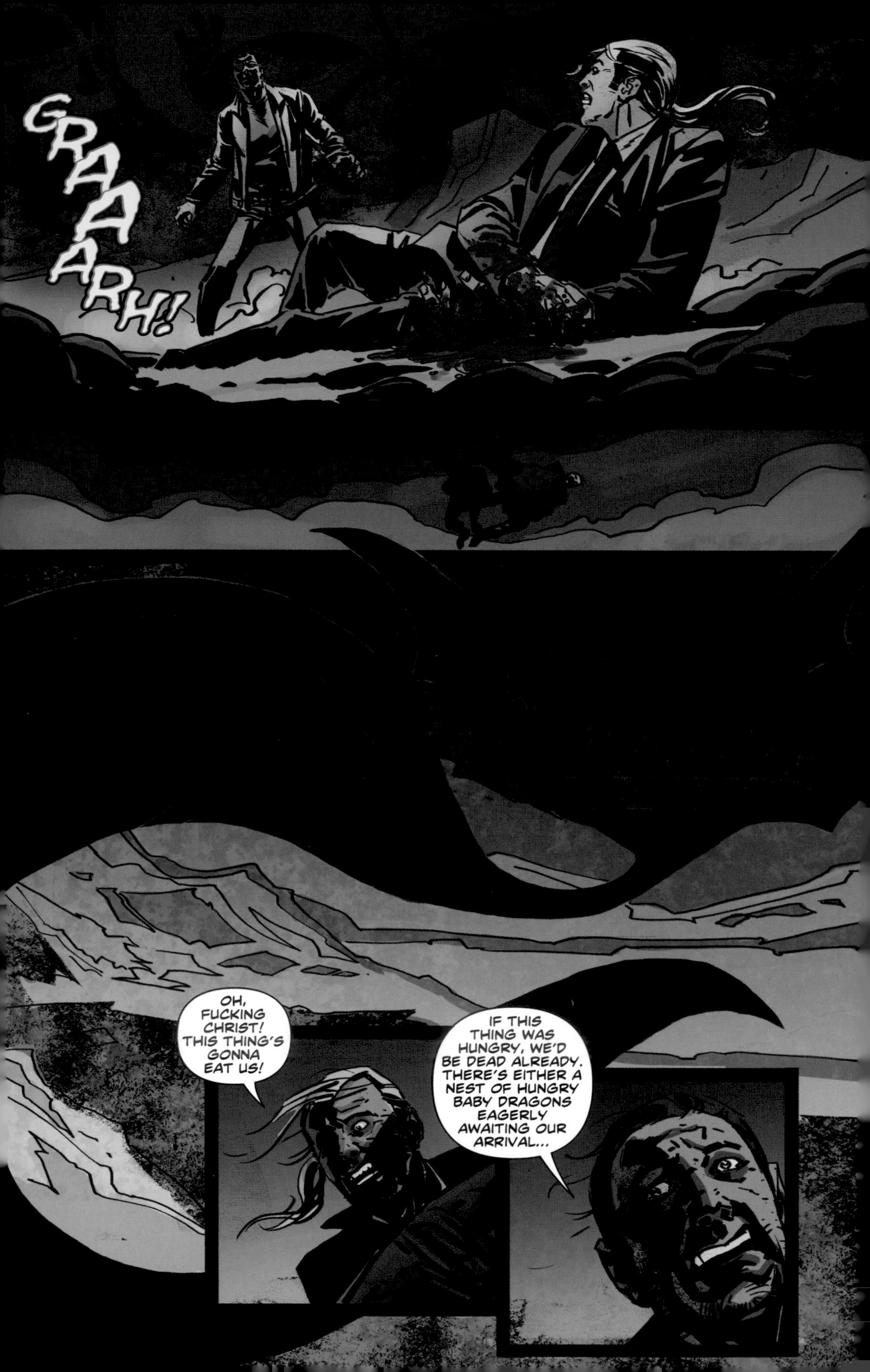
GRAAAARH!
OH, FUCKING CHRIST! THIS THING'S GONNA EAT US!
IF THIS THING WAS HUNGRY, WE'D BE DEAD ALREADY. THERE'S EITHER A NEST OF HUNGRY BABY DRAGONS EAGERLY AWAITING OUR ARRIVAL...

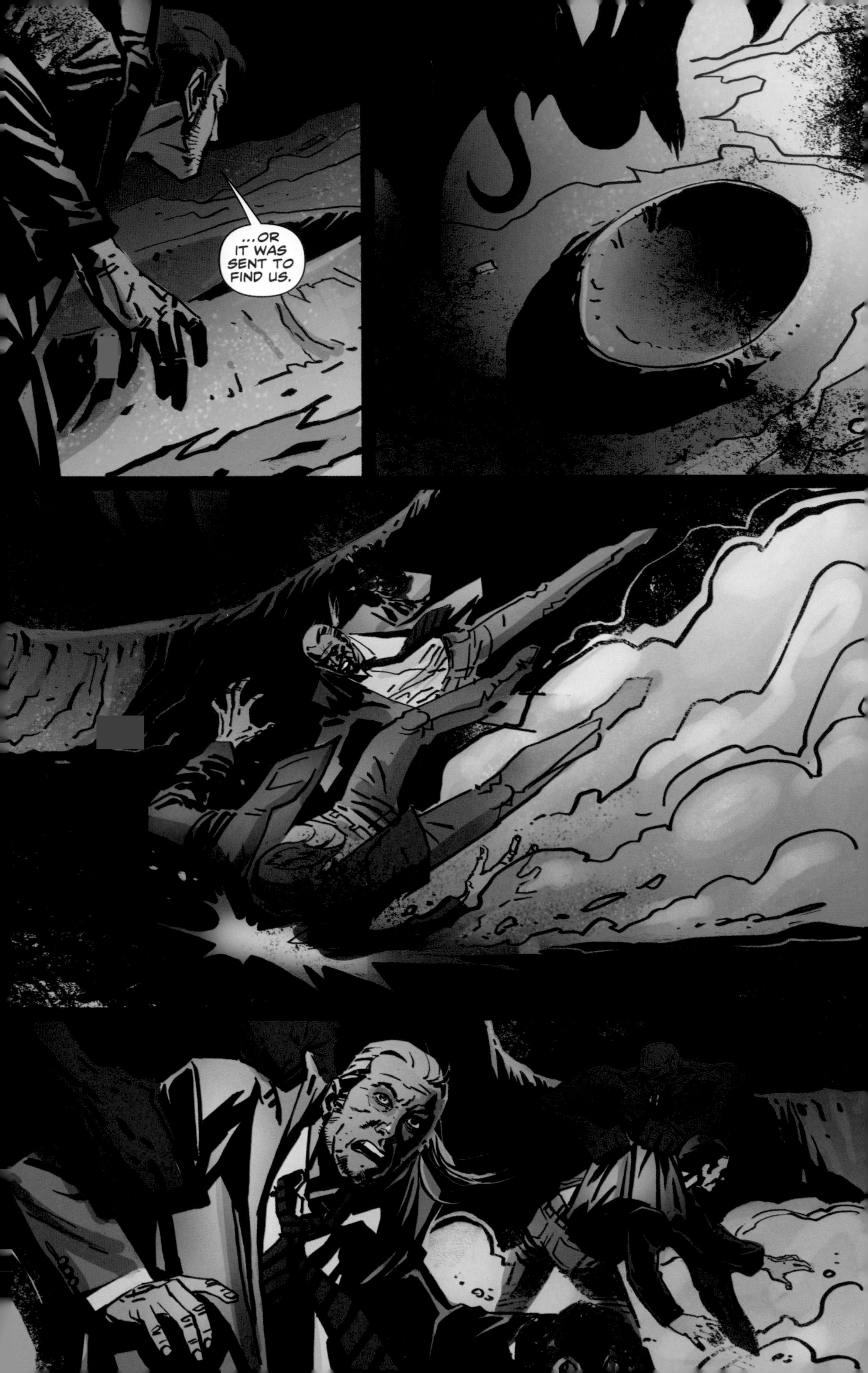
...OR IT WAS SENT TO FIND US.

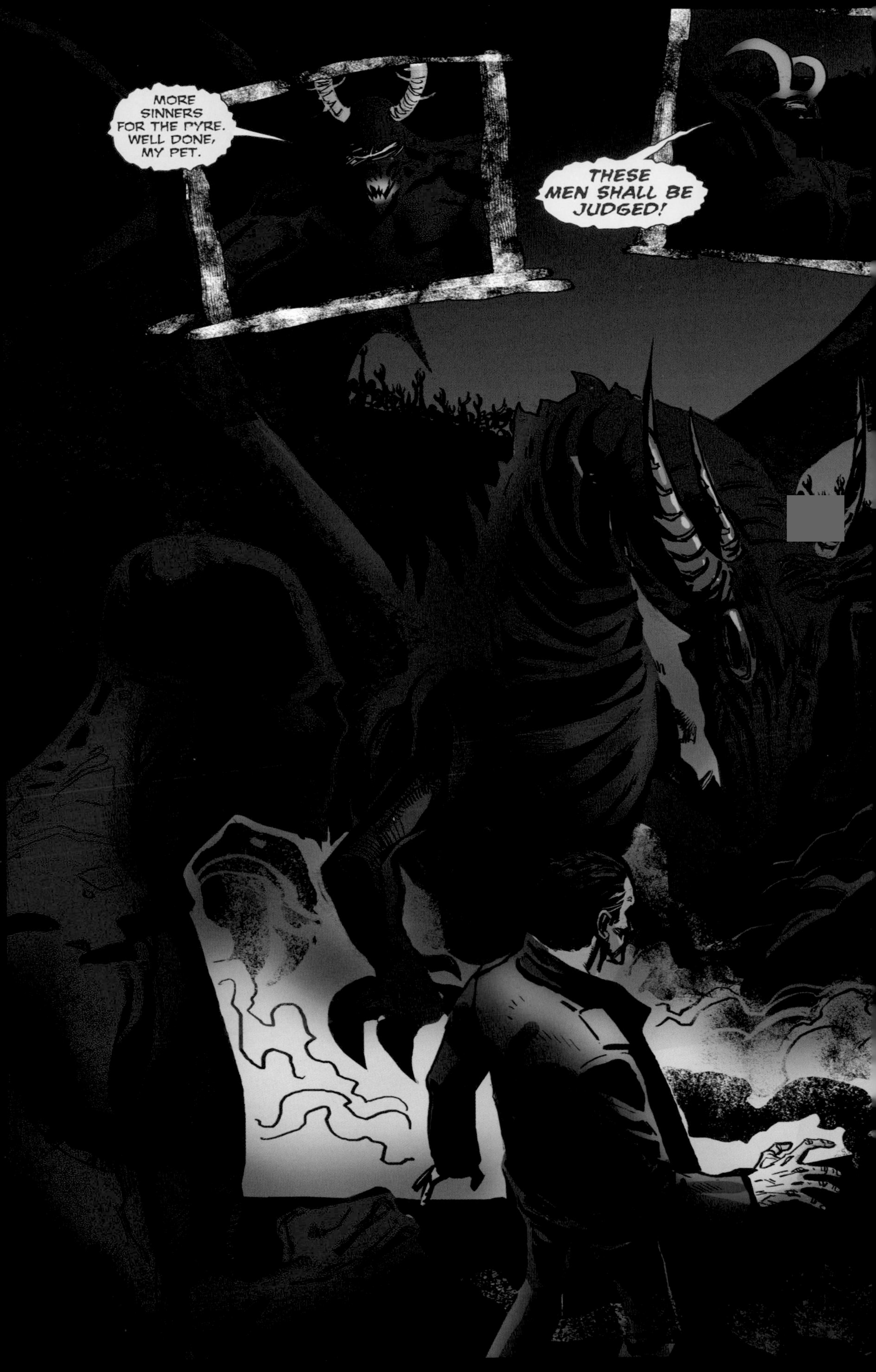
MORE SINNERS FOR THE PYRE. WELL DONE, MY PET.
THESE MEN SHALL BE JUDGED!

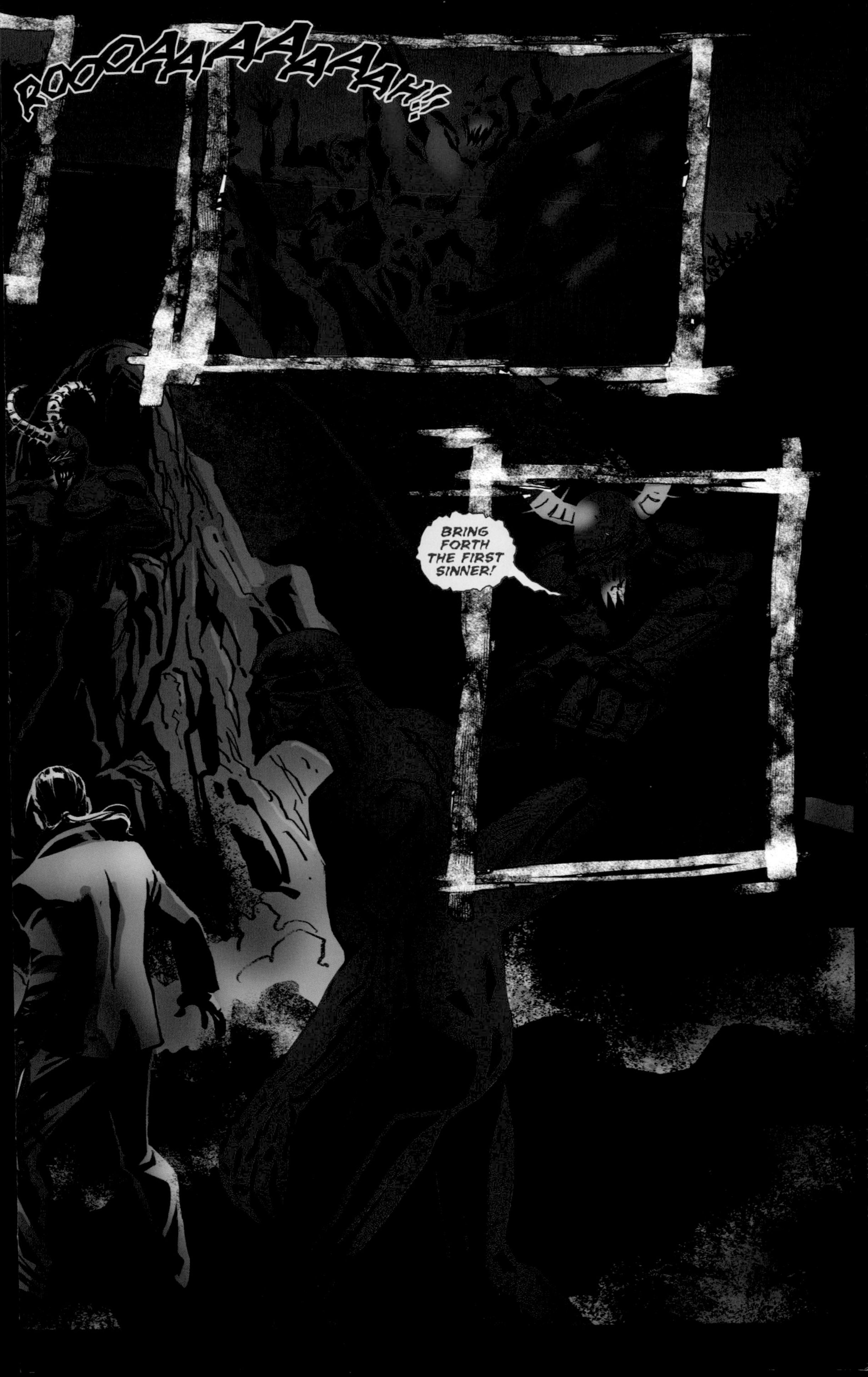
ROOOAAAAAAAAH!!
BRING FORTH THE FIRST SINNER!

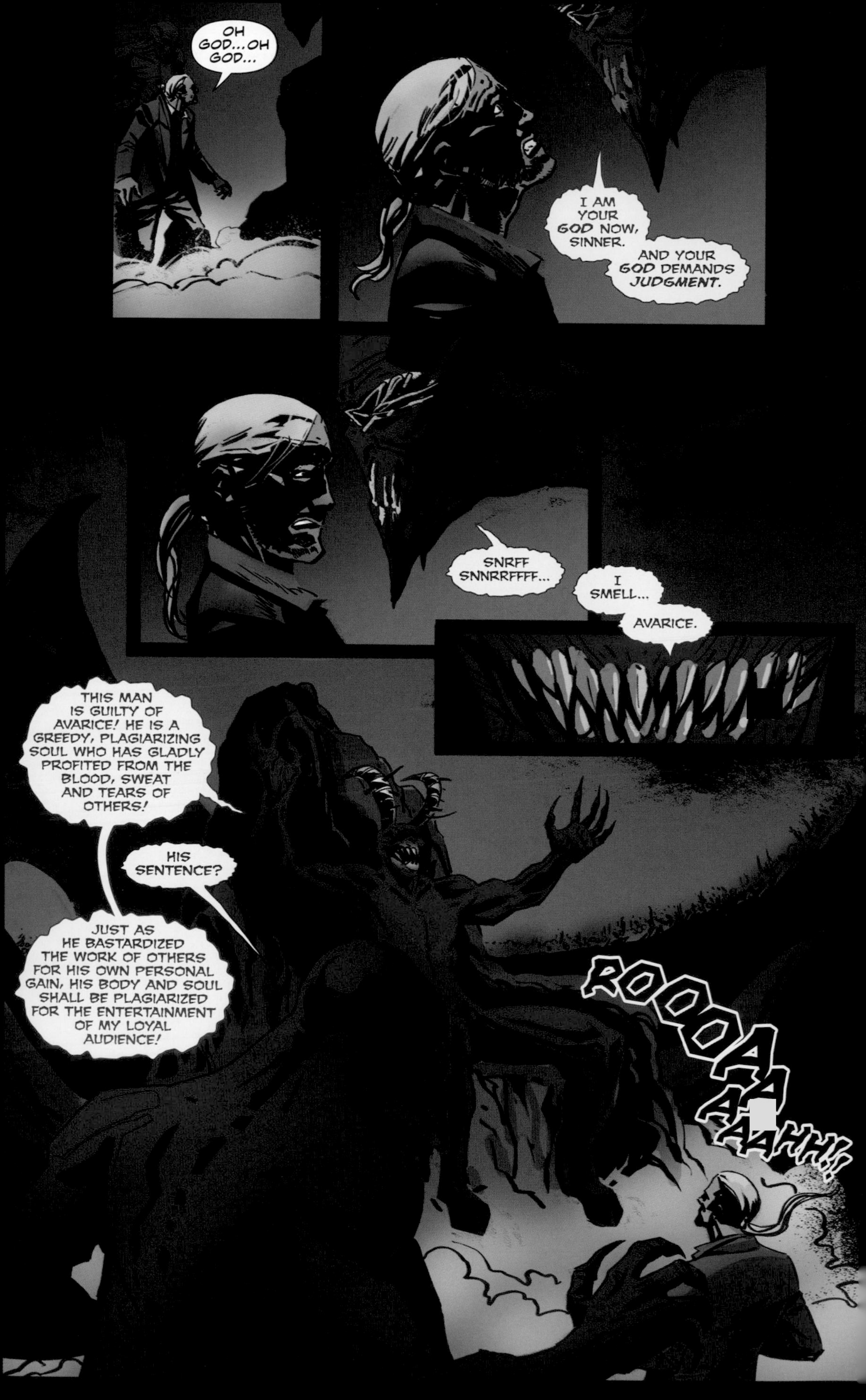
OH GOD...OH GOD...
I AM YOUR GOD NOW, SINNER.
AND YOUR GOD DEMANDS JUDGMENT.
SNRFF SNNRRFFFF...
I SMELL...
AVARICE.
THIS MAN IS GUILTY OF AVARICE! HE IS A GREEDY, PLAGIARIZING SOUL WHO HAS GLADLY PROFITED FROM THE BLOOD, SWEAT AND TEARS OF OTHERS!
HIS SENTENCE?
JUST AS HE BASTARDIZED THE WORK OF OTHERS FOR HIS OWN PERSONAL GAIN, HIS BODY AND SOUL SHALL BE PLAGIARIZED FOR THE ENTERTAINMENT OF MY LOYAL AUDIENCE!
ROOOAAAAAHH!!

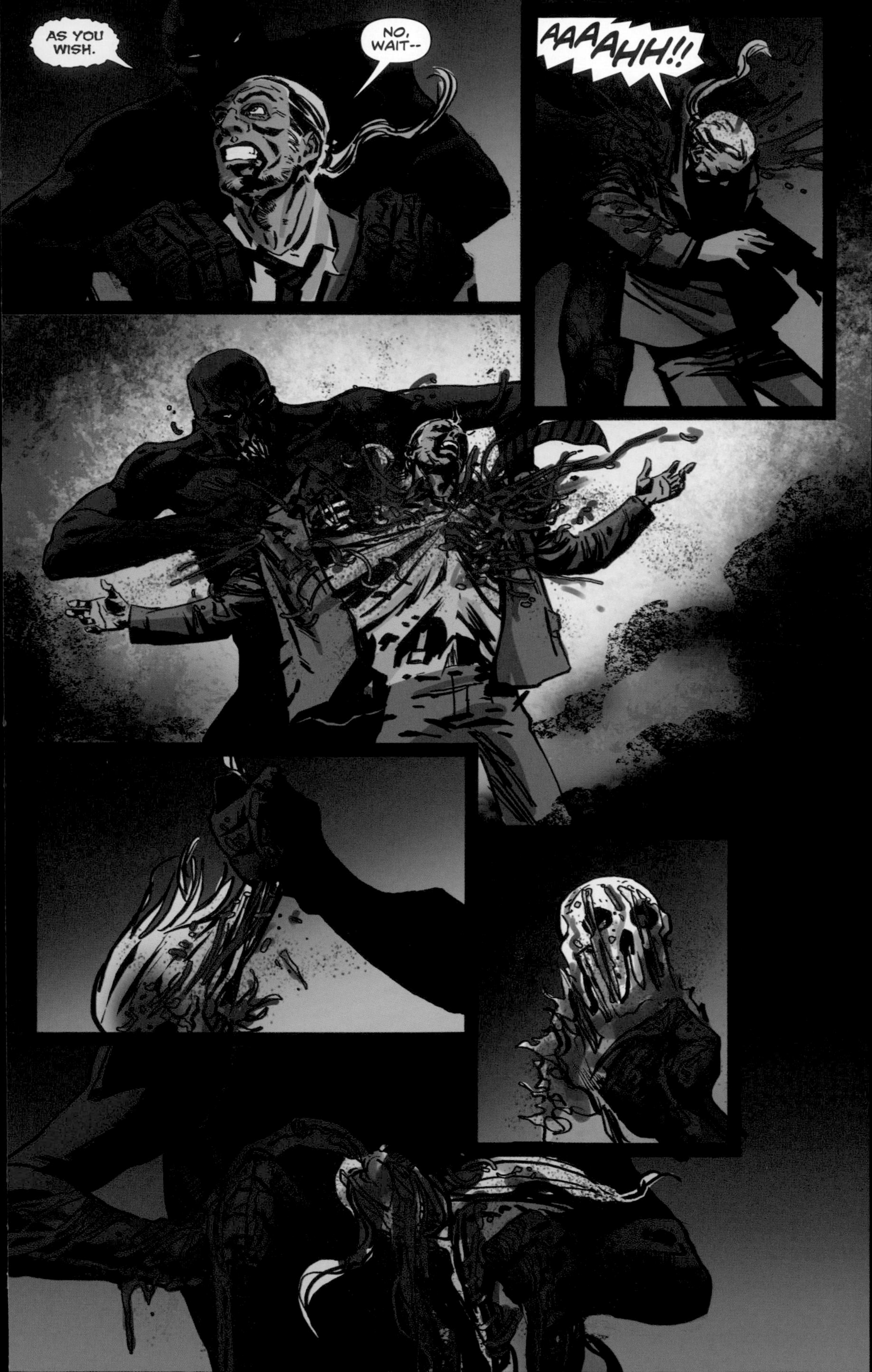
AS YOU WISH.
NO, WAIT--
AAAAAHH!!

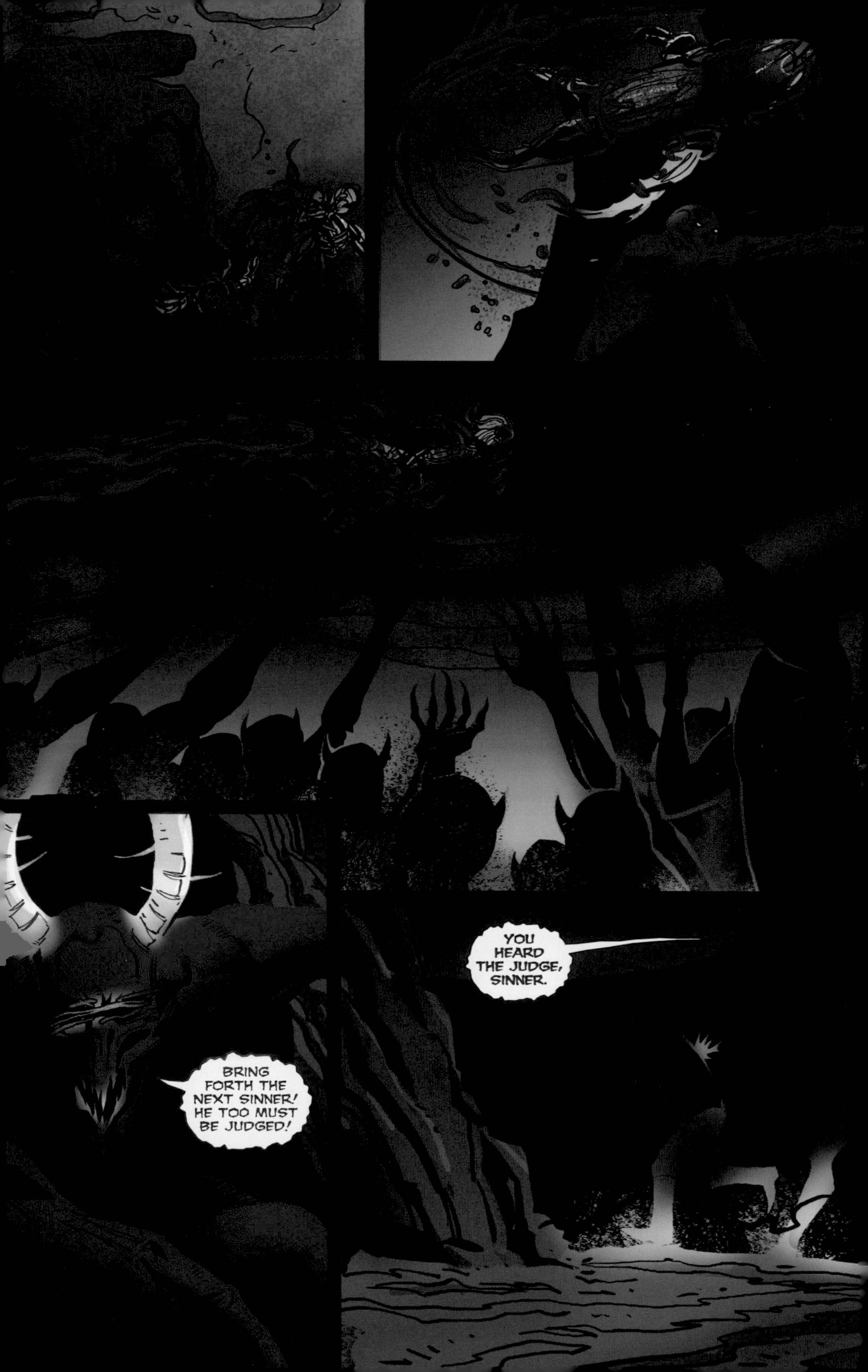
BRING FORTH THE NEXT SINNER! HE TOO MUST BE JUDGED!
YOU HEARD THE JUDGE, SINNER.

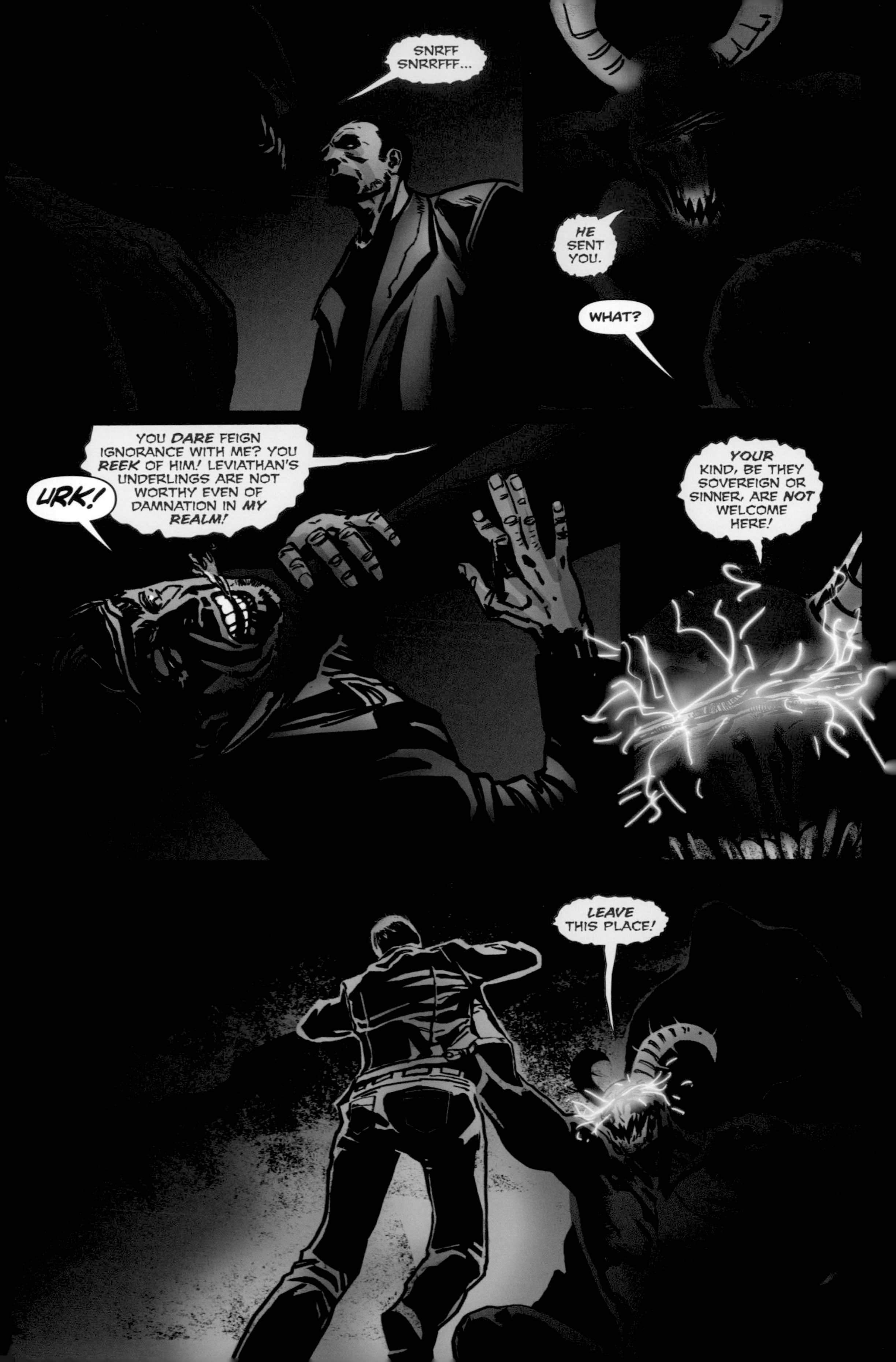
SNRFF SNRRFFF...
HE SENT YOU.
WHAT?
YOU DARE FEIGN IGNORANCE WITH ME? YOU REEK OF HIM! LEVIATHAN'S UNDERLINGS ARE NOT WORTHY EVEN OF DAMNATION IN MY REALM!
URK!
YOUR KIND, BE THEY SOVEREIGN OR SINNER, ARE NOT WELCOME HERE!
LEAVE THIS PLACE!

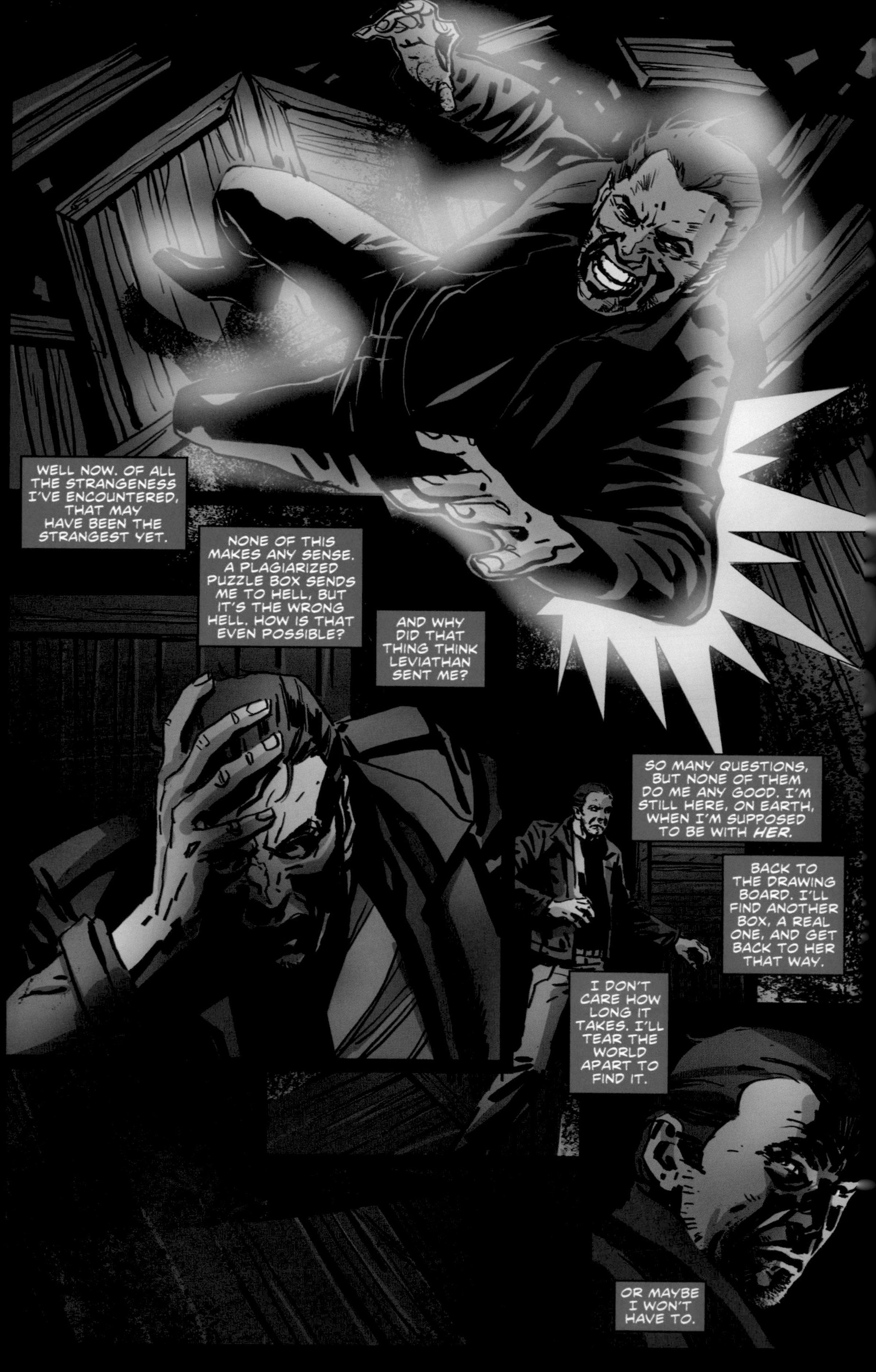
WELL NOW. OF ALL THE STRANGENESS I'VE ENCOUNTERED, THAT MAY HAVE BEEN THE STRANGEST YET.
NONE OF THIS MAKES ANY SENSE. A PLAGIARIZED PUZZLE BOX SENDS ME TO HELL, BUT IT'S THE WRONG HELL. HOW IS THAT EVEN POSSIBLE?
AND WHY DID THAT THING THINK LEVIATHAN SENT ME?
SO MANY QUESTIONS, BUT NONE OF THEM DO ME ANY GOOD. I'M STILL HERE, ON EARTH, WHEN I'M SUPPOSED TO BE WITH *HER*.
BACK TO THE DRAWING BOARD. I'LL FIND ANOTHER BOX, A REAL ONE, AND GET BACK TO HER THAT WAY.
I DON'T CARE HOW LONG IT TAKES. I'LL TEAR THE WORLD APART TO FIND IT.
OR MAYBE I WON'T HAVE TO.

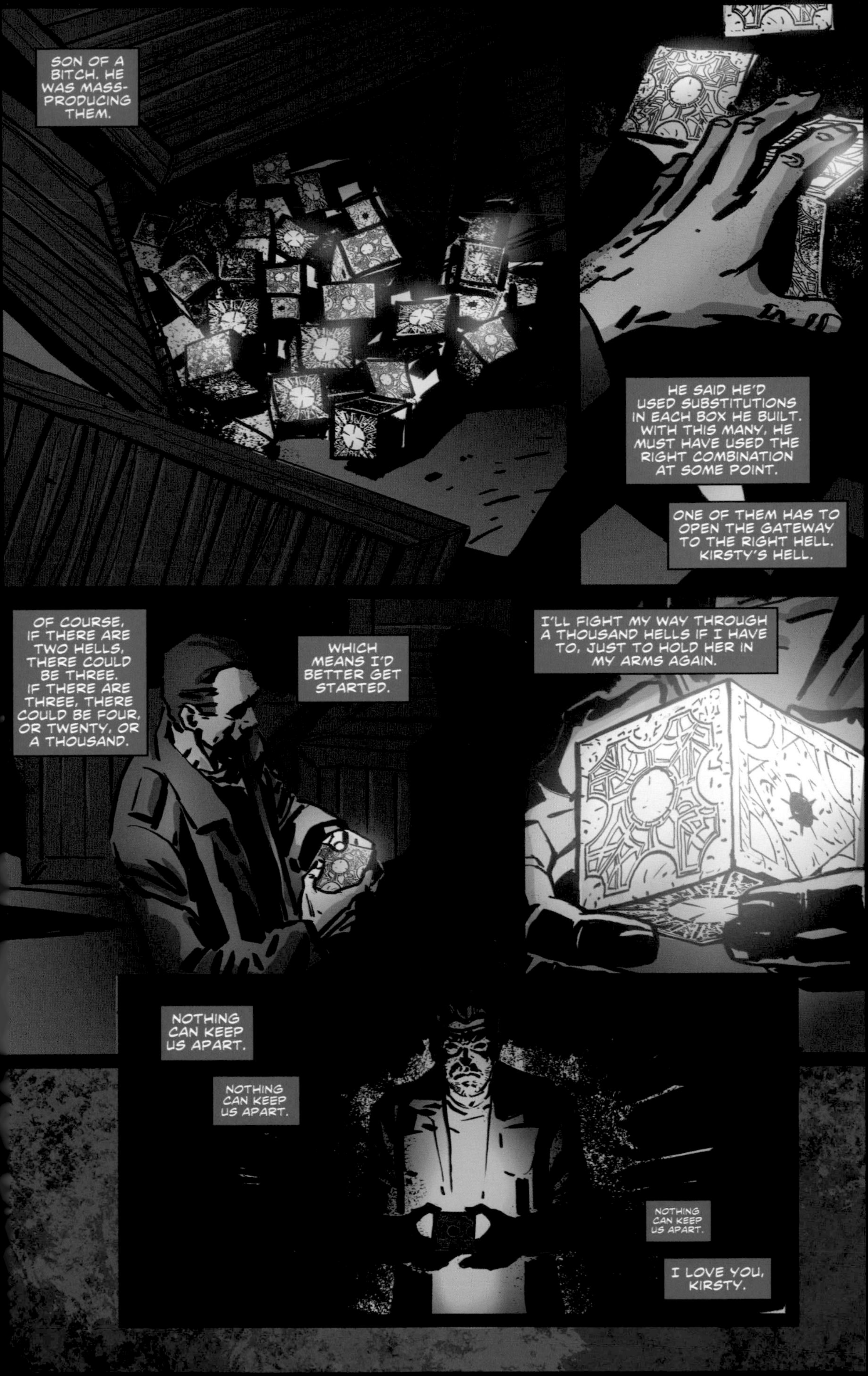
SON OF A BITCH. HE WAS MASS-PRODUCING THEM.
HE SAID HE'D USED SUBSTITUTIONS IN EACH BOX HE BUILT. WITH THIS MANY, HE MUST HAVE USED THE RIGHT COMBINATION AT SOME POINT.
ONE OF THEM HAS TO OPEN THE GATEWAY TO THE RIGHT HELL. KIRSTY'S HELL.
OF COURSE, IF THERE ARE TWO HELLS, THERE COULD BE THREE. IF THERE ARE THREE, THERE COULD BE FOUR, OR TWENTY, OR A THOUSAND.
WHICH MEANS I'D BETTER GET STARTED.
I'LL FIGHT MY WAY THROUGH A THOUSAND HELLS IF I HAVE TO, JUST TO HOLD HER IN MY ARMS AGAIN.
NOTHING CAN KEEP US APART.
NOTHING CAN KEEP US APART.
NOTHING CAN KEEP US APART.
I LOVE YOU, KIRSTY.

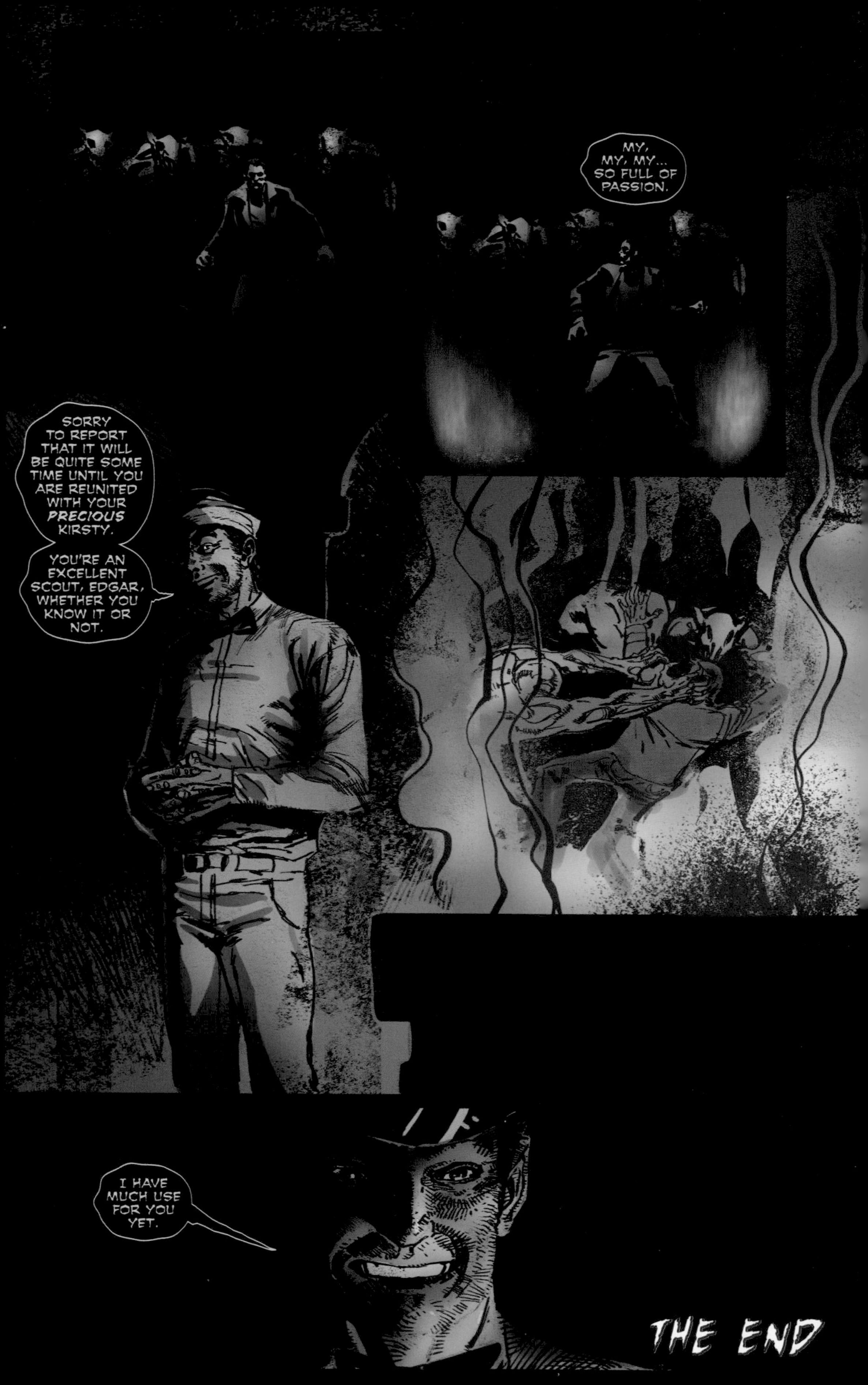
MY, MY, MY... SO FULL OF PASSION.
SORRY TO REPORT THAT IT WILL BE QUITE SOME TIME UNTIL YOU ARE REUNITED WITH YOUR *PRECIOUS* KIRSTY.
YOU'RE AN EXCELLENT SCOUT, EDGAR, WHETHER YOU KNOW IT OR NOT.
I HAVE MUCH USE FOR YOU YET.
THE END

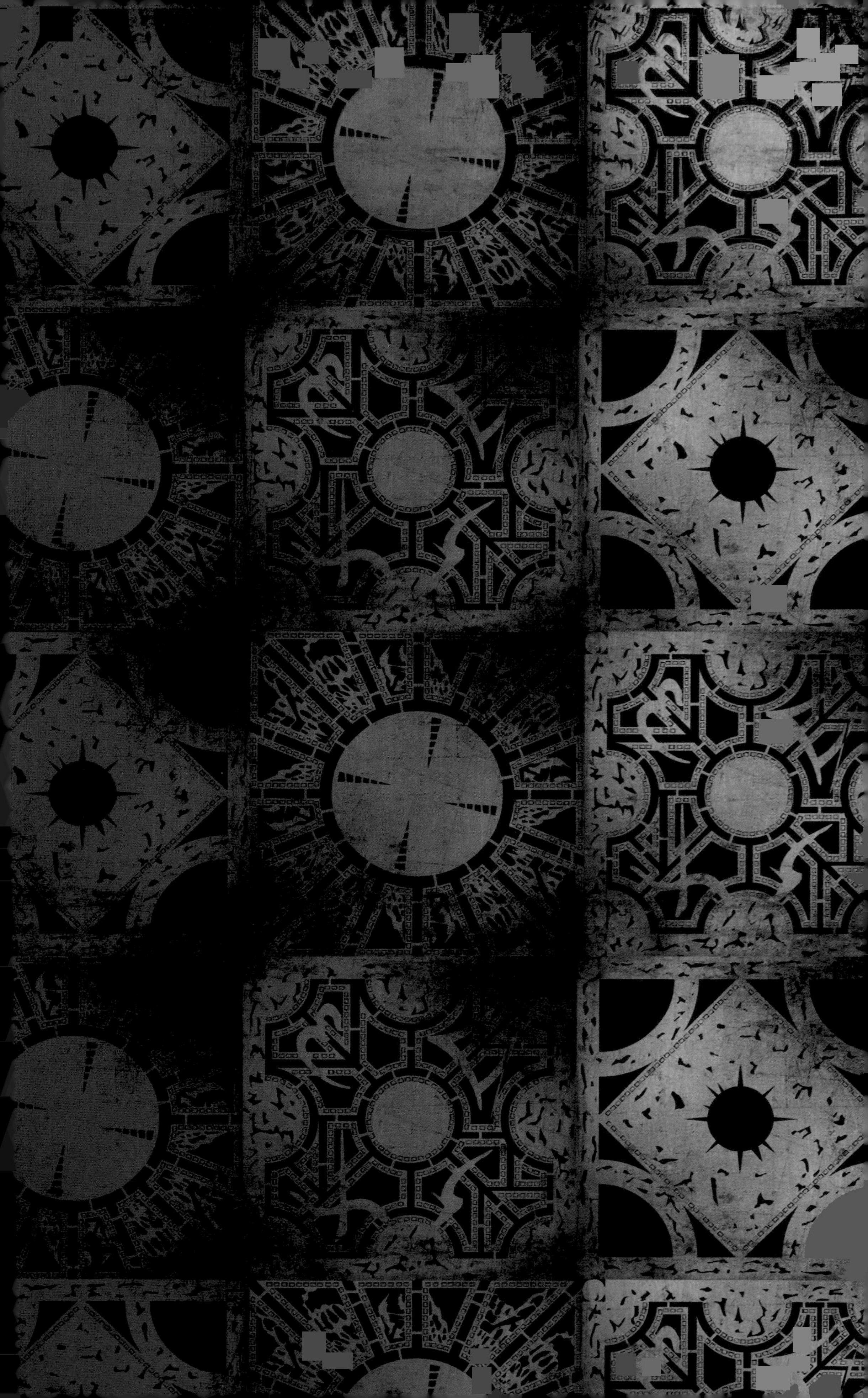

THE DARK WATCH
CHAPTER NINE

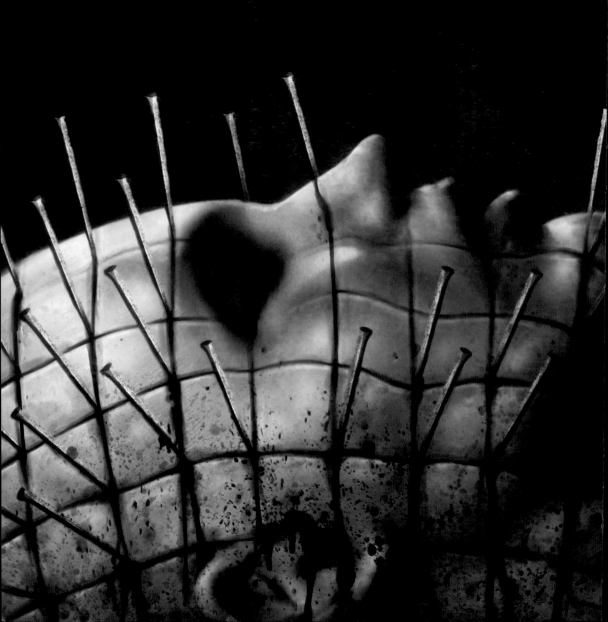

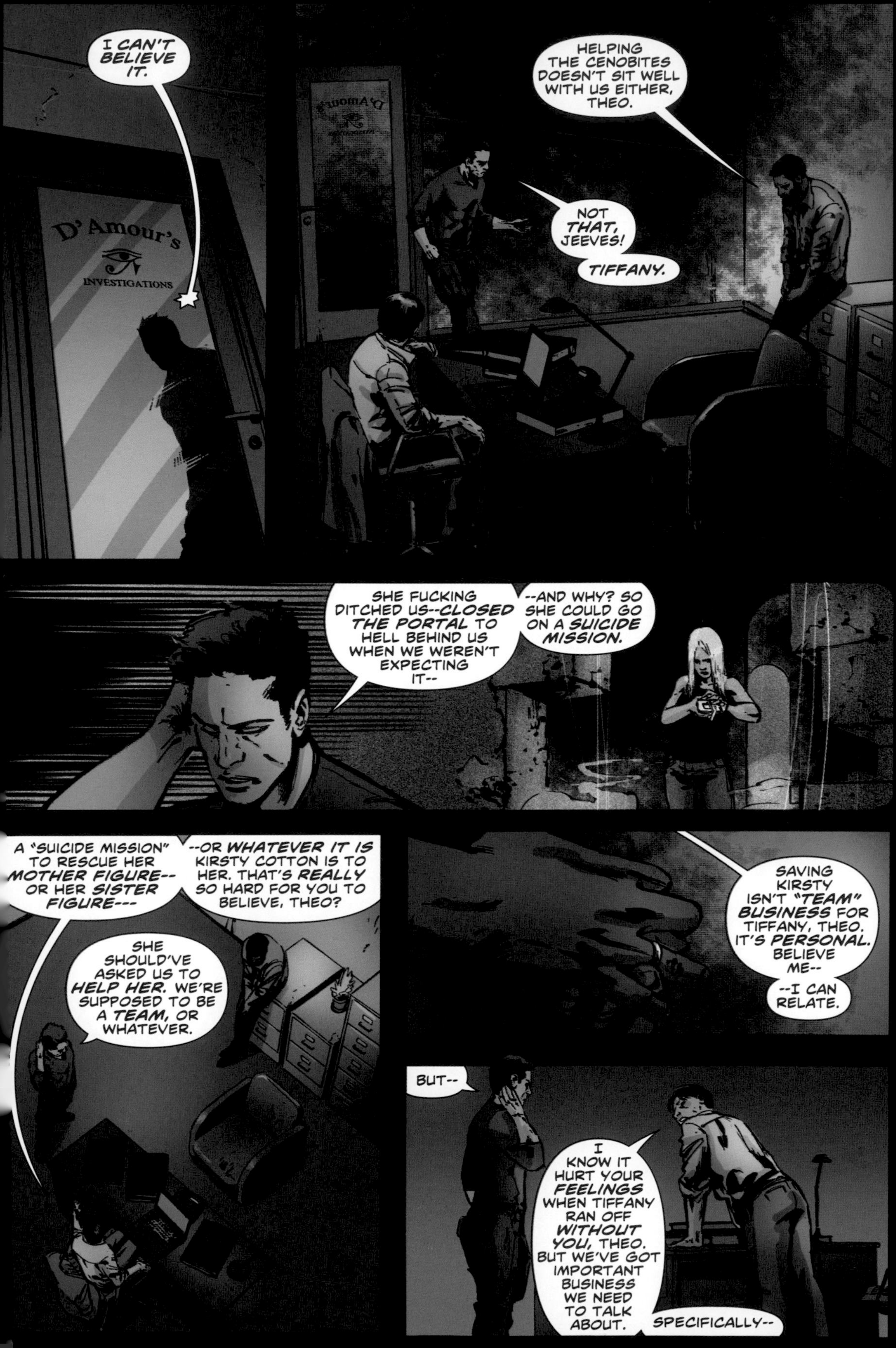

D' Amour's INVESTIGATIONS
I CAN'T BELIEVE IT.
HELPING THE CENOBITES DOESN'T SIT WELL WITH US EITHER, THEO.
NOT THAT, JEEVES!
TIFFANY.
SHE FUCKING DITCHED US--CLOSED THE PORTAL TO HELL BEHIND US WHEN WE WEREN'T EXPECTING IT--
--AND WHY? SO SHE COULD GO ON A SUICIDE MISSION.
A "SUICIDE MISSION" TO RESCUE HER MOTHER FIGURE-- OR HER SISTER FIGURE---
--OR WHATEVER IT IS KIRSTY COTTON IS TO HER. THAT'S REALLY SO HARD FOR YOU TO BELIEVE, THEO?
SHE SHOULD'VE ASKED US TO HELP HER. WE'RE SUPPOSED TO BE A TEAM, OR WHATEVER.
SAVING KIRSTY ISN'T "TEAM" BUSINESS FOR TIFFANY, THEO. IT'S PERSONAL. BELIEVE ME--
--I CAN RELATE.
BUT--
I KNOW IT HURT YOUR FEELINGS WHEN TIFFANY RAN OFF WITHOUT YOU, THEO. BUT WE'VE GOT IMPORTANT BUSINESS WE NEED TO TALK ABOUT.
SPECIFICALLY--

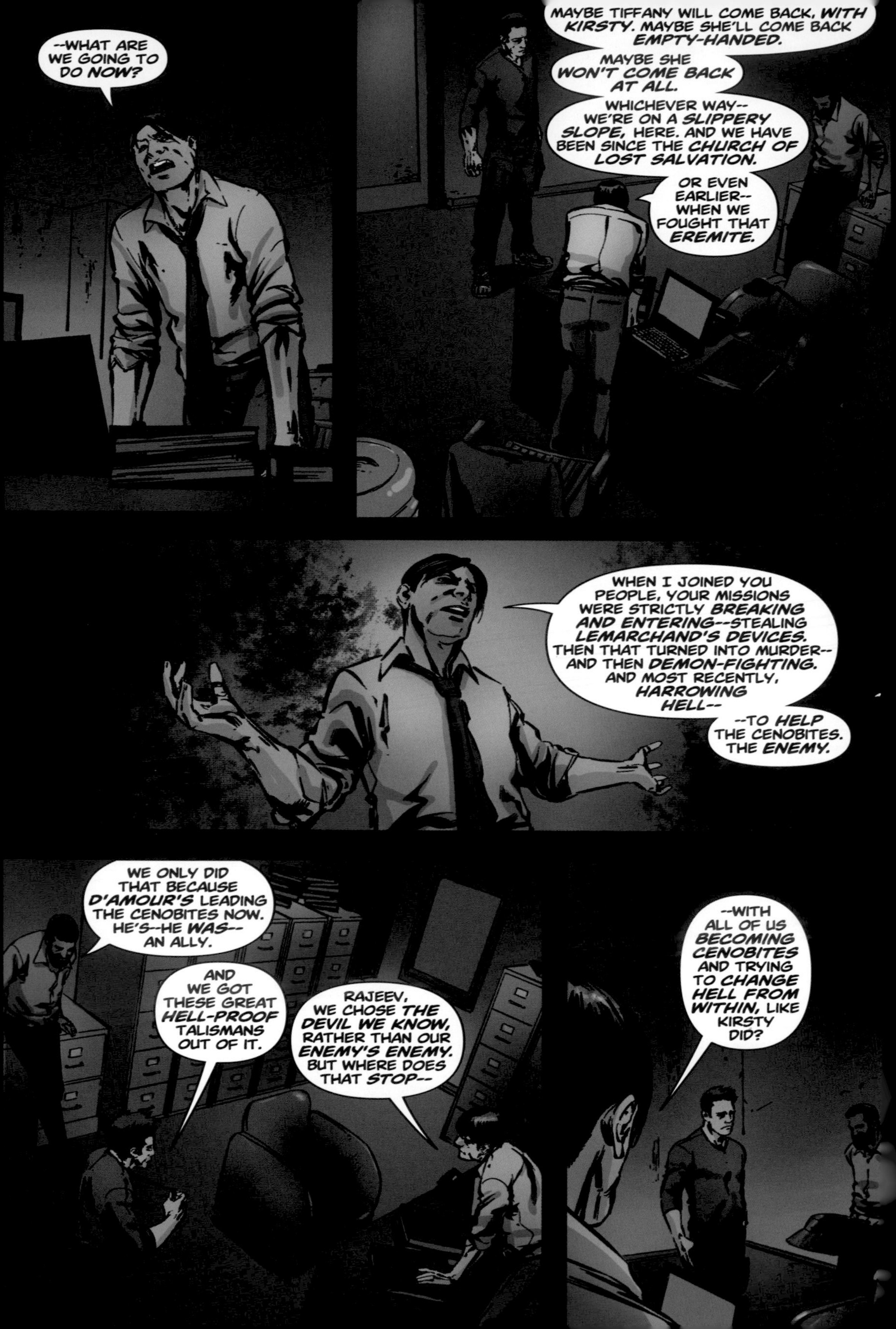
--WHAT ARE WE GOING TO DO NOW?
MAYBE TIFFANY WILL COME BACK, WITH KIRSTY. MAYBE SHE'LL COME BACK EMPTY-HANDED.
MAYBE SHE WON'T COME BACK AT ALL.
WHICHEVER WAY-- WE'RE ON A SLIPPERY SLOPE, HERE. AND WE HAVE BEEN SINCE THE CHURCH OF LOST SALVATION.
OR EVEN EARLIER-- WHEN WE FOUGHT THAT EREMITE.
WHEN I JOINED YOU PEOPLE, YOUR MISSIONS WERE STRICTLY BREAKING AND ENTERING--STEALING LEMARCHAND'S DEVICES. THEN THAT TURNED INTO MURDER-- AND THEN DEMON-FIGHTING. AND MOST RECENTLY, HARROWING HELL--
--TO HELP THE CENOBITES. THE ENEMY.
WE ONLY DID THAT BECAUSE D'AMOUR'S LEADING THE CENOBITES NOW. HE'S--HE WAS-- AN ALLY.
AND WE GOT THESE GREAT HELL-PROOF TALISMANS OUT OF IT.
RAJEEV, WE CHOSE THE DEVIL WE KNOW, RATHER THAN OUR ENEMY'S ENEMY. BUT WHERE DOES THAT STOP--
--WITH ALL OF US BECOMING CENOBITES AND TRYING TO CHANGE HELL FROM WITHIN, LIKE KIRSTY DID?

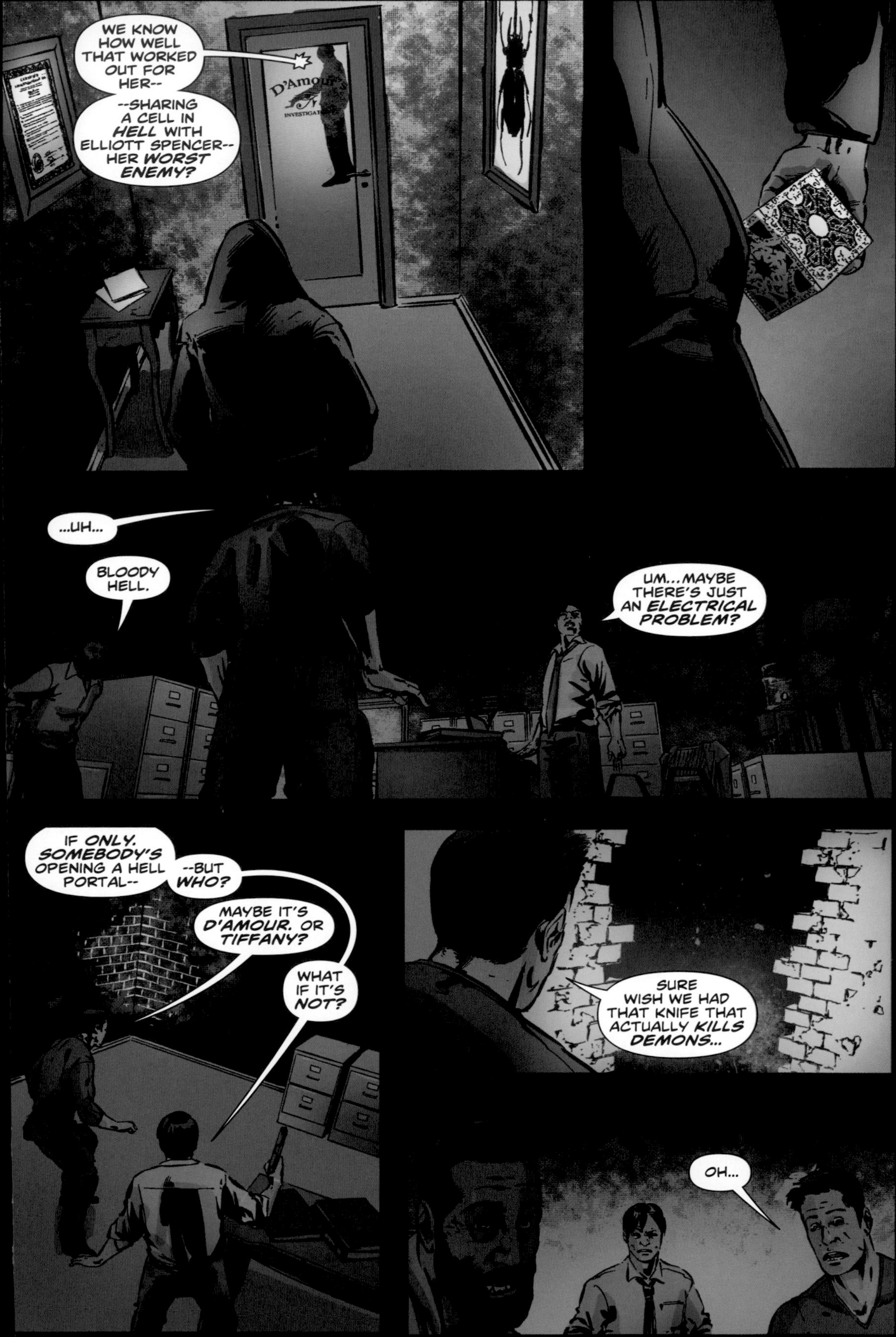
WE KNOW HOW WELL THAT WORKED OUT FOR HER--
--SHARING A CELL IN HELL WITH ELLIOTT SPENCER--HER WORST ENEMY?
...UH...
BLOODY HELL.
UM...MAYBE THERE'S JUST AN ELECTRICAL PROBLEM?
IF ONLY. SOMEBODY'S OPENING A HELL PORTAL--
--BUT WHO?
MAYBE IT'S D'AMOUR. OR TIFFANY?
WHAT IF IT'S NOT?
SURE WISH WE HAD THAT KNIFE THAT ACTUALLY KILLS DEMONS...
OH...

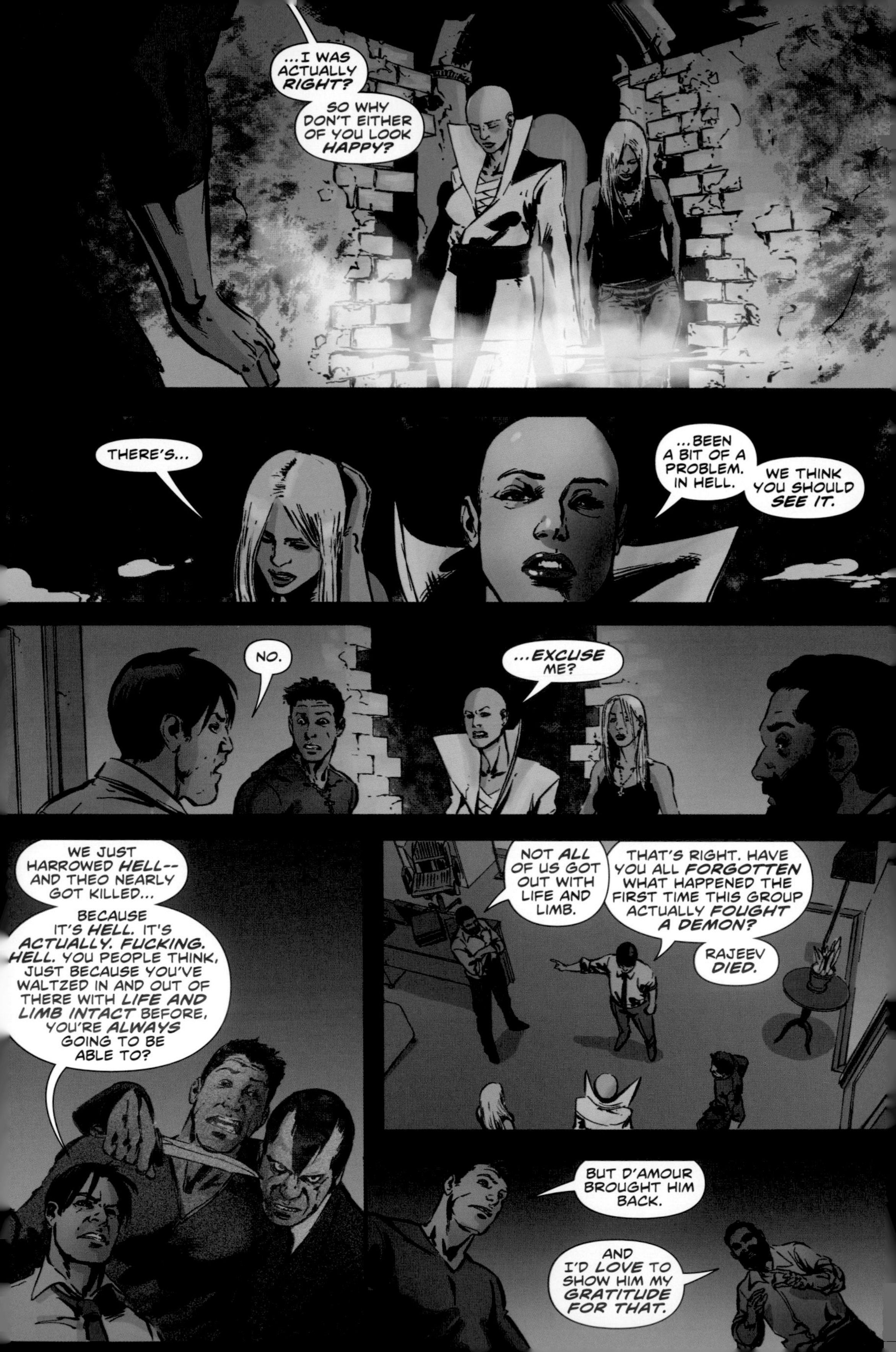
...I WAS ACTUALLY RIGHT?
SO WHY DON'T EITHER OF YOU LOOK HAPPY?
THERE'S...
...BEEN A BIT OF A PROBLEM. IN HELL.
WE THINK YOU SHOULD SEE IT.
NO.
...EXCUSE ME?
WE JUST HARROWED HELL-- AND THEO NEARLY GOT KILLED...
BECAUSE IT'S HELL. IT'S ACTUALLY. FUCKING. HELL. YOU PEOPLE THINK, JUST BECAUSE YOU'VE WALTZED IN AND OUT OF THERE WITH LIFE AND LIMB INTACT BEFORE, YOU'RE ALWAYS GOING TO BE ABLE TO?
NOT ALL OF US GOT OUT WITH LIFE AND LIMB.
THAT'S RIGHT. HAVE YOU ALL FORGOTTEN WHAT HAPPENED THE FIRST TIME THIS GROUP ACTUALLY FOUGHT A DEMON?
RAJEEV DIED.
BUT D'AMOUR BROUGHT HIM BACK.
AND I'D LOVE TO SHOW HIM MY GRATITUDE FOR THAT.

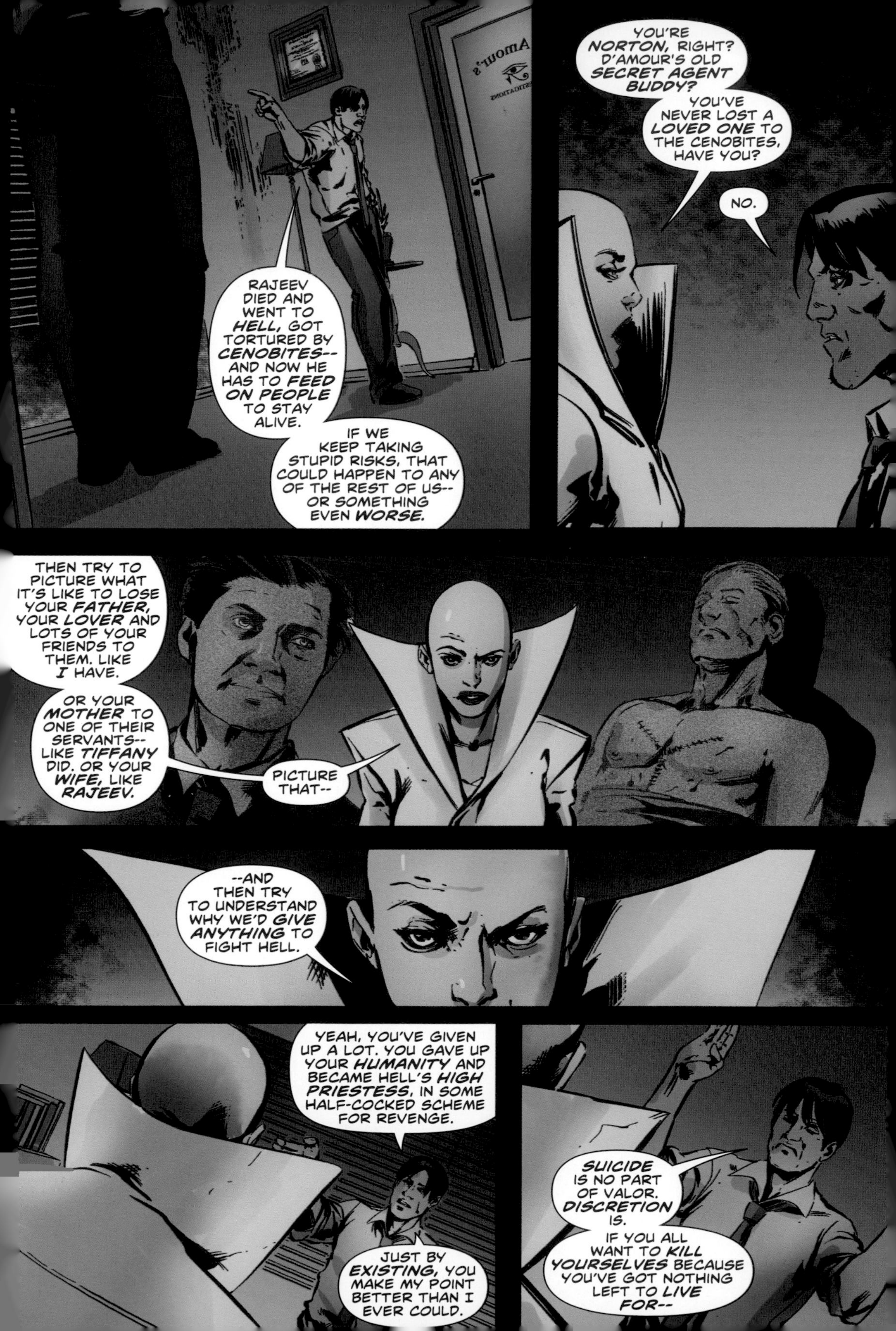
RAJEEV DIED AND WENT TO HELL, GOT TORTURED BY CENOBITES-- AND NOW HE HAS TO FEED ON PEOPLE TO STAY ALIVE.
IF WE KEEP TAKING STUPID RISKS, THAT COULD HAPPEN TO ANY OF THE REST OF US-- OR SOMETHING EVEN WORSE.
YOU'RE NORTON, RIGHT? D'AMOUR'S OLD SECRET AGENT BUDDY?
YOU'VE NEVER LOST A LOVED ONE TO THE CENOBITES, HAVE YOU?
NO.
THEN TRY TO PICTURE WHAT IT'S LIKE TO LOSE YOUR FATHER, YOUR LOVER AND LOTS OF YOUR FRIENDS TO THEM. LIKE I HAVE.
OR YOUR MOTHER TO ONE OF THEIR SERVANTS-- LIKE TIFFANY DID. OR YOUR WIFE, LIKE RAJEEV.
PICTURE THAT--
--AND THEN TRY TO UNDERSTAND WHY WE'D GIVE ANYTHING TO FIGHT HELL.
YEAH, YOU'VE GIVEN UP A LOT. YOU GAVE UP YOUR HUMANITY AND BECAME HELL'S HIGH PRIESTESS, IN SOME HALF-COCKED SCHEME FOR REVENGE.
JUST BY EXISTING, YOU MAKE MY POINT BETTER THAN I EVER COULD.
SUICIDE IS NO PART OF VALOR. DISCRETION IS.
IF YOU ALL WANT TO KILL YOURSELVES BECAUSE YOU'VE GOT NOTHING LEFT TO LIVE FOR--

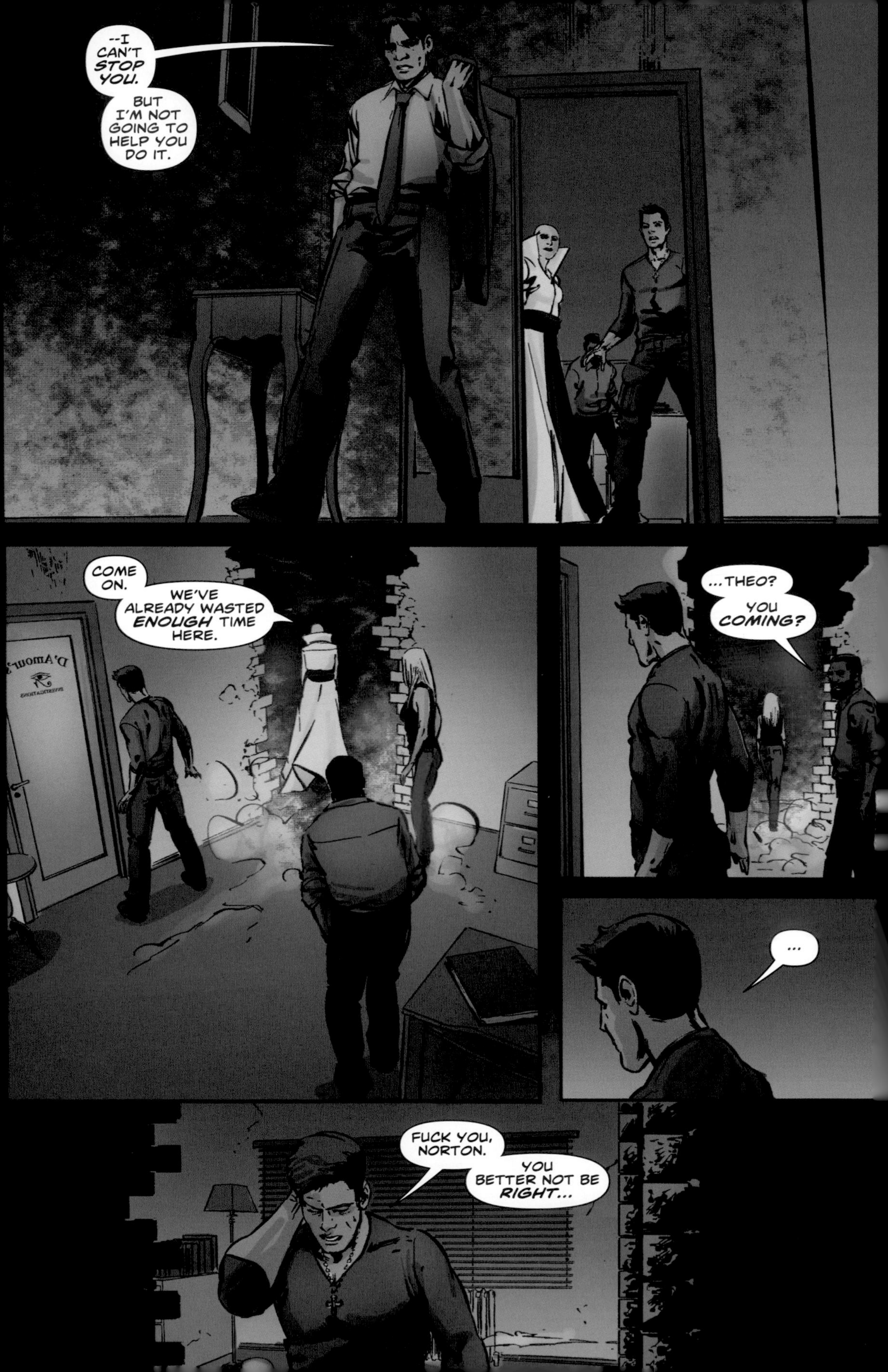
--I CAN'T STOP YOU.
BUT I'M NOT GOING TO HELP YOU DO IT.
COME ON.
WE'VE ALREADY WASTED ENOUGH TIME HERE.
...THEO?
YOU COMING?
...
FUCK YOU, NORTON.
YOU BETTER NOT BE RIGHT...

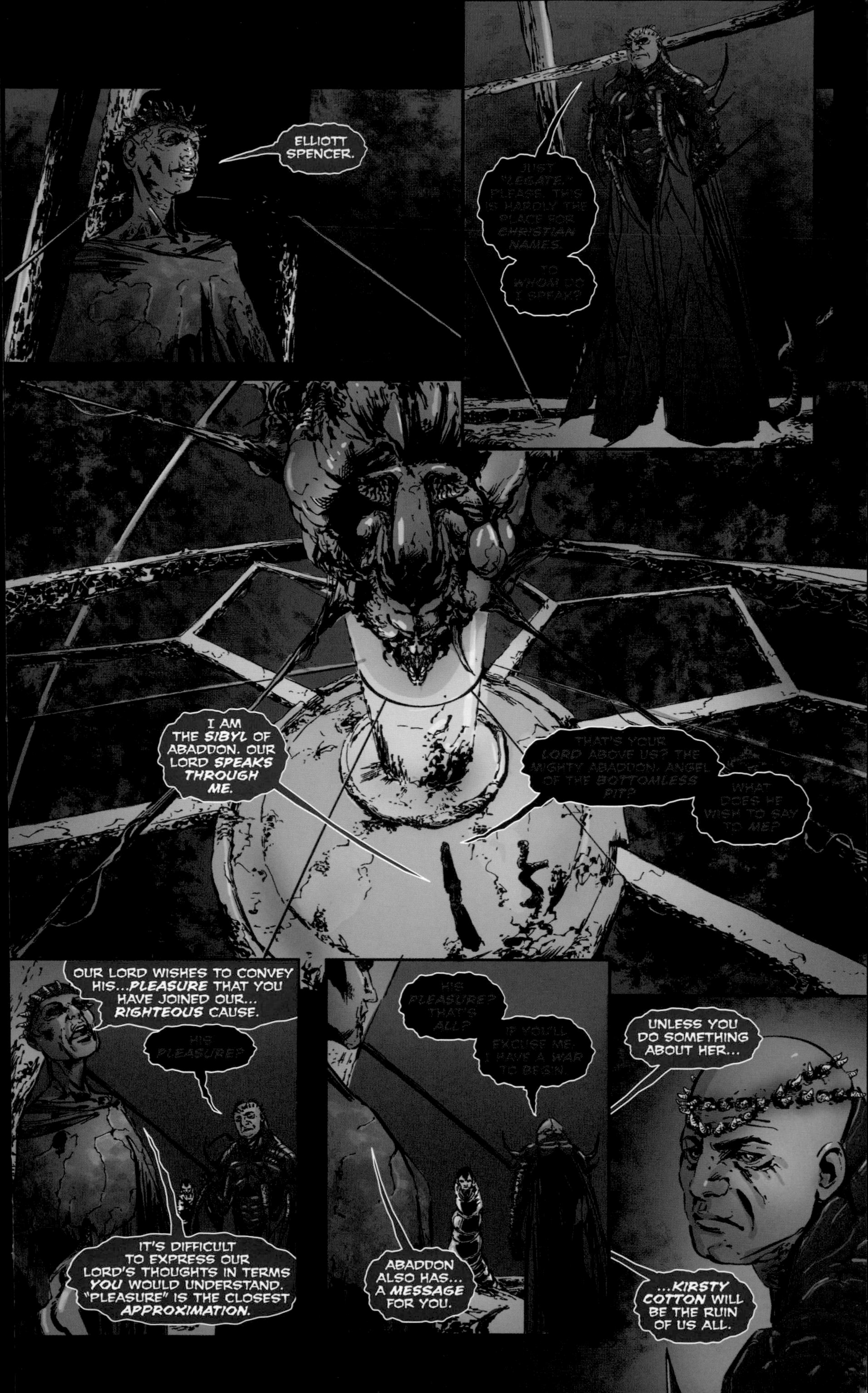
ELLIOTT SPENCER.
JUST "LEGATE," PLEASE. THIS IS HARDLY THE PLACE FOR *CHRISTIAN NAMES.*
TO WHOM DO I SPEAK?
I AM THE ***SIBYL*** OF ABADDON. OUR LORD ***SPEAKS THROUGH*** ME.
THAT'S YOUR *LORD* ABOVE US? THE MIGHTY ABADDON, ANGEL OF THE *BOTTOMLESS PIT?*
WHAT DOES HE WISH TO SAY TO *ME?*
OUR LORD WISHES TO CONVEY HIS...***PLEASURE*** THAT YOU HAVE JOINED OUR... ***RIGHTEOUS*** CAUSE.
HIS *PLEASURE?*
IT'S DIFFICULT TO EXPRESS OUR LORD'S THOUGHTS IN TERMS ***YOU*** WOULD UNDERSTAND. "PLEASURE" IS THE CLOSEST ***APPROXIMATION.***
HIS *PLEASURE?* THAT'S *ALL?*
IF YOU'LL EXCUSE ME, I HAVE A *WAR* TO BEGIN.
ABADDON ALSO HAS... A ***MESSAGE*** FOR YOU.
UNLESS YOU DO SOMETHING ABOUT HER...
...***KIRSTY COTTON*** WILL BE THE RUIN OF US ALL.

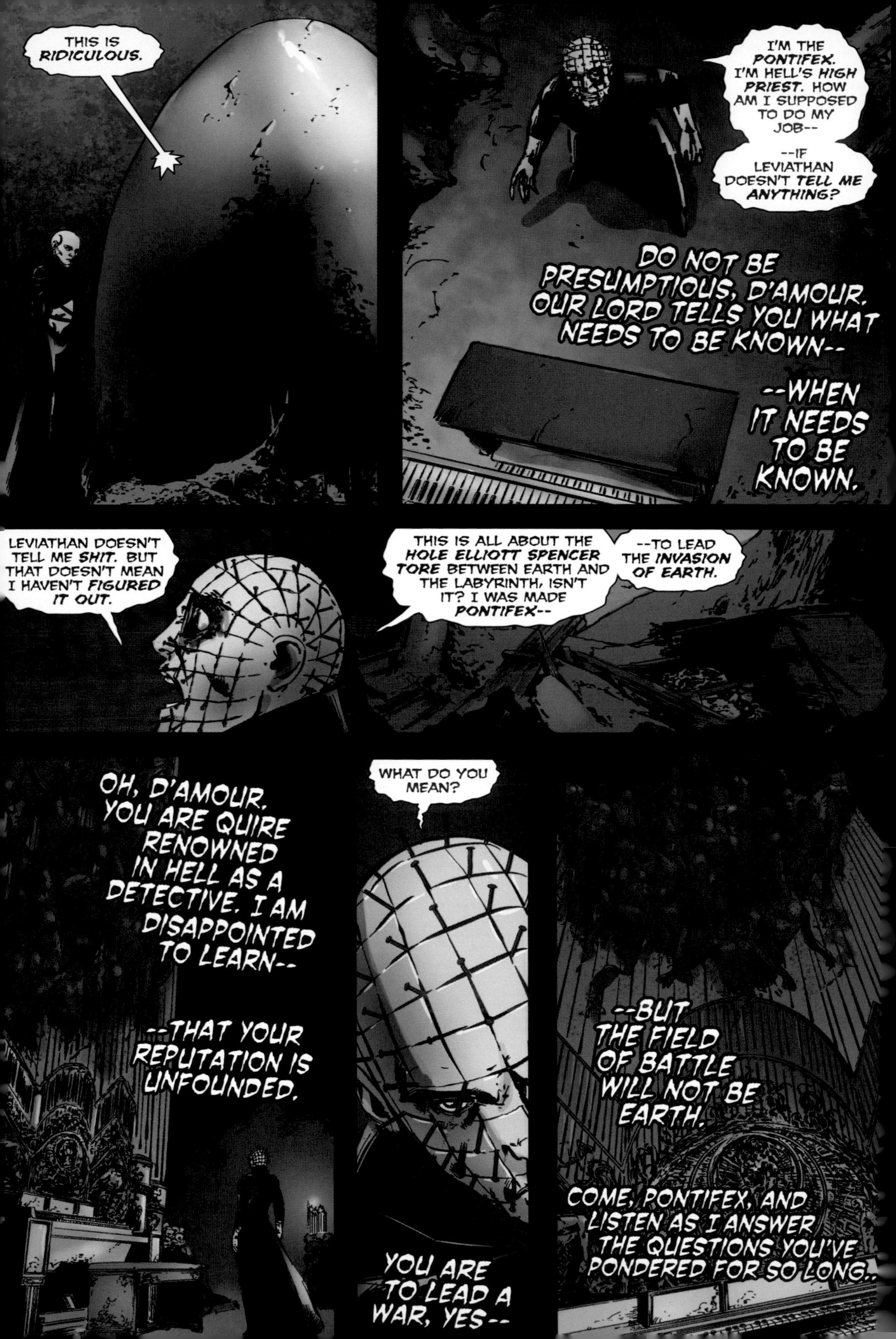
THIS IS RIDICULOUS.
I'M THE PONTIFEX. I'M HELL'S HIGH PRIEST. HOW AM I SUPPOSED TO DO MY JOB--
--IF LEVIATHAN DOESN'T TELL ME ANYTHING?
DO NOT BE PRESUMPTIOUS, D'AMOUR. OUR LORD TELLS YOU WHAT NEEDS TO BE KNOWN--
--WHEN IT NEEDS TO BE KNOWN.
LEVIATHAN DOESN'T TELL ME SHIT. BUT THAT DOESN'T MEAN I HAVEN'T FIGURED IT OUT.
THIS IS ALL ABOUT THE HOLE ELLIOTT SPENCER TORE BETWEEN EARTH AND THE LABYRINTH, ISN'T IT? I WAS MADE PONTIFEX--
--TO LEAD THE INVASION OF EARTH.
OH, D'AMOUR. YOU ARE QUIRE RENOWNED IN HELL AS A DETECTIVE. I AM DISAPPOINTED TO LEARN--
--THAT YOUR REPUTATION IS UNFOUNDED.
WHAT DO YOU MEAN?
YOU ARE TO LEAD A WAR, YES--
--BUT THE FIELD OF BATTLE WILL NOT BE EARTH.
COME, PONTIFEX, AND LISTEN AS I ANSWER THE QUESTIONS YOU'VE PONDERED FOR SO LONG.

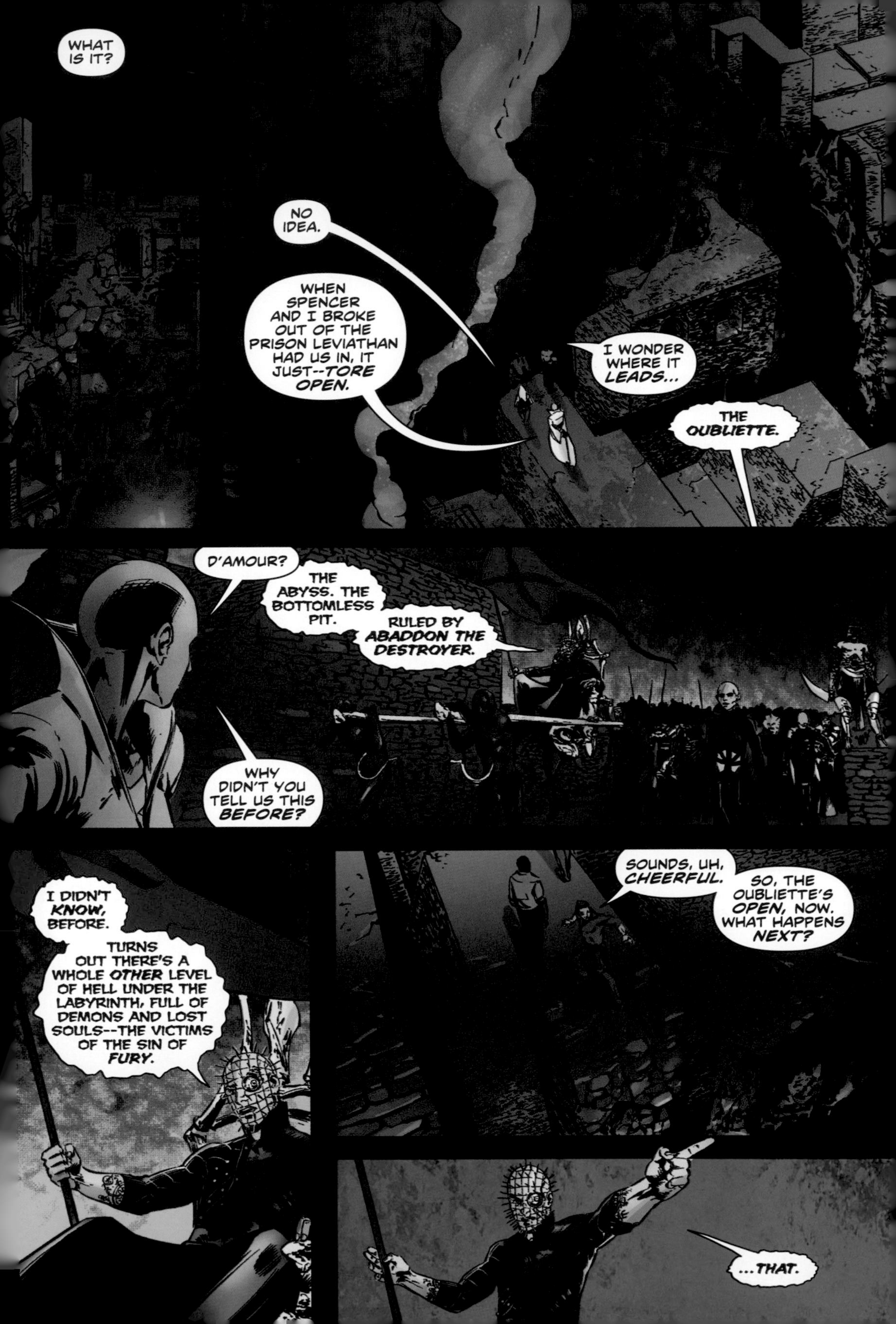
WHAT IS IT?
NO IDEA.
WHEN SPENCER AND I BROKE OUT OF THE PRISON LEVIATHAN HAD US IN, IT JUST--*TORE OPEN.*
I WONDER WHERE IT *LEADS...*
THE *OUBLIETTE.*
D'AMOUR?
THE ABYSS. THE BOTTOMLESS PIT.
RULED BY *ABADDON THE DESTROYER.*
WHY DIDN'T YOU TELL US THIS *BEFORE?*
I DIDN'T *KNOW,* BEFORE.
TURNS OUT THERE'S A WHOLE *OTHER* LEVEL OF HELL UNDER THE LABYRINTH, FULL OF DEMONS AND LOST SOULS--THE VICTIMS OF THE SIN OF *FURY.*
SOUNDS, UH, *CHEERFUL.*
SO, THE OUBLIETTE'S *OPEN,* NOW. WHAT HAPPENS *NEXT?*
...THAT.

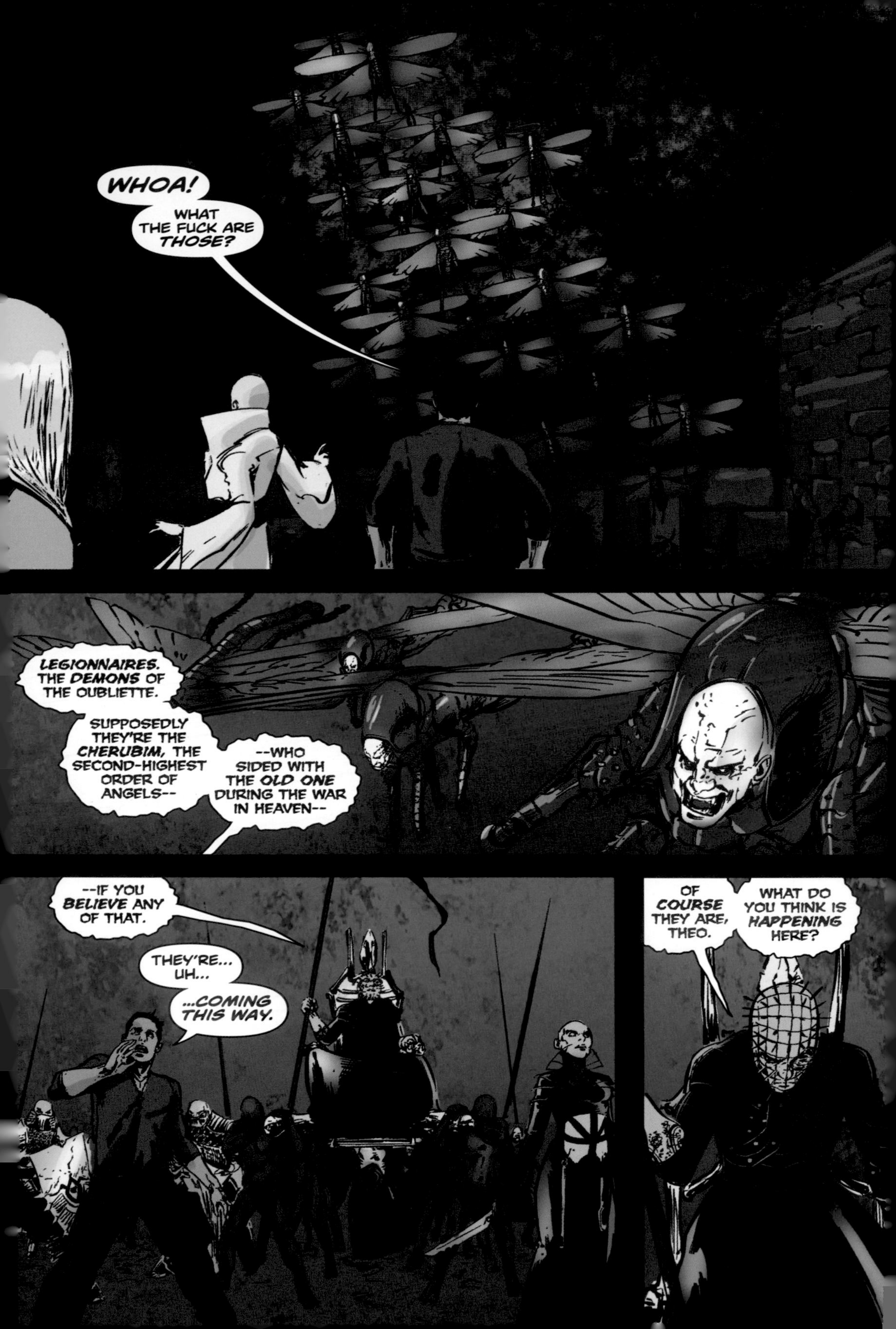
WHOA!
WHAT THE FUCK ARE THOSE?
LEGIONNAIRES. THE DEMONS OF THE OUBLIETTE.
SUPPOSEDLY THEY'RE THE CHERUBIM, THE SECOND-HIGHEST ORDER OF ANGELS--
--WHO SIDED WITH THE OLD ONE DURING THE WAR IN HEAVEN--
--IF YOU BELIEVE ANY OF THAT.
THEY'RE... UH...
...COMING THIS WAY.
OF COURSE THEY ARE, THEO.
WHAT DO YOU THINK IS HAPPENING HERE?

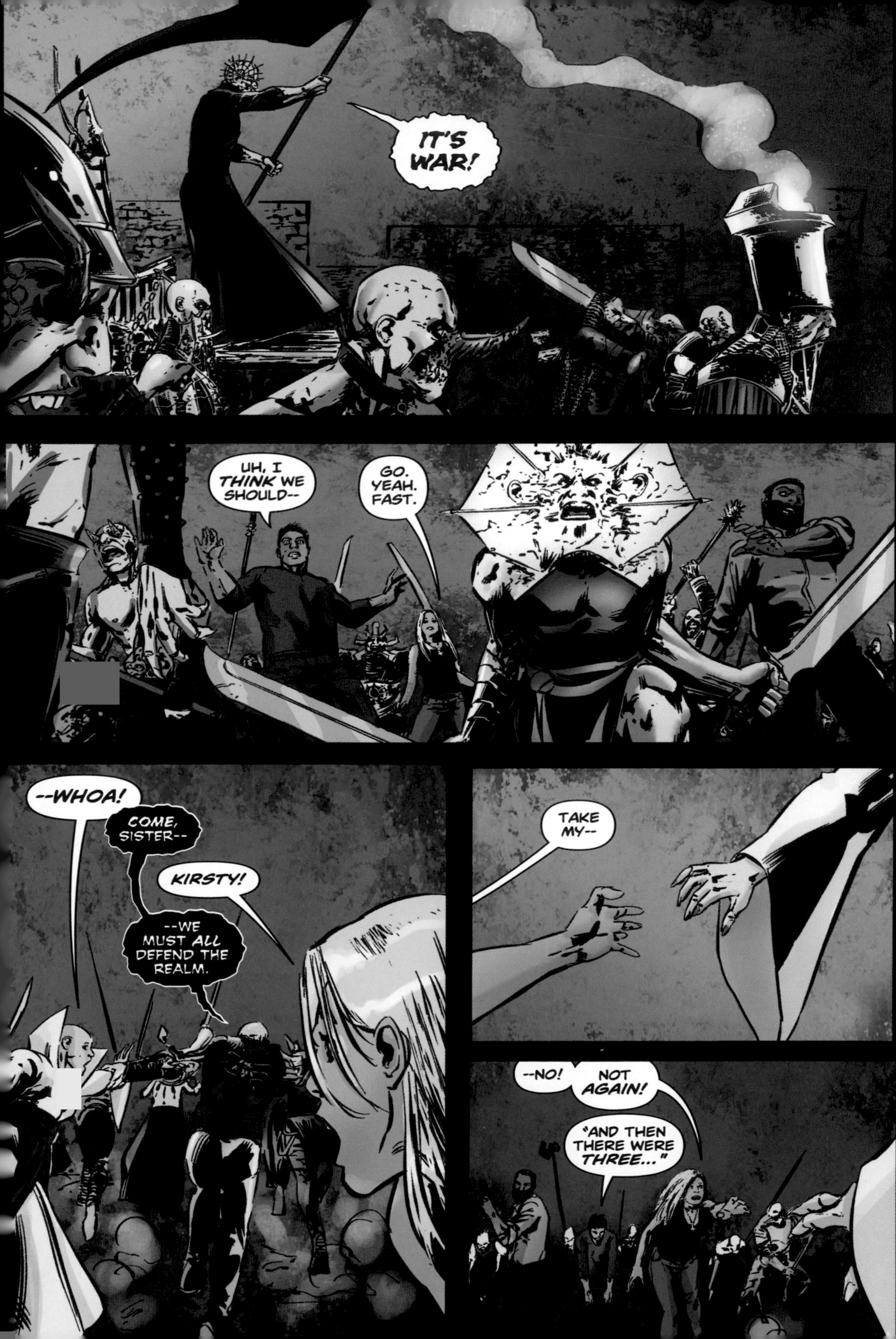
IT'S WAR!
UH, I THINK WE SHOULD--
GO. YEAH. FAST.
--WHOA!
COME, SISTER--
KIRSTY!
--WE MUST ALL DEFEND THE REALM.
TAKE MY--
--NO!
NOT AGAIN!
"AND THEN THERE WERE THREE..."

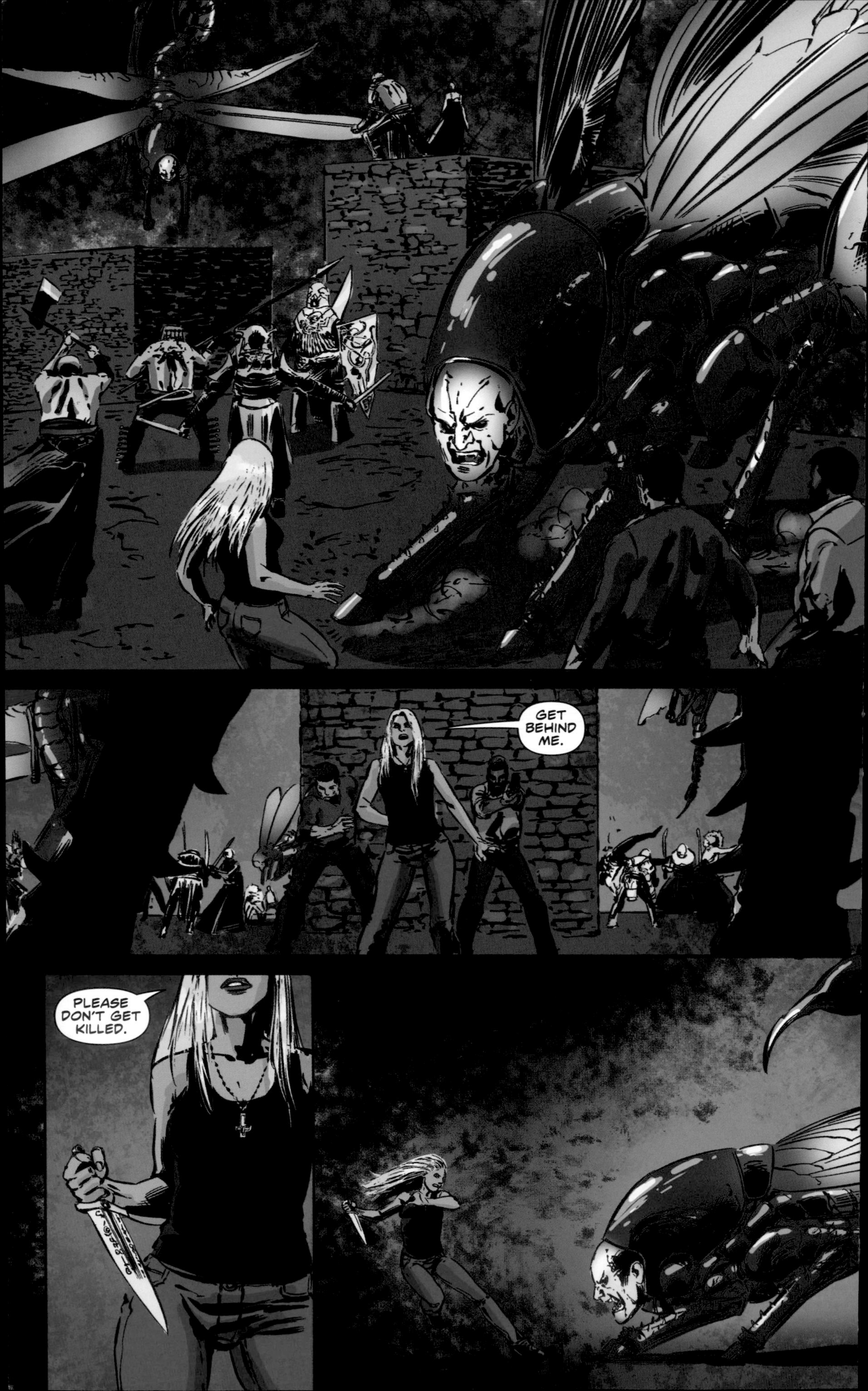
GET BEHIND ME.
PLEASE DON'T GET KILLED.

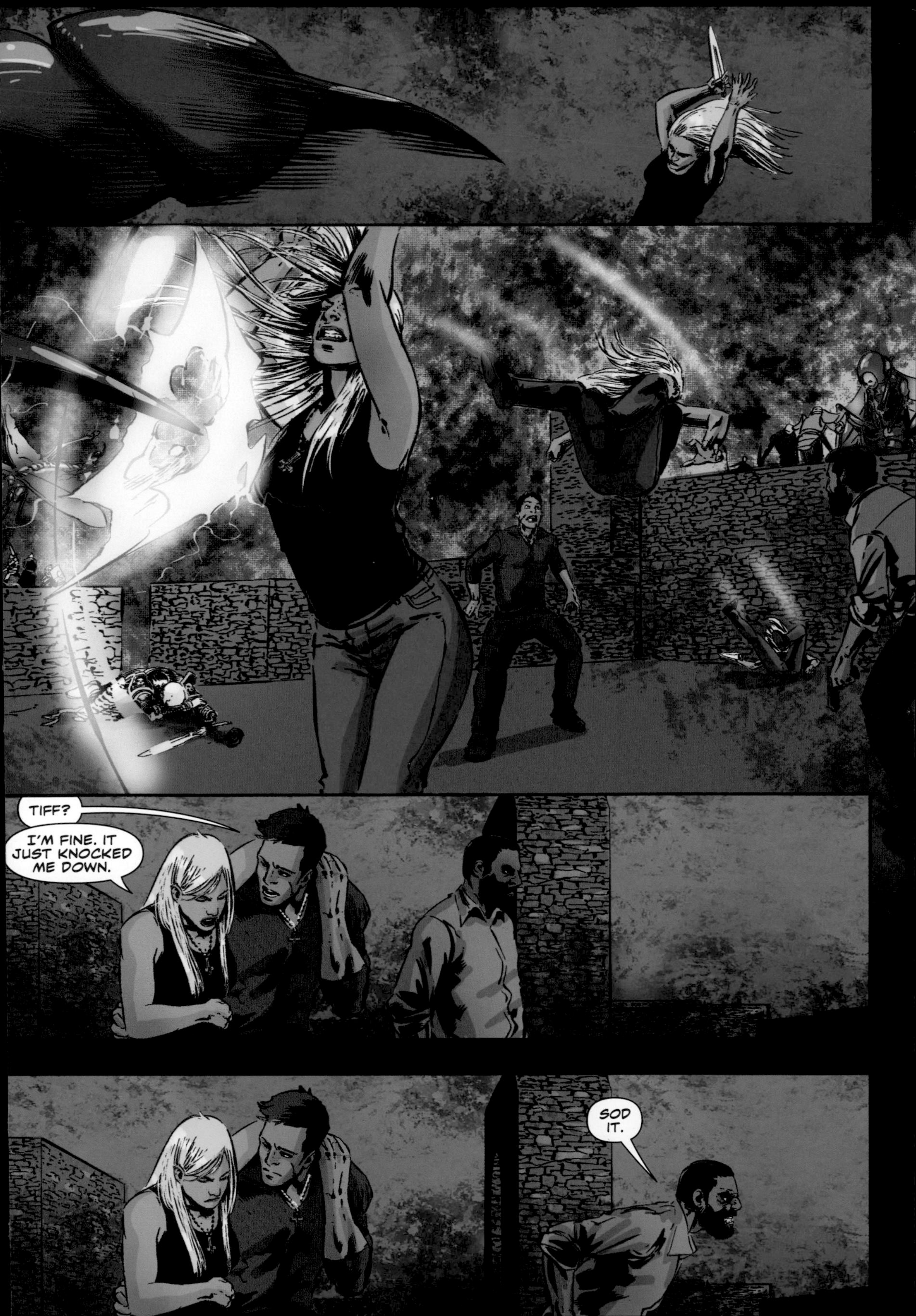
TIFF?
I'M FINE. IT JUST KNOCKED ME DOWN.
SOD IT.

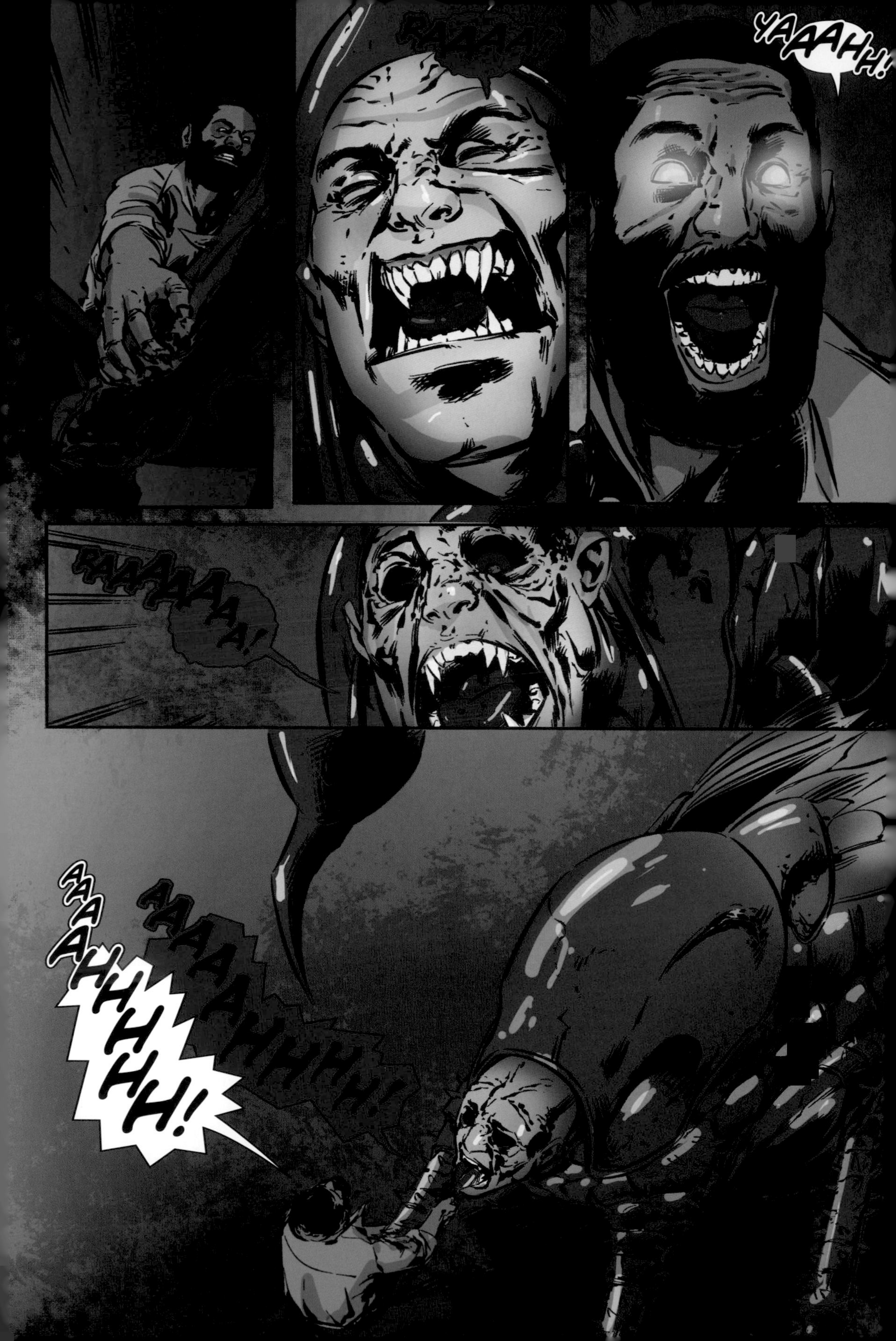
RAAAAA!
YAAAHH!
RAAAAAAAA!
AAAAHHHHHH!
AAAAAAHHHHHH!

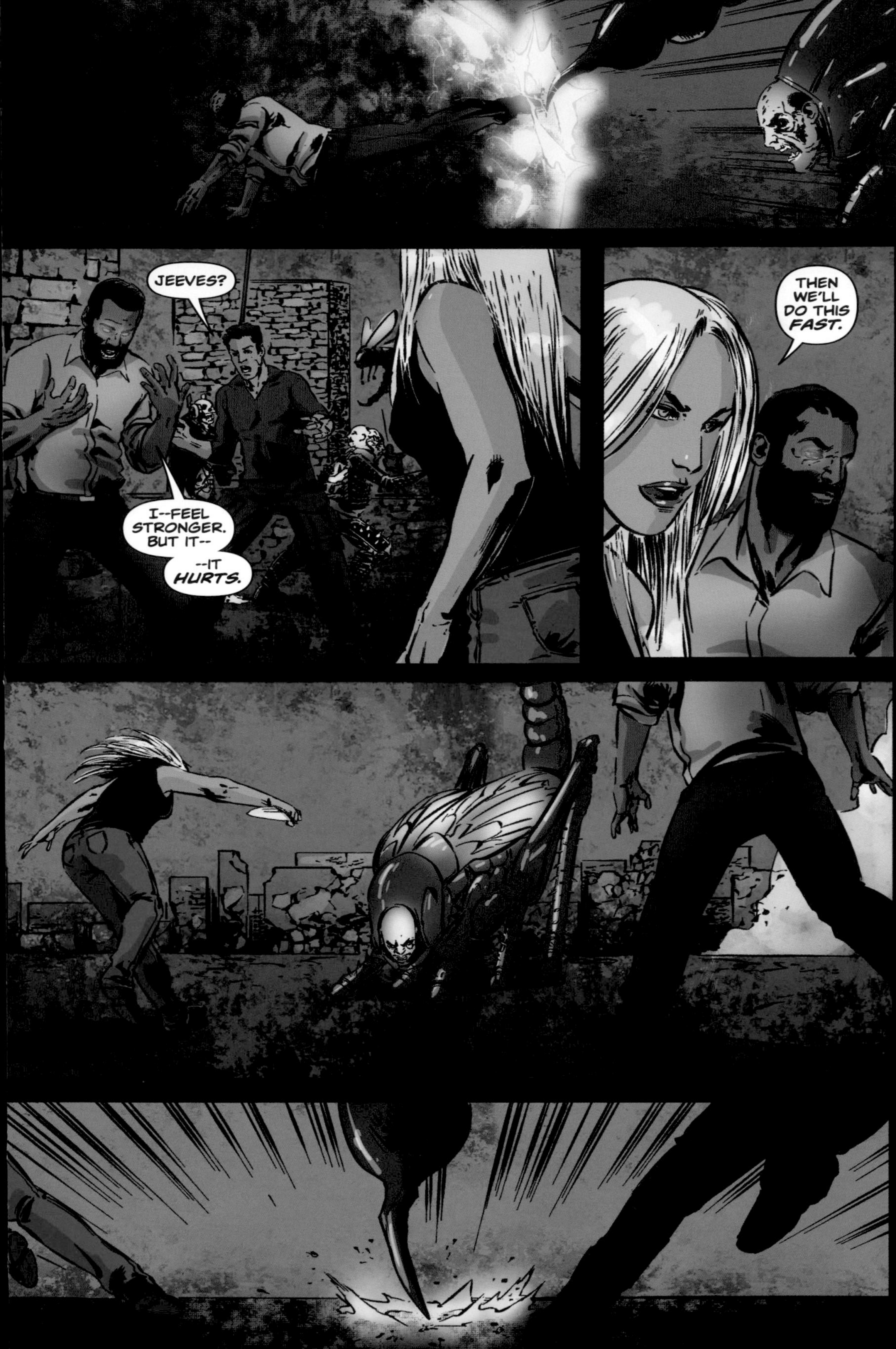
JEEVES?
I--FEEL STRONGER. BUT IT--
--IT HURTS.
THEN WE'LL DO THIS FAST.

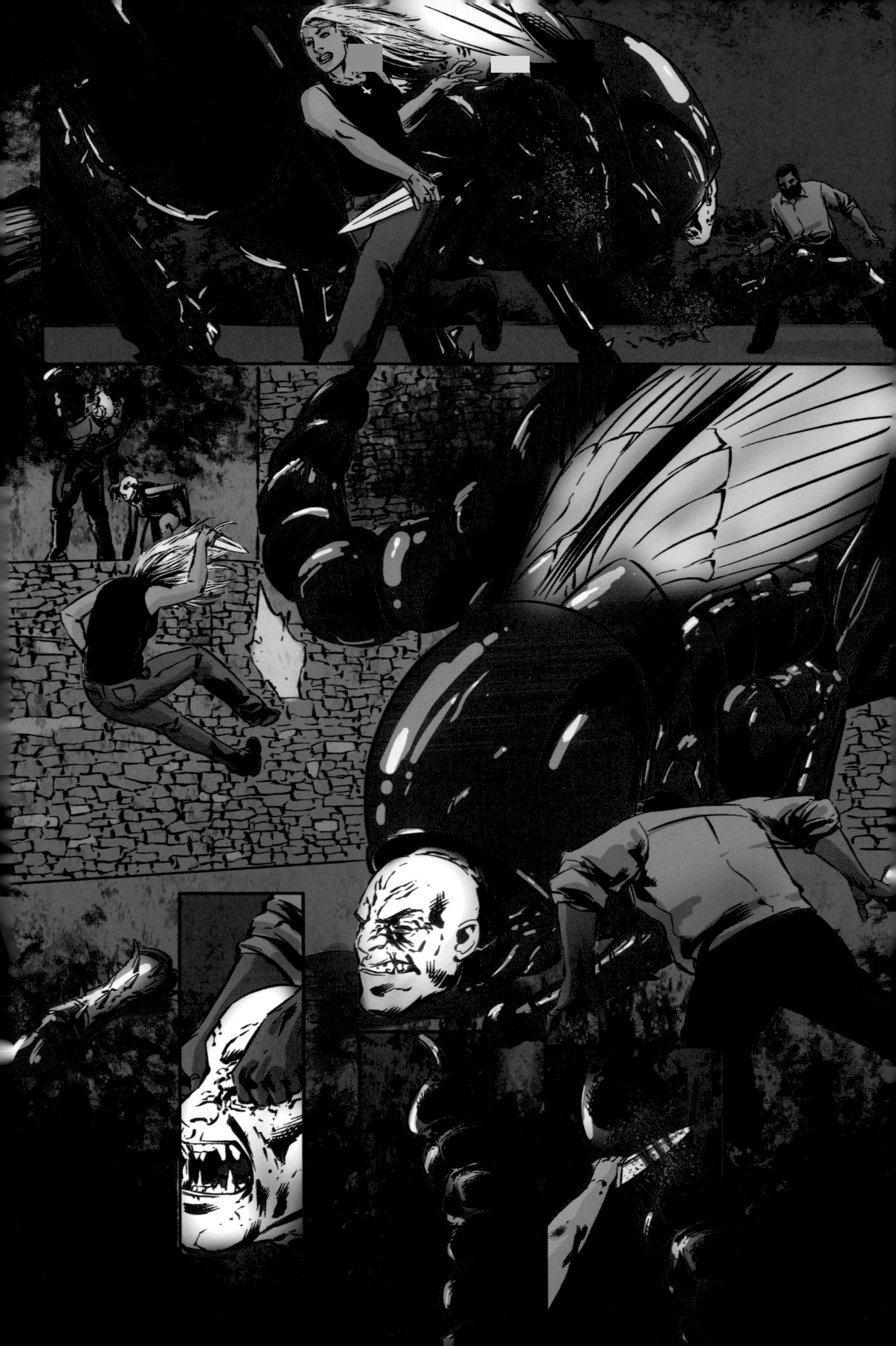

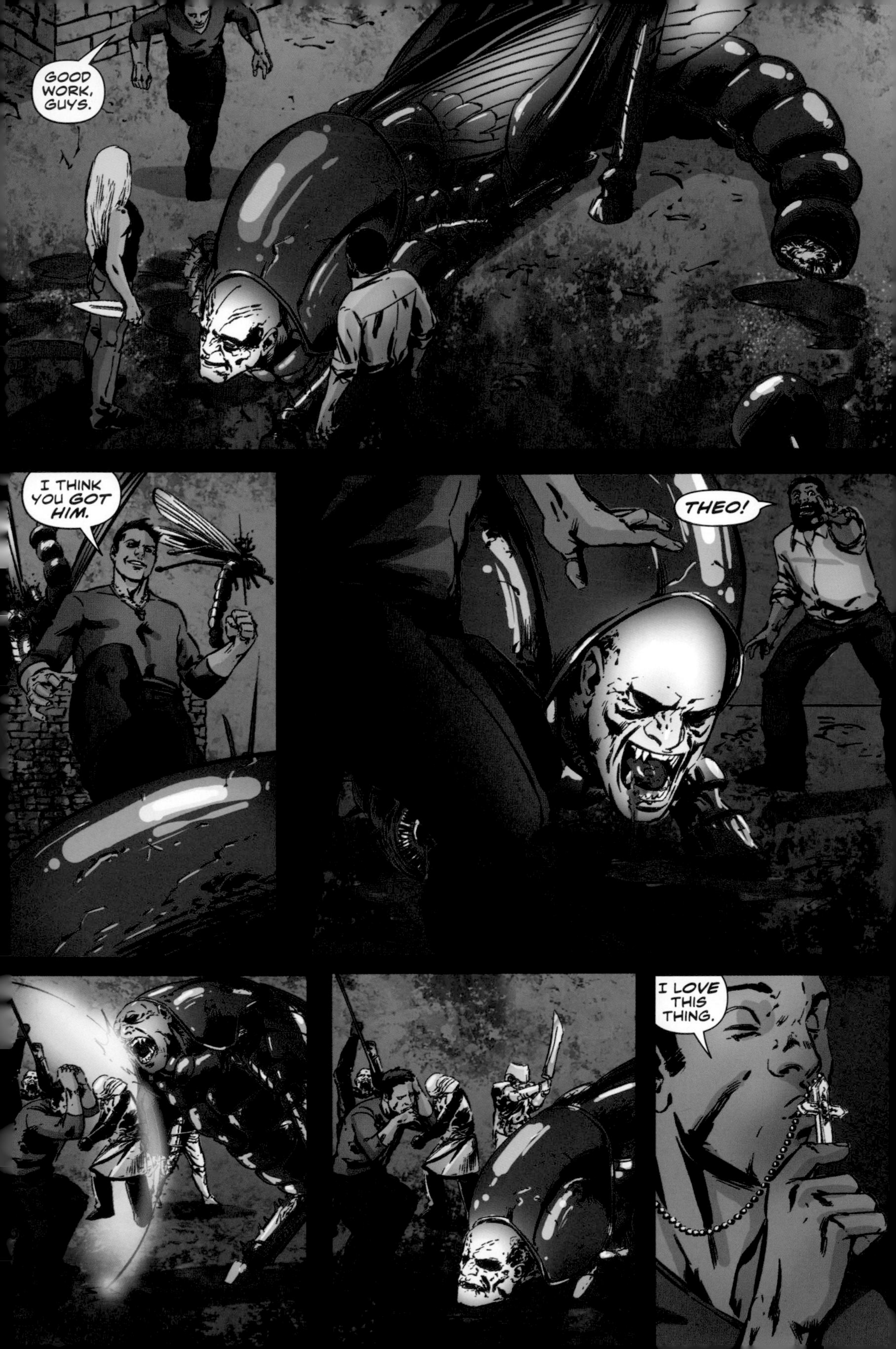
GOOD WORK, GUYS.
I THINK YOU GOT HIM.
THEO!
I LOVE THIS THING.

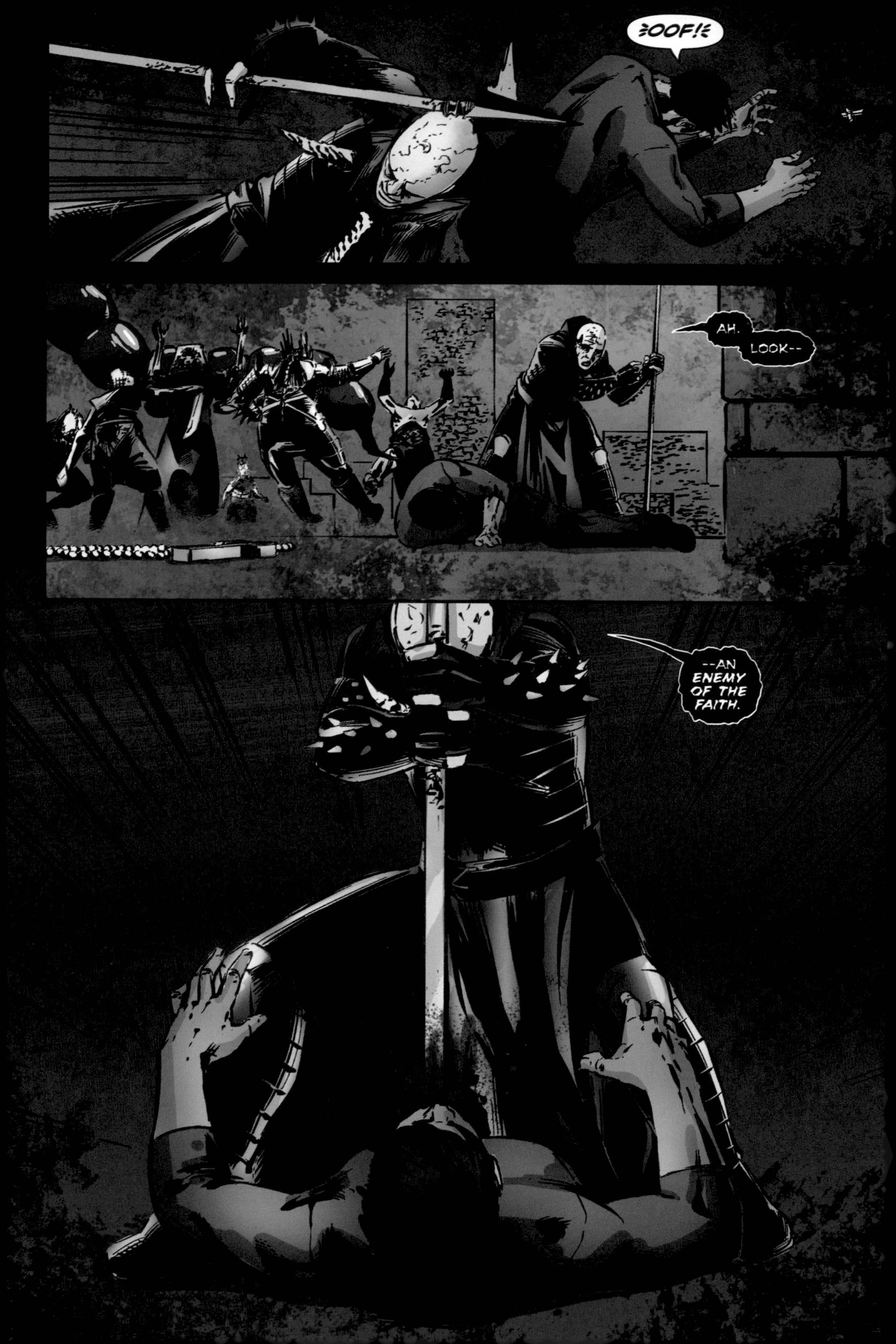
OOF!
AH.
LOOK--
--AN ENEMY OF THE FAITH.

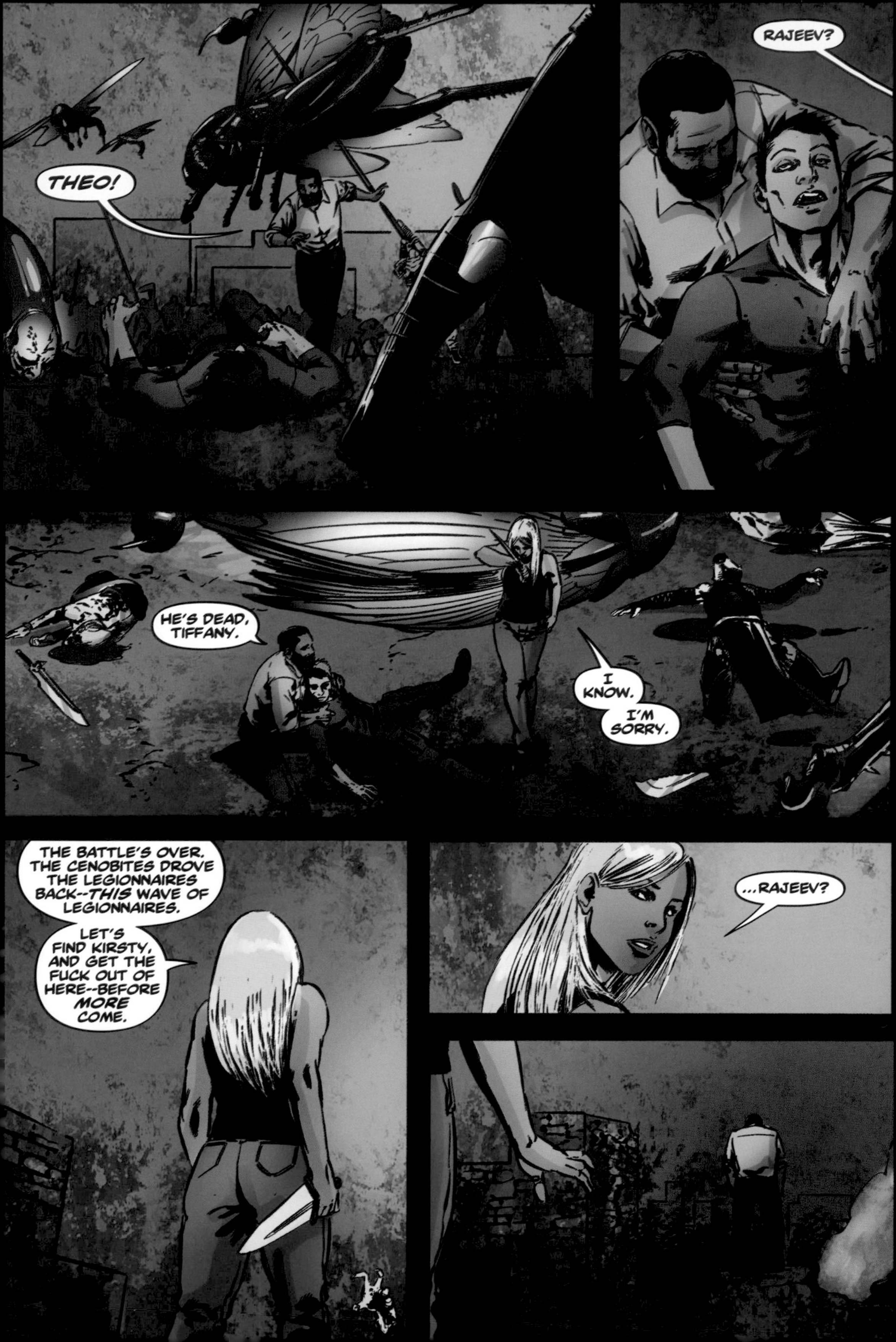
THEO!
RAJEEV?
HE'S DEAD, TIFFANY.
I KNOW. I'M SORRY.
THE BATTLE'S OVER. THE CENOBITES DROVE THE LEGIONNAIRES BACK--THIS WAVE OF LEGIONNAIRES.
LET'S FIND KIRSTY, AND GET THE FUCK OUT OF HERE--BEFORE MORE COME.
...RAJEEV?

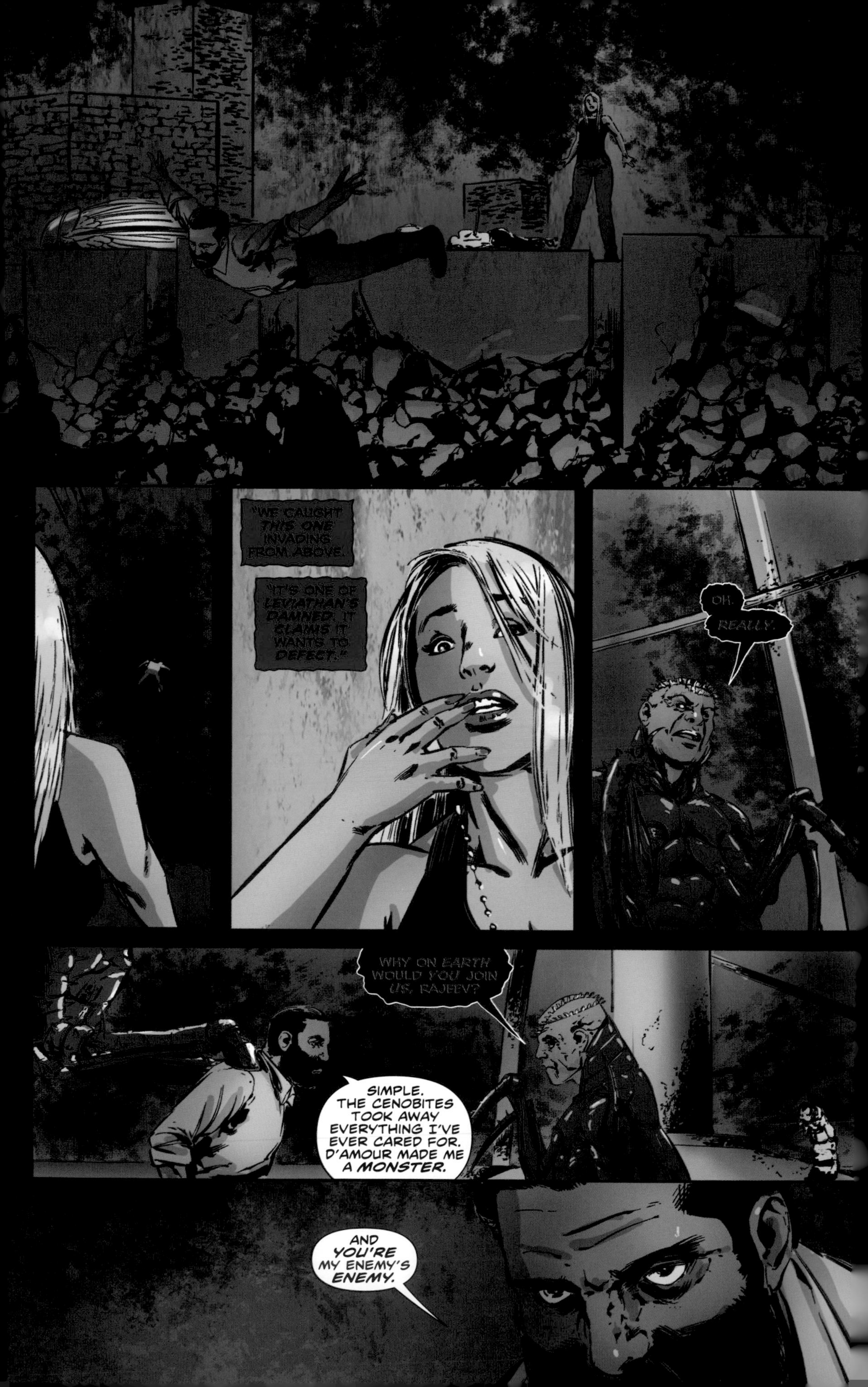
"WE CAUGHT THIS ONE INVADING FROM ABOVE.
"IT'S ONE OF LEVIATHAN'S DAMNED. IT CLAIMS IT WANTS TO DEFECT."
OH. REALLY.
WHY ON EARTH WOULD YOU JOIN US, RAJEEV?
SIMPLE. THE CENOBITES TOOK AWAY EVERYTHING I'VE EVER CARED FOR. D'AMOUR MADE ME A MONSTER.
AND YOU'RE MY ENEMY'S ENEMY.

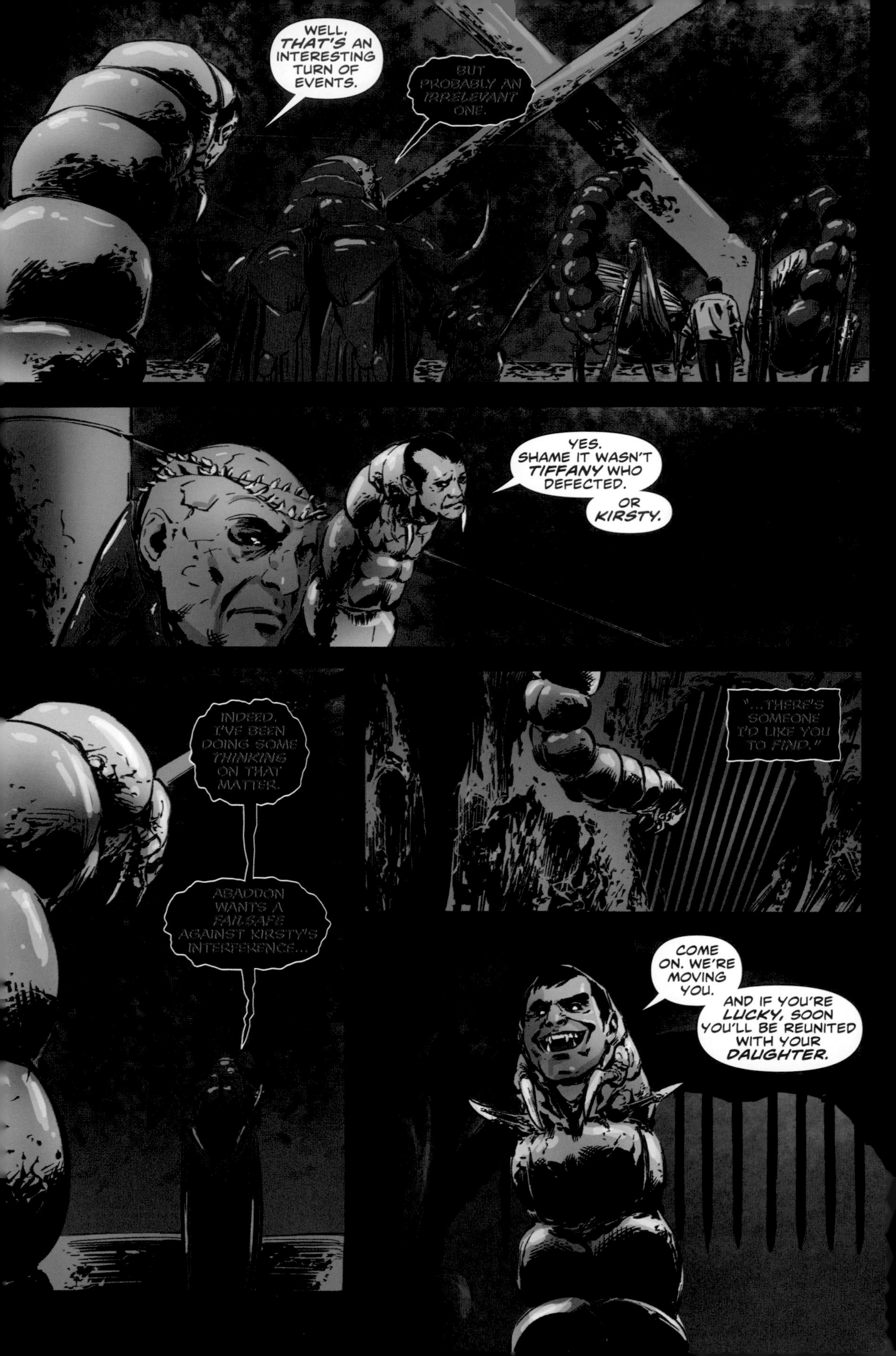
WELL, THAT'S AN INTERESTING TURN OF EVENTS.
BUT PROBABLY AN IRRELEVANT ONE.
YES. SHAME IT WASN'T TIFFANY WHO DEFECTED.
OR KIRSTY.
INDEED. I'VE BEEN DOING SOME THINKING ON THAT MATTER.
ABADDON WANTS A FAILSAFE AGAINST KIRSTY'S INTERFERENCE...
"...THERE'S SOMEONE I'D LIKE YOU TO FIND."
COME ON. WE'RE MOVING YOU.
AND IF YOU'RE LUCKY, SOON YOU'LL BE REUNITED WITH YOUR DAUGHTER.

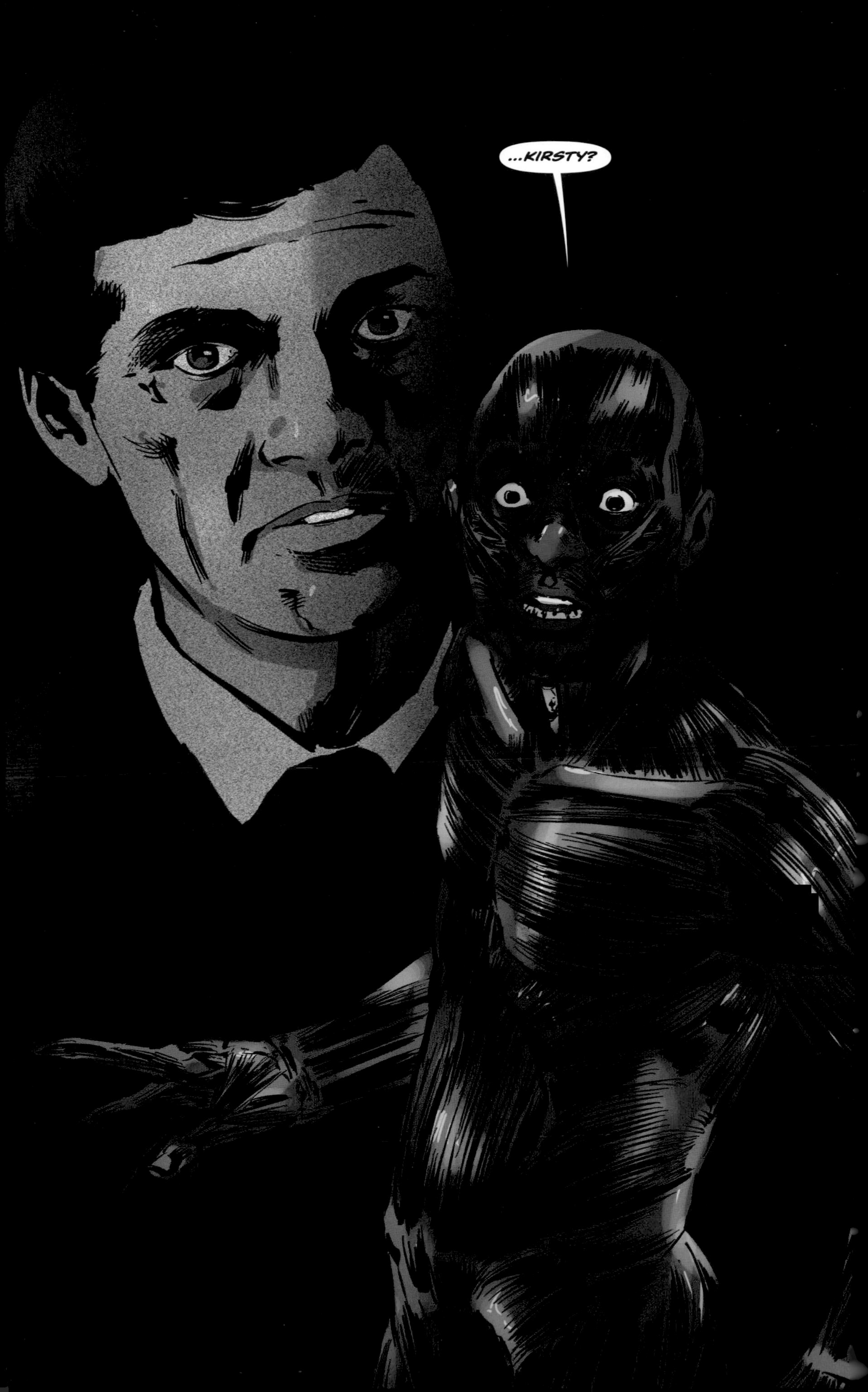
...KIRSTY?

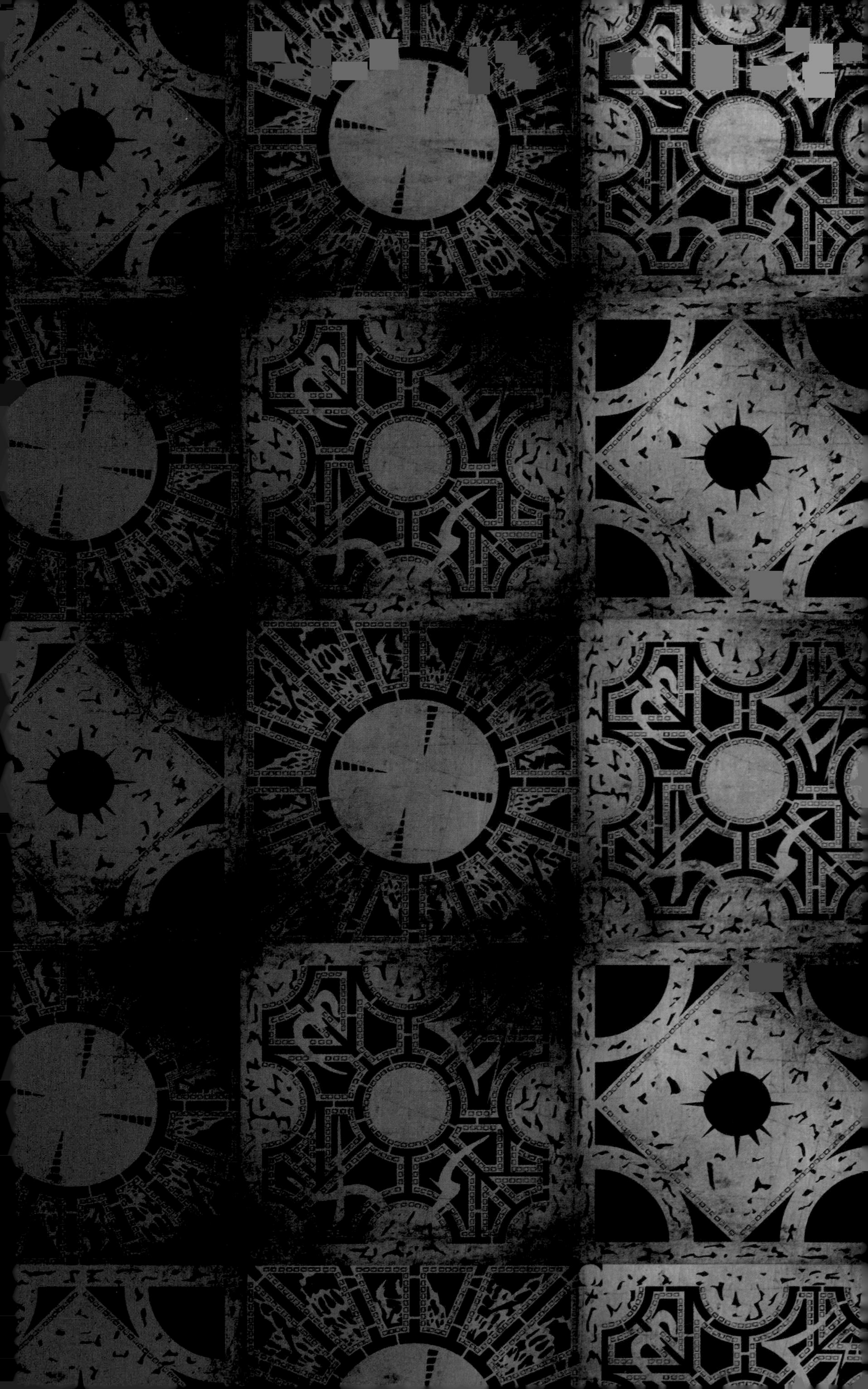

CHAPTER TEN

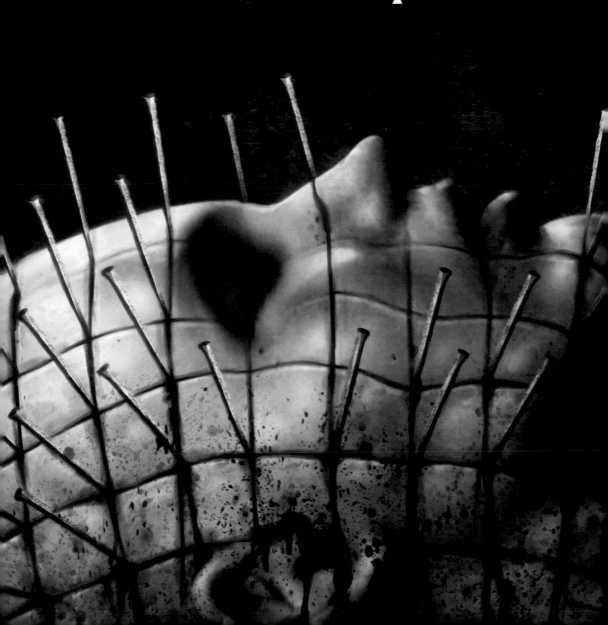

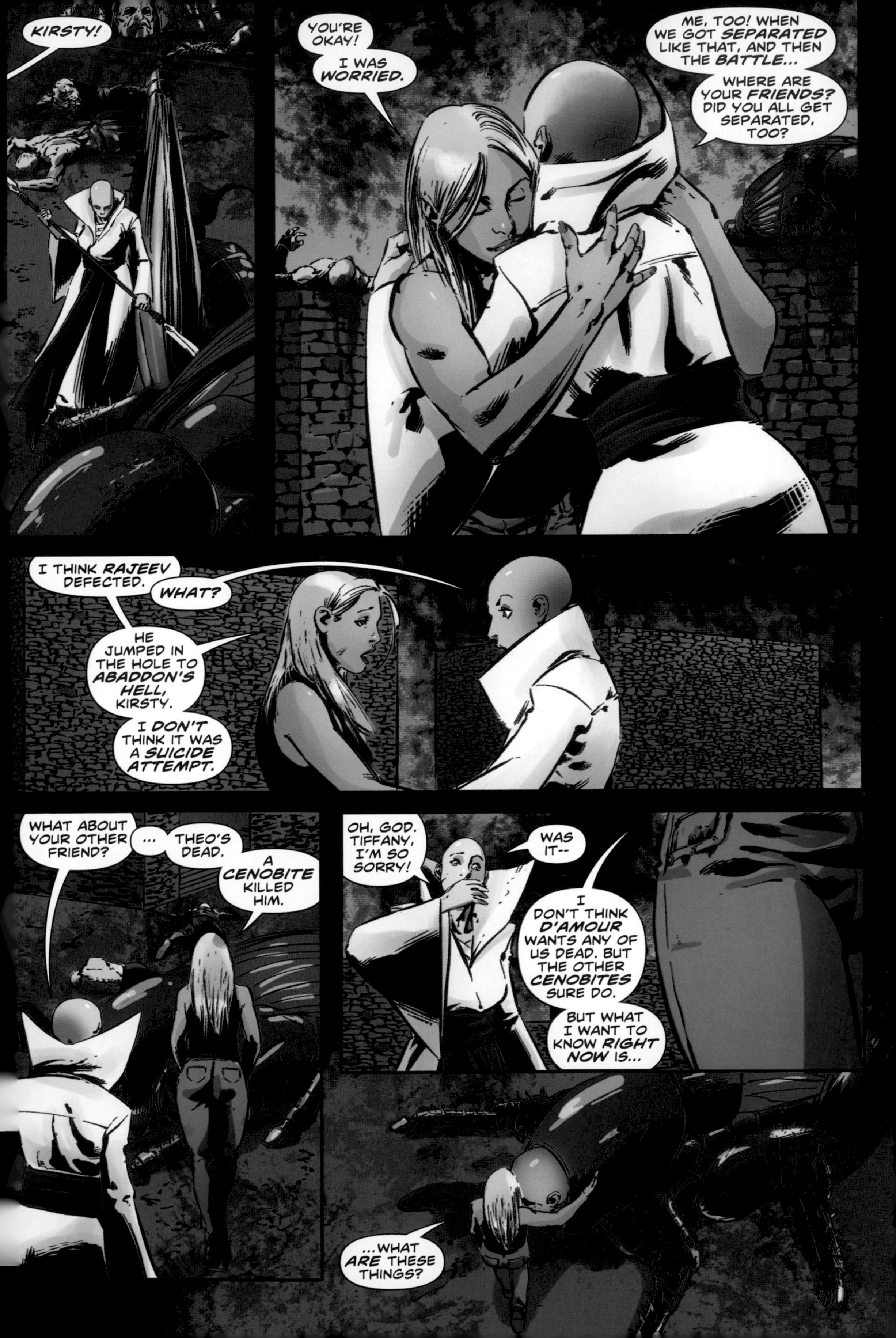

KIRSTY!
YOU'RE OKAY!
I WAS WORRIED.
ME, TOO! WHEN WE GOT SEPARATED LIKE THAT, AND THEN THE BATTLE...
WHERE ARE YOUR FRIENDS? DID YOU ALL GET SEPARATED, TOO?
I THINK RAJEEV DEFECTED.
WHAT?
HE JUMPED IN THE HOLE TO ABADDON'S HELL, KIRSTY.
I DON'T THINK IT WAS A SUICIDE ATTEMPT.
WHAT ABOUT YOUR OTHER FRIEND?
...
THEO'S DEAD.
A CENOBITE KILLED HIM.
OH, GOD. TIFFANY, I'M SO SORRY!
WAS IT--
I DON'T THINK D'AMOUR WANTS ANY OF US DEAD. BUT THE OTHER CENOBITES SURE DO.
BUT WHAT I WANT TO KNOW RIGHT NOW IS...
...WHAT ARE THESE THINGS?

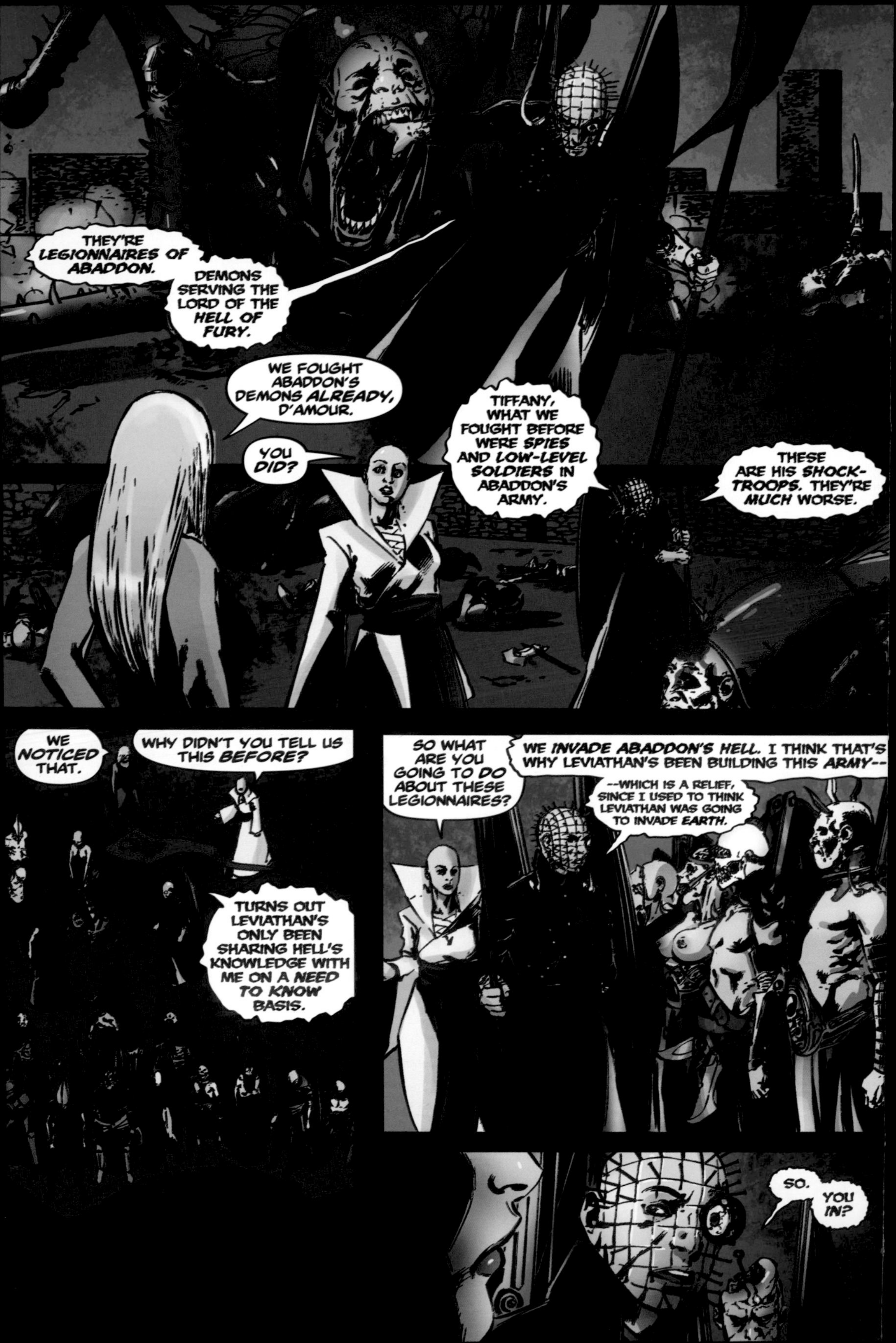
THEY'RE LEGIONNAIRES OF ABADDON.
DEMONS SERVING THE LORD OF THE HELL OF FURY.
WE FOUGHT ABADDON'S DEMONS ALREADY, D'AMOUR.
YOU DID?
TIFFANY, WHAT WE FOUGHT BEFORE WERE SPIES AND LOW-LEVEL SOLDIERS IN ABADDON'S ARMY.
THESE ARE HIS SHOCK-TROOPS. THEY'RE MUCH WORSE.
WE NOTICED THAT.
WHY DIDN'T YOU TELL US THIS BEFORE?
TURNS OUT LEVIATHAN'S ONLY BEEN SHARING HELL'S KNOWLEDGE WITH ME ON A NEED TO KNOW BASIS.
SO WHAT ARE YOU GOING TO DO ABOUT THESE LEGIONNAIRES?
WE INVADE ABADDON'S HELL. I THINK THAT'S WHY LEVIATHAN'S BEEN BUILDING THIS ARMY--
--WHICH IS A RELIEF, SINCE I USED TO THINK LEVIATHAN WAS GOING TO INVADE EARTH.
SO. YOU IN?

...UH...

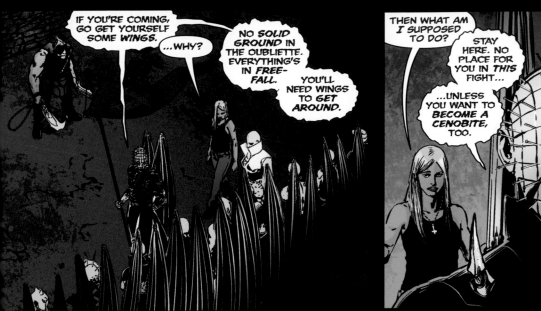

IF YOU'RE COMING, GO GET YOURSELF SOME *WINGS*.

...WHY?

NO *SOLID GROUND* IN THE OUBLIETTE. EVERYTHING'S IN *FREE-FALL*. YOU'LL NEED WINGS TO *GET AROUND*.

THEN WHAT AM *I* SUPPOSED TO DO?

STAY *HERE*. NO PLACE FOR YOU IN *THIS* FIGHT...

...UNLESS YOU WANT TO *BECOME A CENOBITE*, TOO.

UH, UH.

JESUS, D'AMOUR.

DON'T *LYNCH* ME FOR BEING PRACTICAL.

TIFFANY, YOU'RE IN THE MIDDLE OF THE *DEMON WAR*. ALL BEING HUMAN GETS YOU ON A BATTLEFIELD IN HELL IS *KILLED*.

WE GO IN *TEN MINUTES*. WHATEVER YOU'RE DOING--

--BETTER DO IT *FAST*.

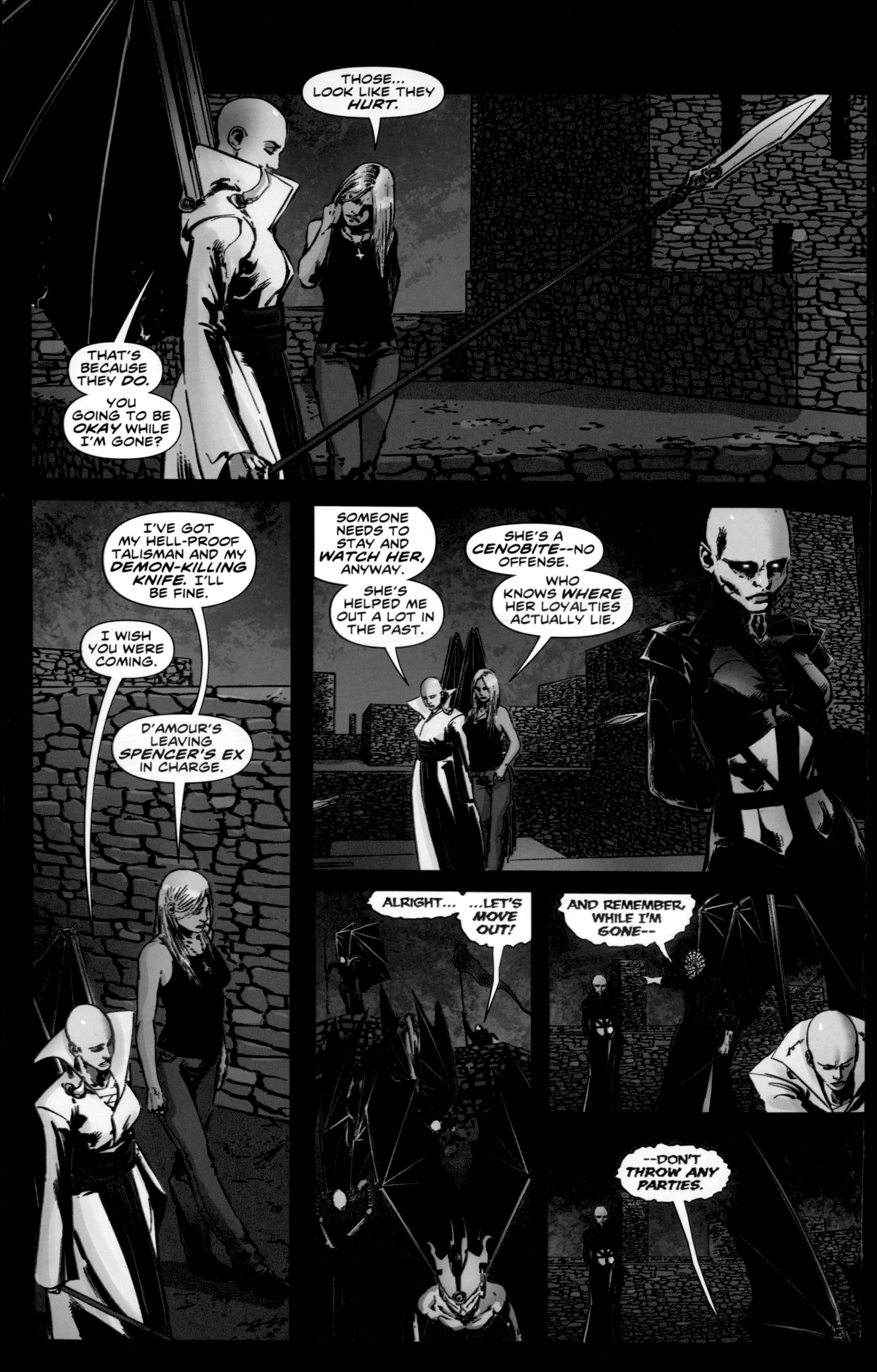
THOSE... LOOK LIKE THEY *HURT*.
THAT'S BECAUSE THEY *DO*.
YOU GOING TO BE *OKAY* WHILE I'M GONE?
I'VE GOT MY HELL-PROOF TALISMAN AND MY ***DEMON-KILLING KNIFE***. I'LL BE FINE.
I WISH YOU WERE COMING.
D'AMOUR'S LEAVING ***SPENCER'S EX*** IN CHARGE.
SOMEONE NEEDS TO STAY AND ***WATCH HER***, ANYWAY.
SHE'S HELPED ME OUT A LOT IN THE PAST.
SHE'S A ***CENOBITE***--NO OFFENSE.
WHO KNOWS ***WHERE*** HER LOYALTIES ACTUALLY LIE.
ALRIGHT...
...LET'S ***MOVE OUT!***
AND REMEMBER, WHILE I'M GONE--
--DON'T ***THROW ANY PARTIES***.

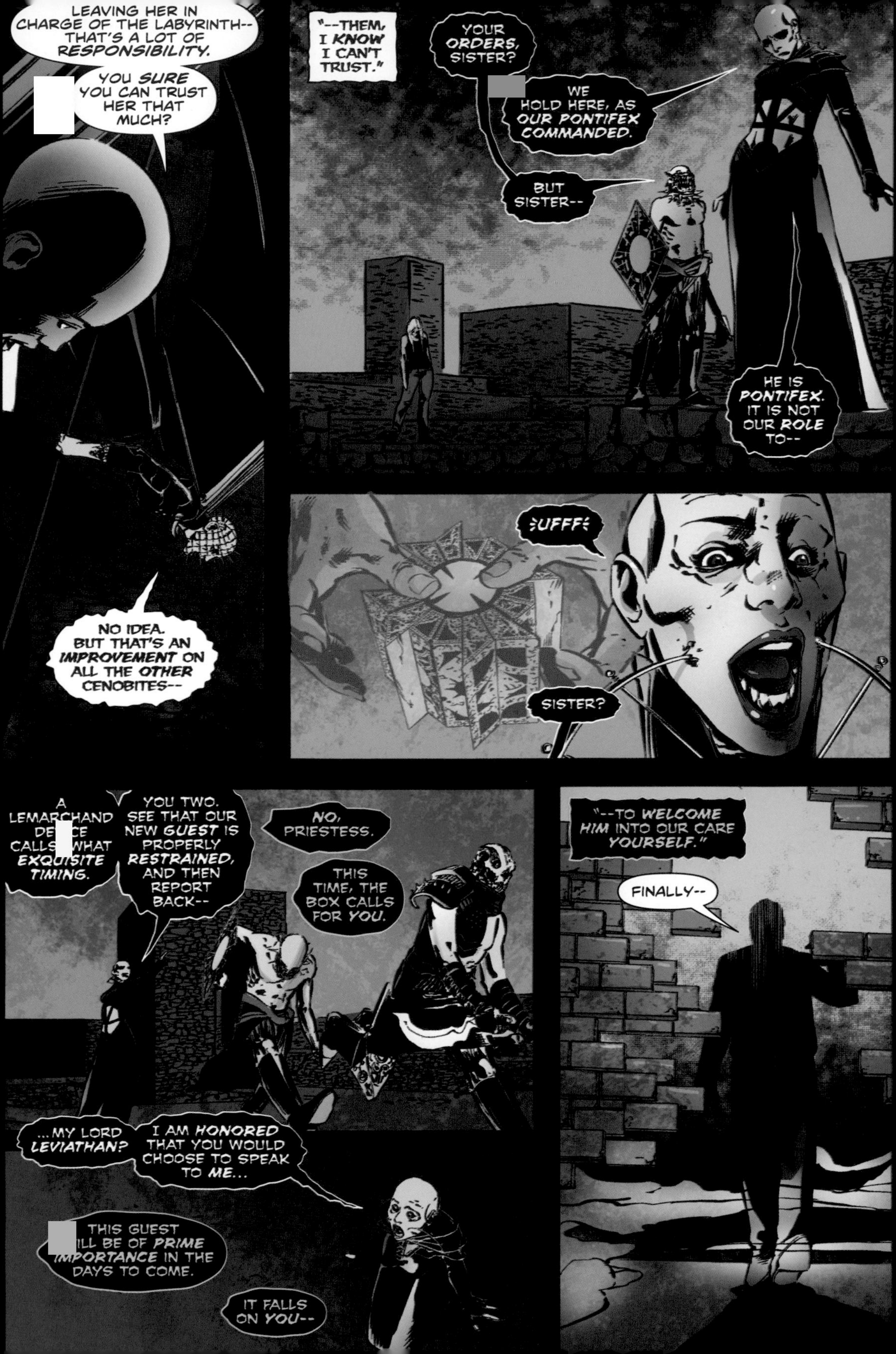
LEAVING HER IN CHARGE OF THE LABYRINTH-- THAT'S A LOT OF RESPONSIBILITY.
YOU SURE YOU CAN TRUST HER THAT MUCH?
NO IDEA. BUT THAT'S AN IMPROVEMENT ON ALL THE OTHER CENOBITES--
"--THEM, I KNOW I CAN'T TRUST."
YOUR ORDERS, SISTER?
WE HOLD HERE, AS OUR PONTIFEX COMMANDED.
BUT SISTER--
HE IS PONTIFEX. IT IS NOT OUR ROLE TO--
UFFF
SISTER?
A LEMARCHAND DE CE CALLS WHAT EXQUISITE TIMING.
YOU TWO. SEE THAT OUR NEW GUEST IS PROPERLY RESTRAINED, AND THEN REPORT BACK--
NO, PRIESTESS.
THIS TIME, THE BOX CALLS FOR YOU.
...MY LORD LEVIATHAN?
I AM HONORED THAT YOU WOULD CHOOSE TO SPEAK TO ME...
THIS GUEST ILL BE OF PRIME IMPORTANCE IN THE DAYS TO COME.
IT FALLS ON YOU--
"--TO WELCOME HIM INTO OUR CARE YOURSELF."
FINALLY--

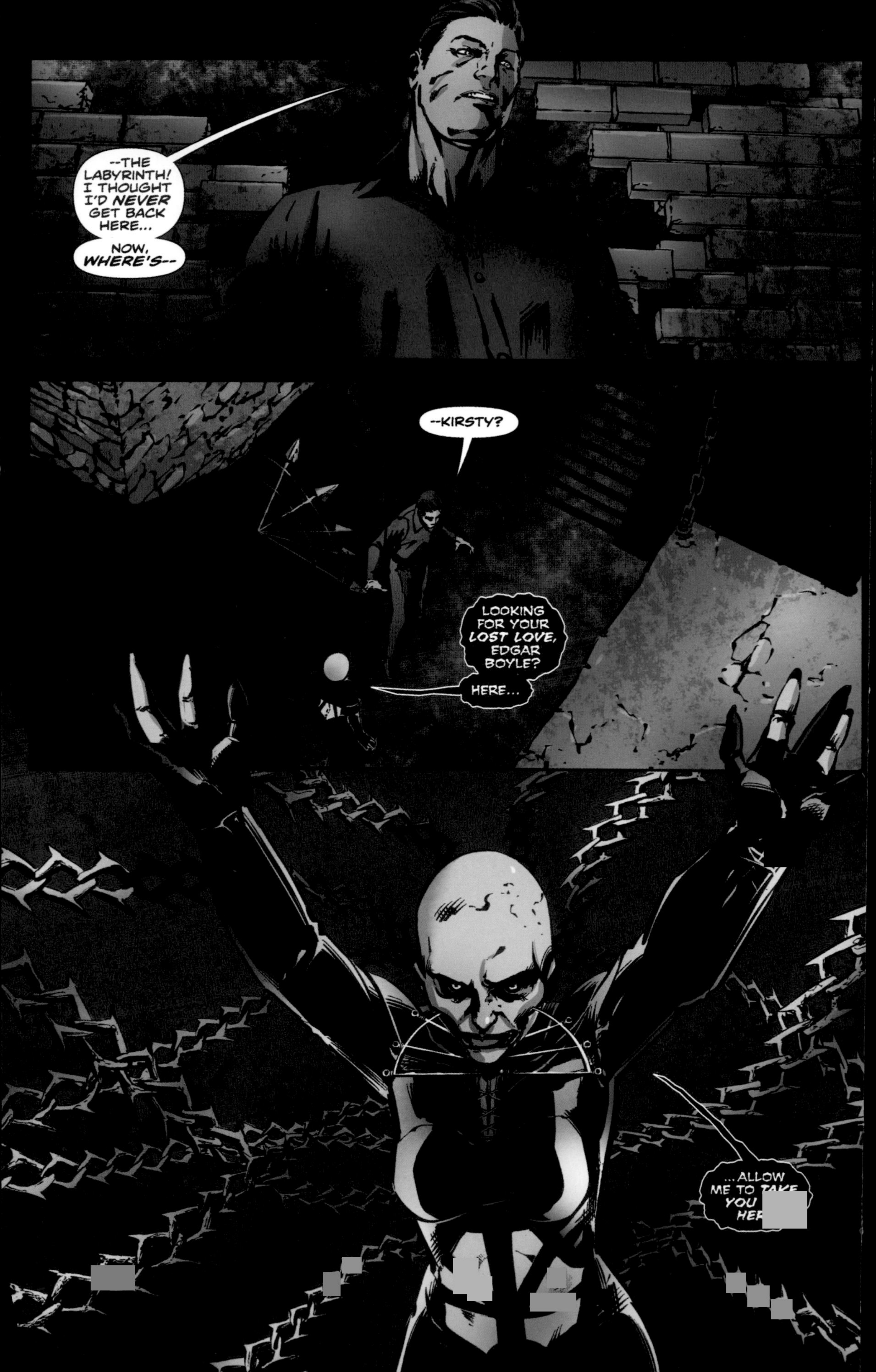
--THE LABYRINTH! I THOUGHT I'D NEVER GET BACK HERE...
NOW, WHERE'S--
--KIRSTY?
LOOKING FOR YOUR LOST LOVE, EDGAR BOYLE?
HERE...
...ALLOW ME TO TAKE YOU

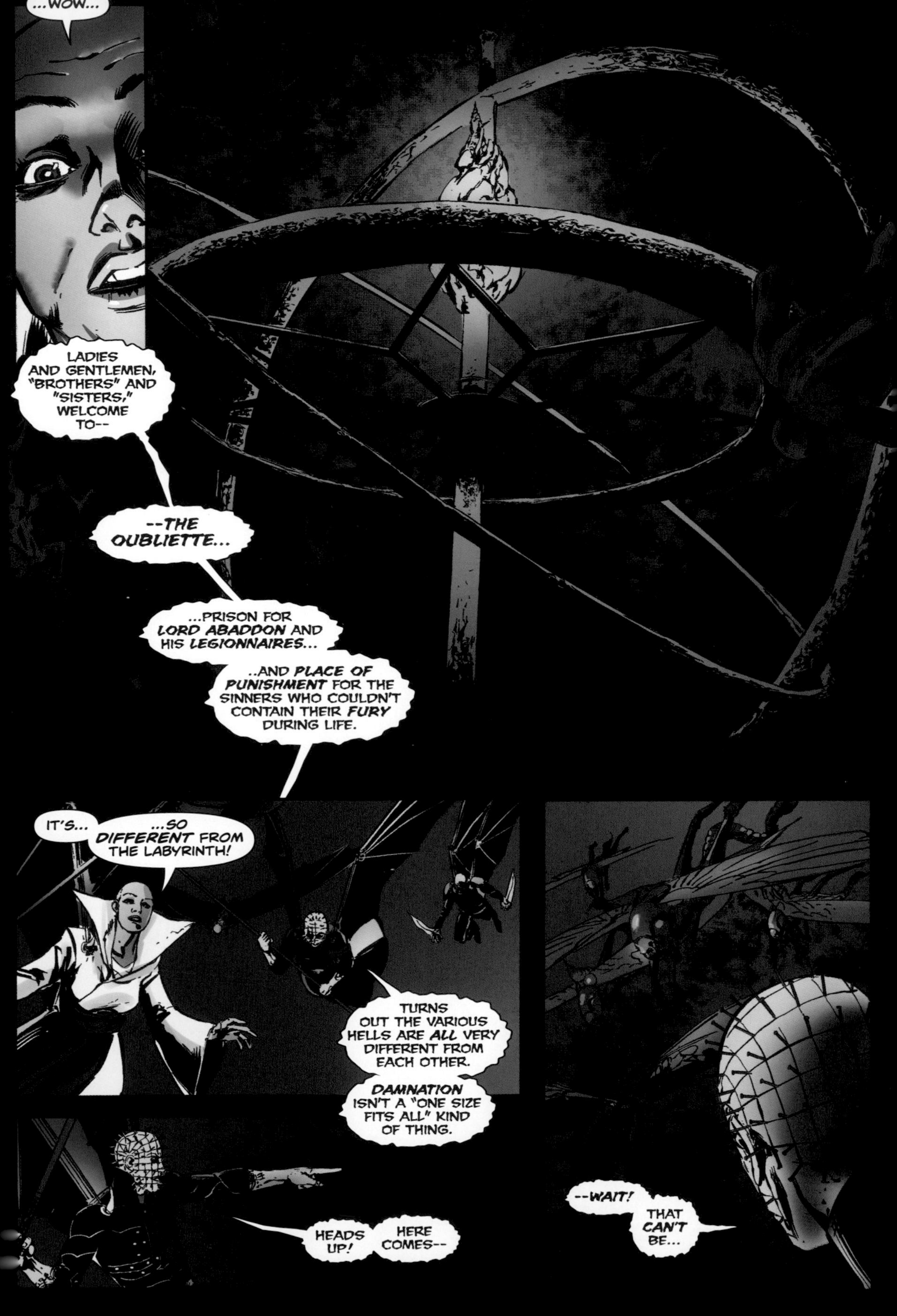
...WOW...
LADIES AND GENTLEMEN, "BROTHERS" AND "SISTERS," WELCOME TO--
--THE OUBLIETTE...
...PRISON FOR LORD ABADDON AND HIS LEGIONNAIRES...
..AND PLACE OF PUNISHMENT FOR THE SINNERS WHO COULDN'T CONTAIN THEIR FURY DURING LIFE.
IT'S...
...SO DIFFERENT FROM THE LABYRINTH!
TURNS OUT THE VARIOUS HELLS ARE ALL VERY DIFFERENT FROM EACH OTHER.
DAMNATION ISN'T A "ONE SIZE FITS ALL" KIND OF THING.
HEADS UP!
HERE COMES--
--WAIT!
THAT CAN'T BE...

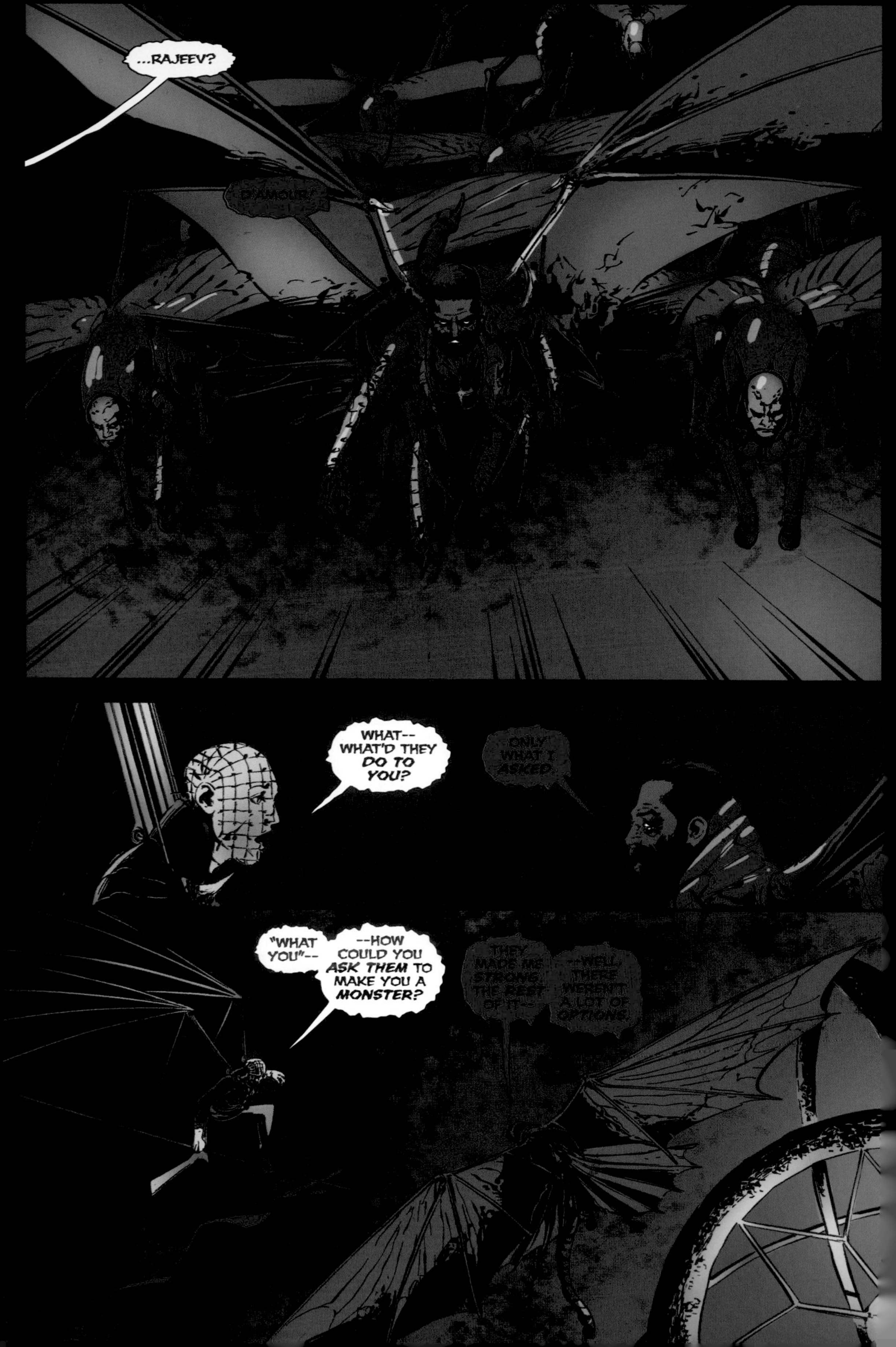
...RAJEEV?
DIAMOUR?
WHAT-- WHAT'D THEY DO TO YOU?
...ONLY WHAT I ASKED.
"WHAT YOU"--
--HOW COULD YOU ASK THEM TO MAKE YOU A MONSTER?
THEY MADE ME STRONG. THE REST OF IT--
--WELL, THERE WEREN'T A LOT OF OPTIONS.

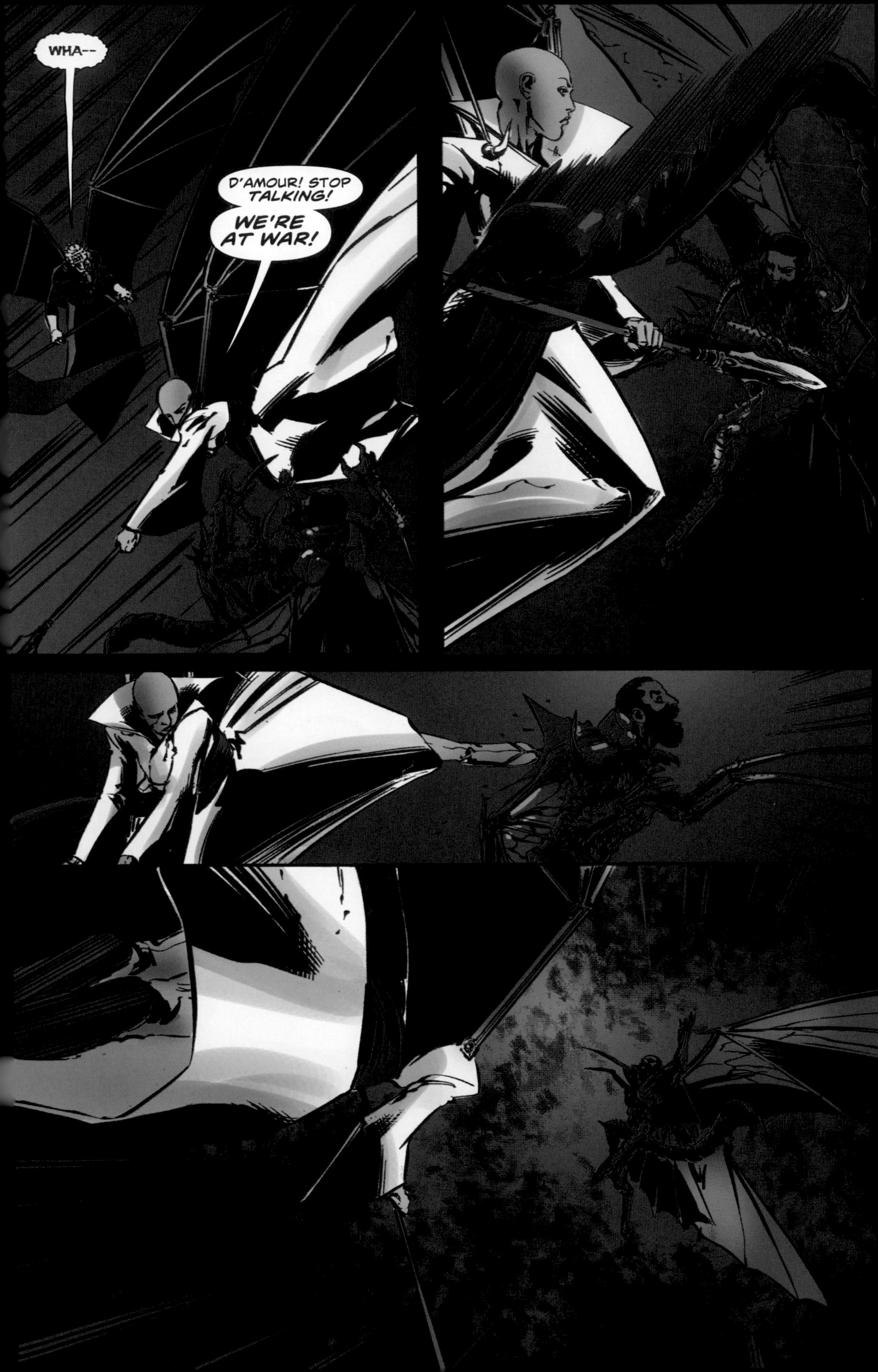
WHA--
D'AMOUR! STOP TALKING!
WE'RE AT WAR!

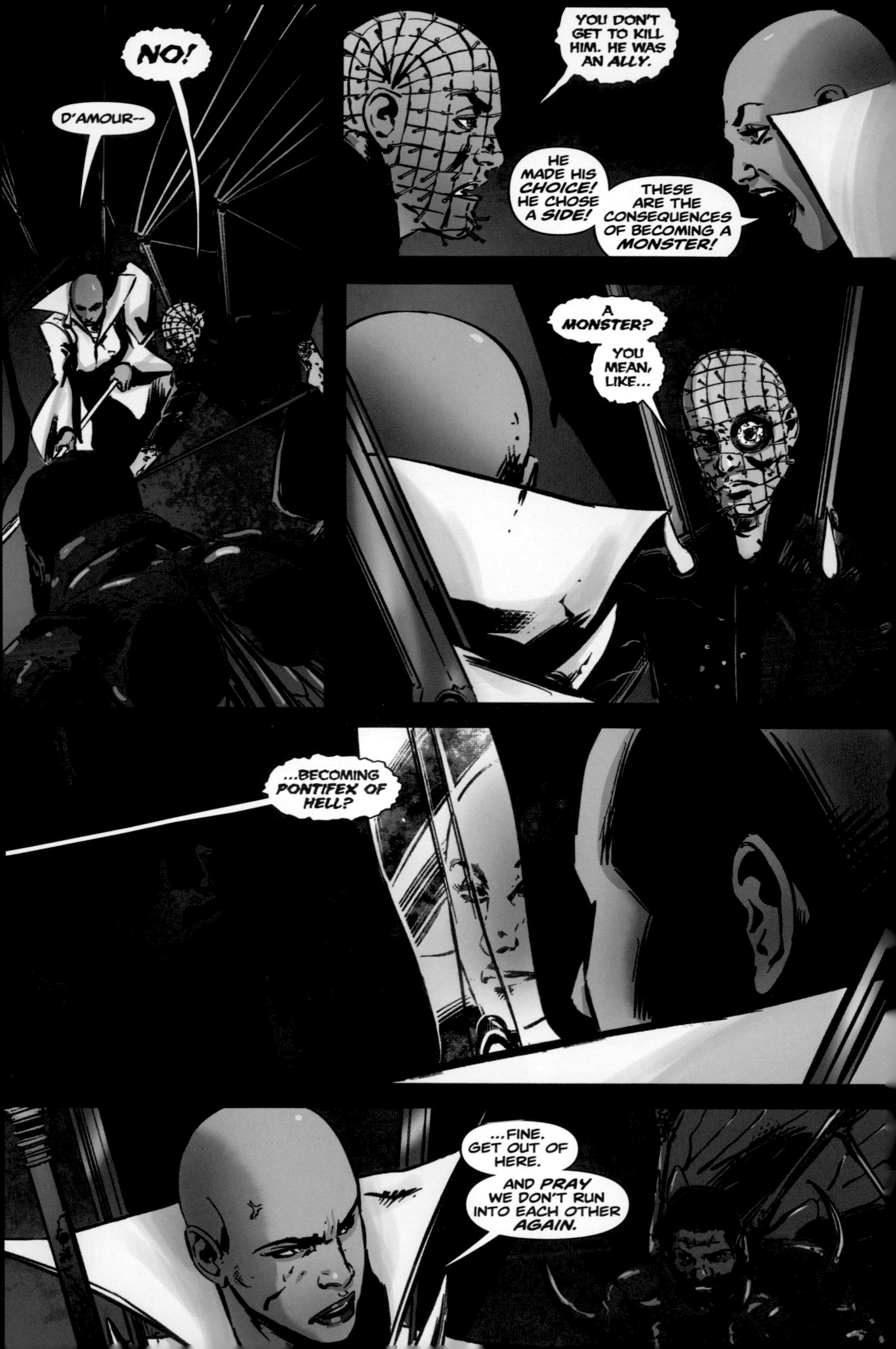
NO!
D'AMOUR--
YOU DON'T GET TO KILL HIM. HE WAS AN *ALLY*.
HE MADE HIS *CHOICE!* HE CHOSE A *SIDE!*
THESE ARE THE CONSEQUENCES OF BECOMING A *MONSTER!*
A *MONSTER?*
YOU MEAN, LIKE...
...BECOMING *PONTIFEX OF HELL?*
...FINE. GET OUT OF HERE.
AND *PRAY* WE DON'T RUN INTO EACH OTHER *AGAIN*.

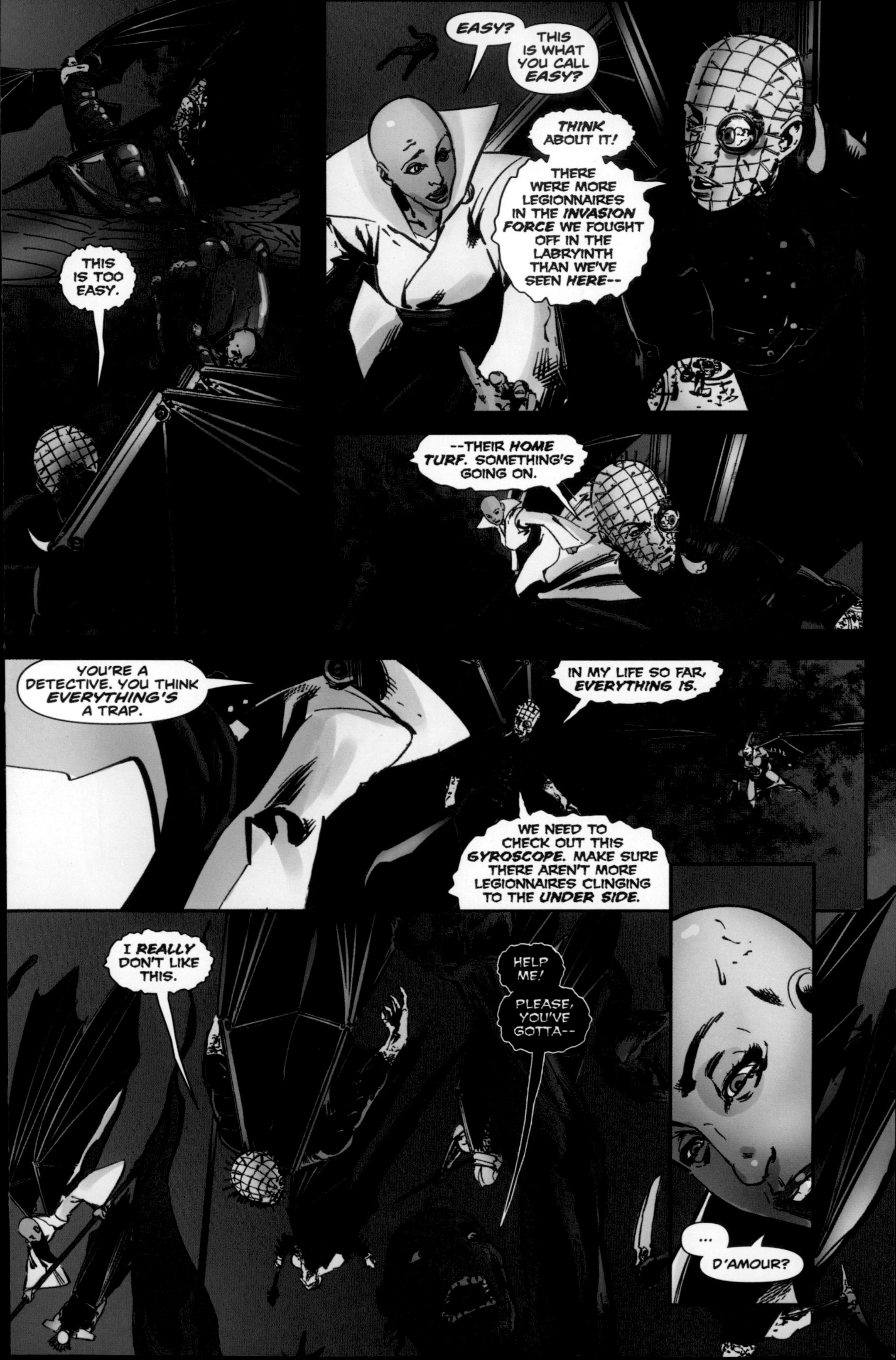
THIS IS TOO EASY.
EASY? THIS IS WHAT YOU CALL EASY?
THINK ABOUT IT!
THERE WERE MORE LEGIONNAIRES IN THE INVASION FORCE WE FOUGHT OFF IN THE LABRYINTH THAN WE'VE SEEN HERE--
--THEIR HOME TURF. SOMETHING'S GOING ON.
YOU'RE A DETECTIVE. YOU THINK EVERYTHING'S A TRAP.
IN MY LIFE SO FAR, EVERYTHING IS.
WE NEED TO CHECK OUT THIS GYROSCOPE. MAKE SURE THERE AREN'T MORE LEGIONNAIRES CLINGING TO THE UNDER SIDE.
I REALLY DON'T LIKE THIS.
HELP ME!
PLEASE, YOU'VE GOTTA--
...
D'AMOUR?

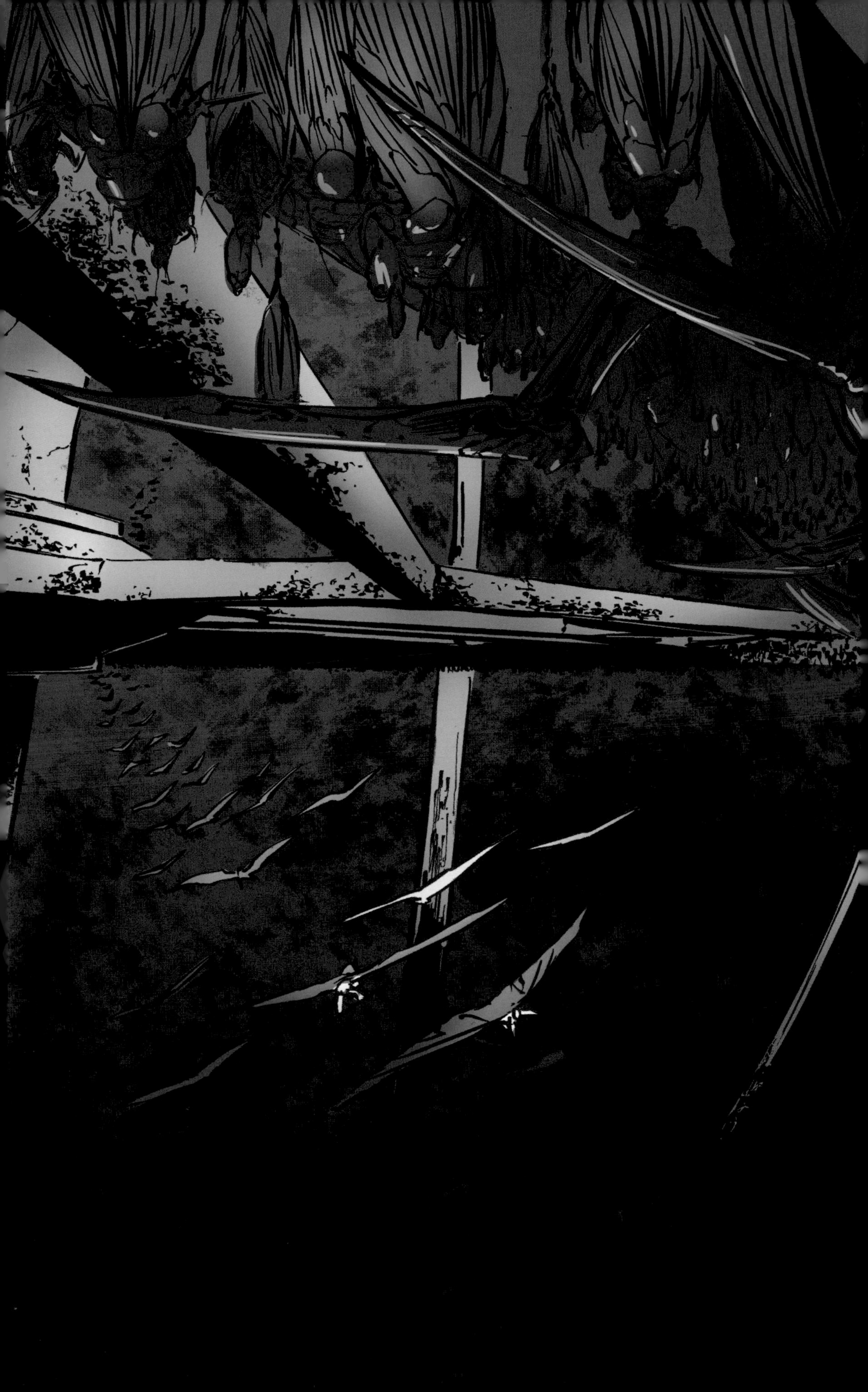

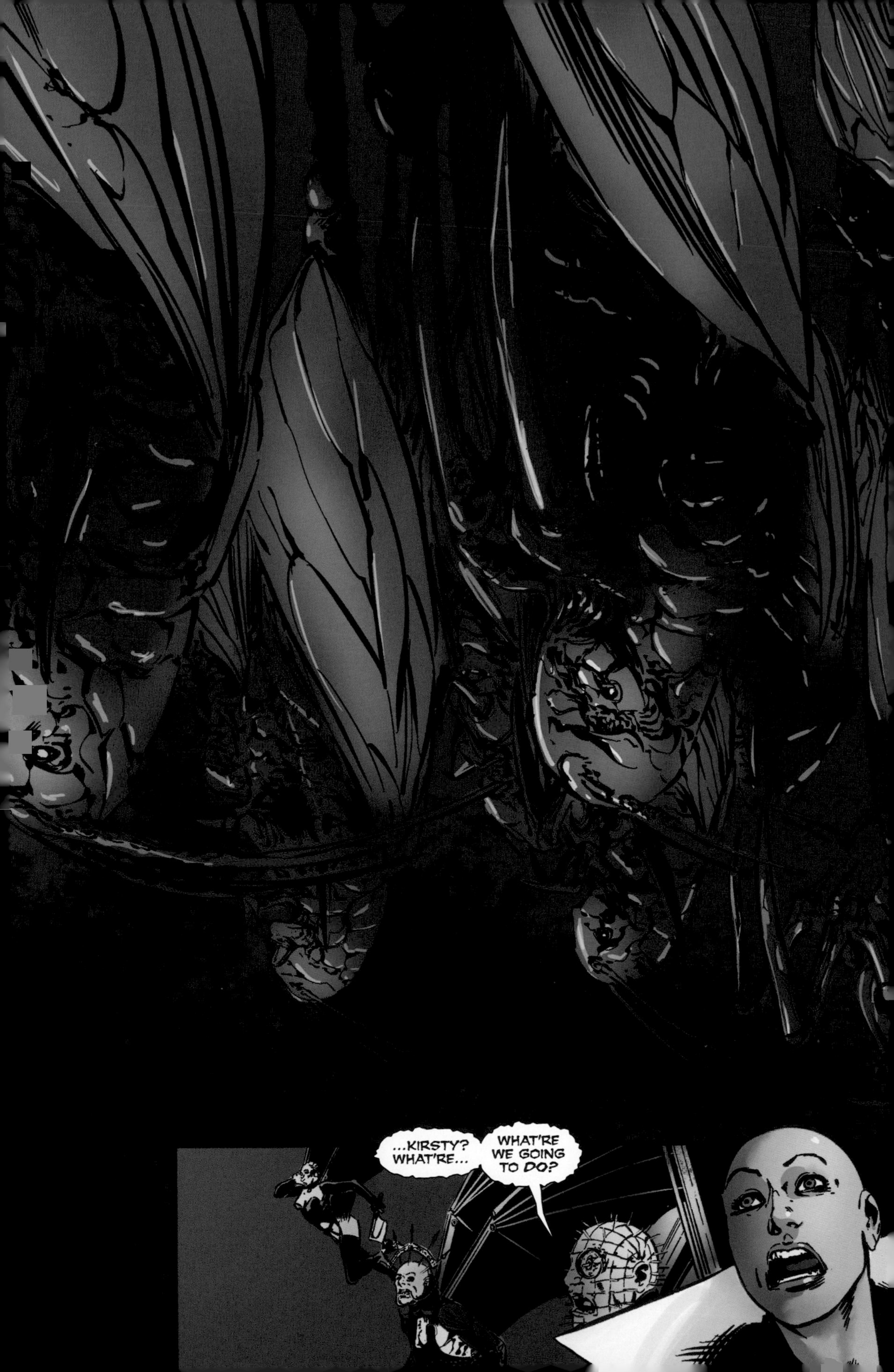
...KIRSTY? WHAT'RE...
WHAT'RE WE GOING TO DO?

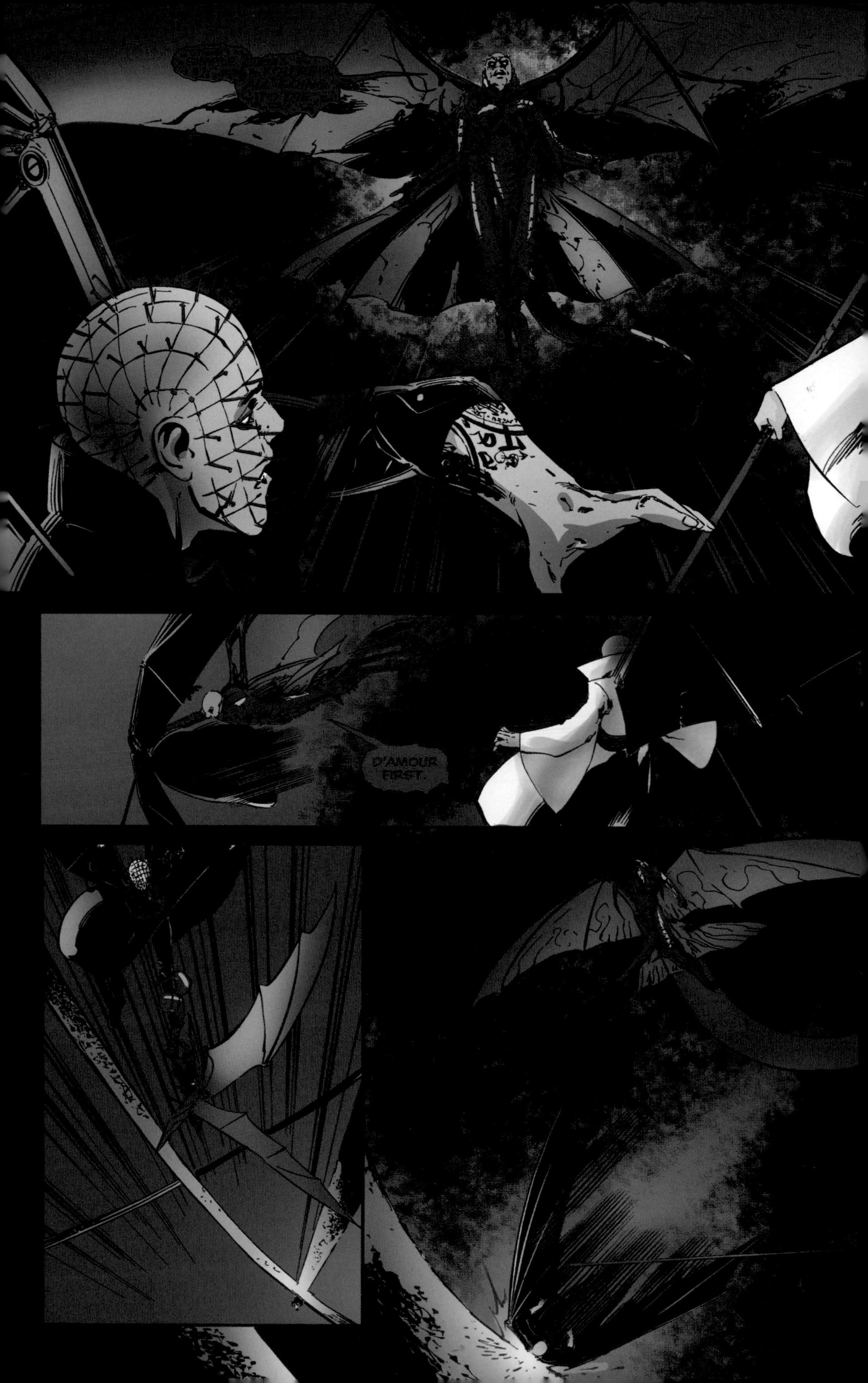
D'AMOUR FIRST.

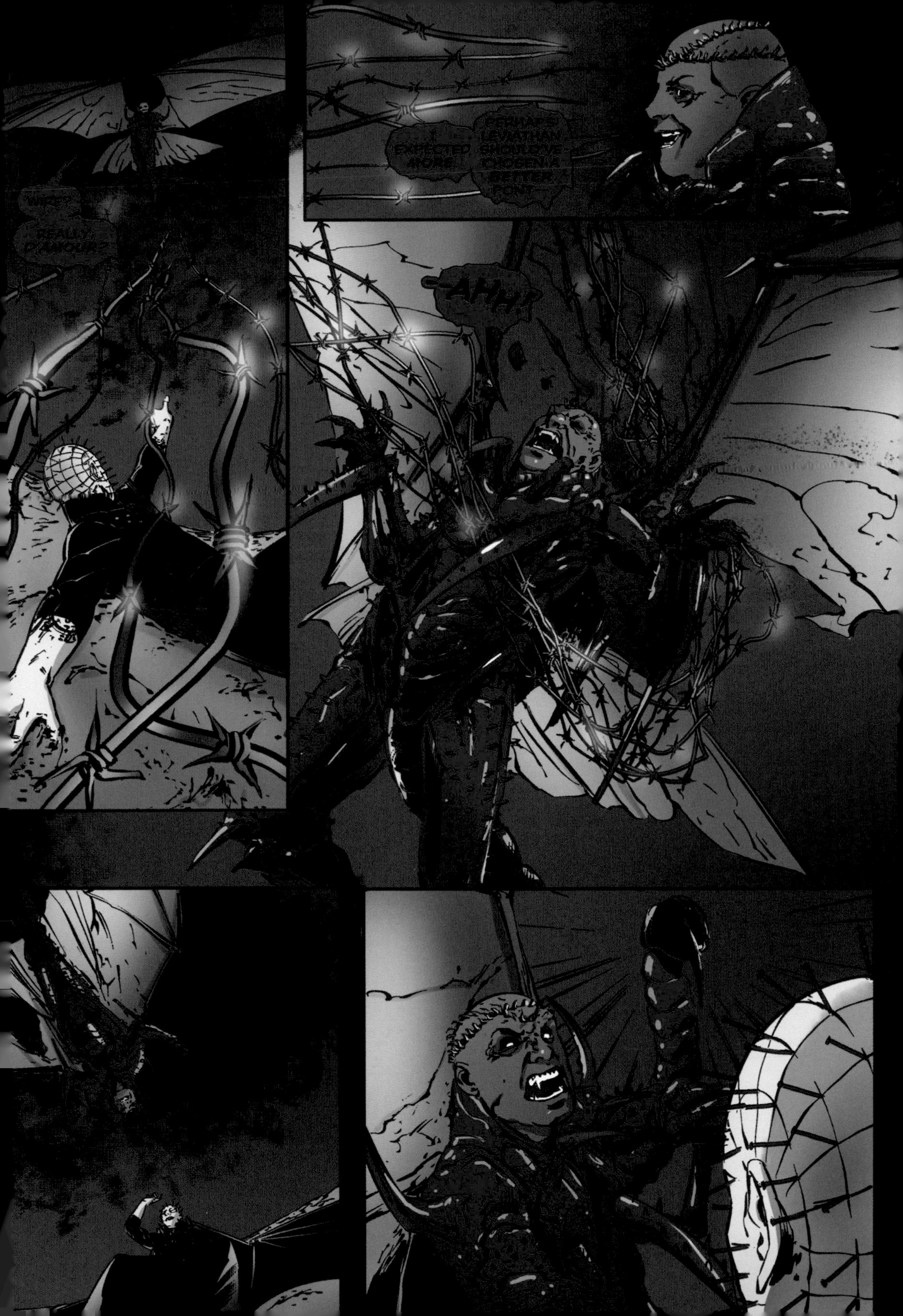
WIRE?
REALLY, D'AMOUR?
I EXPECTED MORE
PERHAPS LEVIATHAN SHOULD'VE CHOSEN A BETTER
AHH!

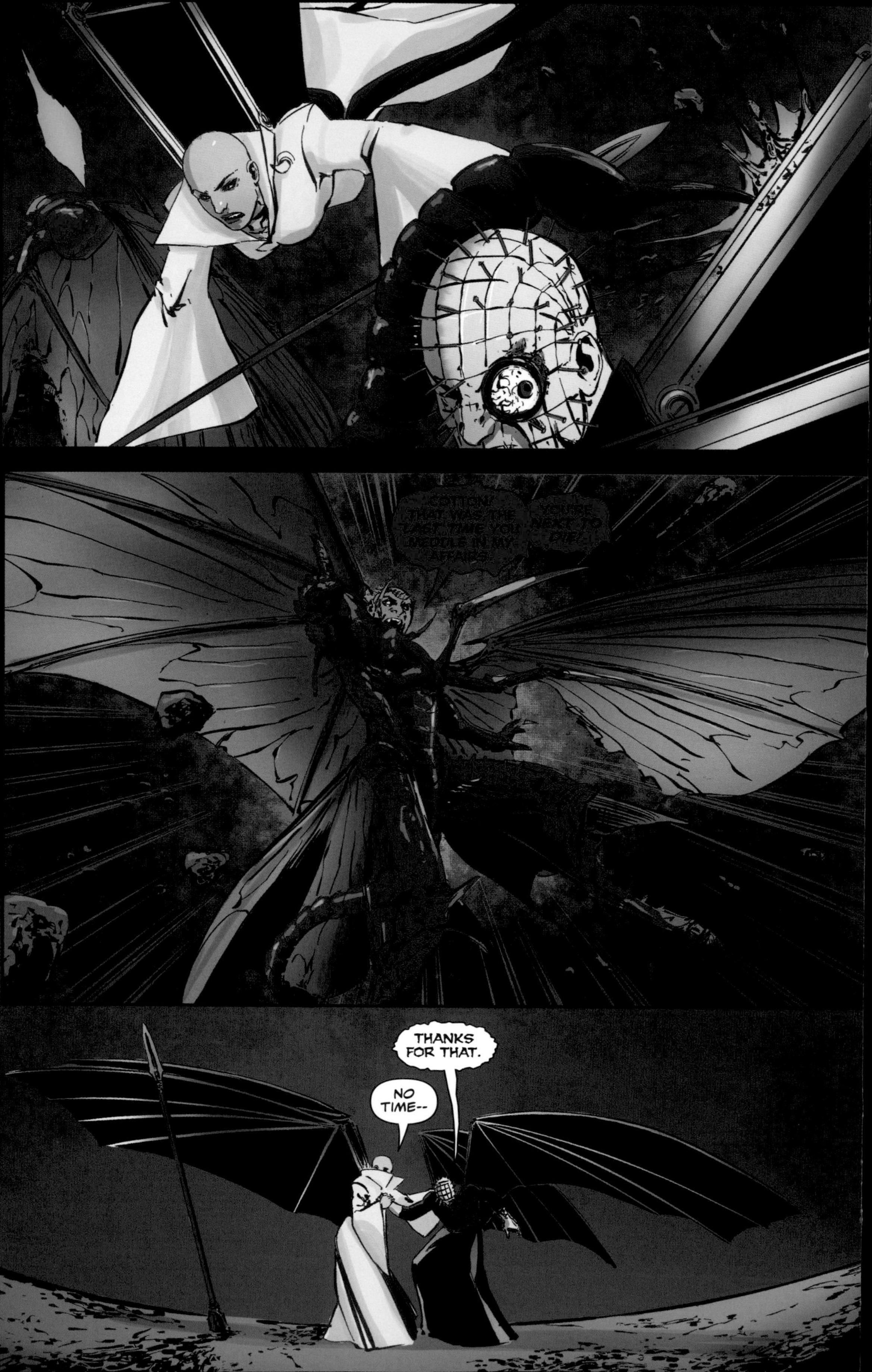
COTTON! THAT WAS THE LAST TIME YOU MEDDLE IN MY AFFAIRS.
YOU'RE NEXT TO DIE!
NO TIME--
THANKS FOR THAT.

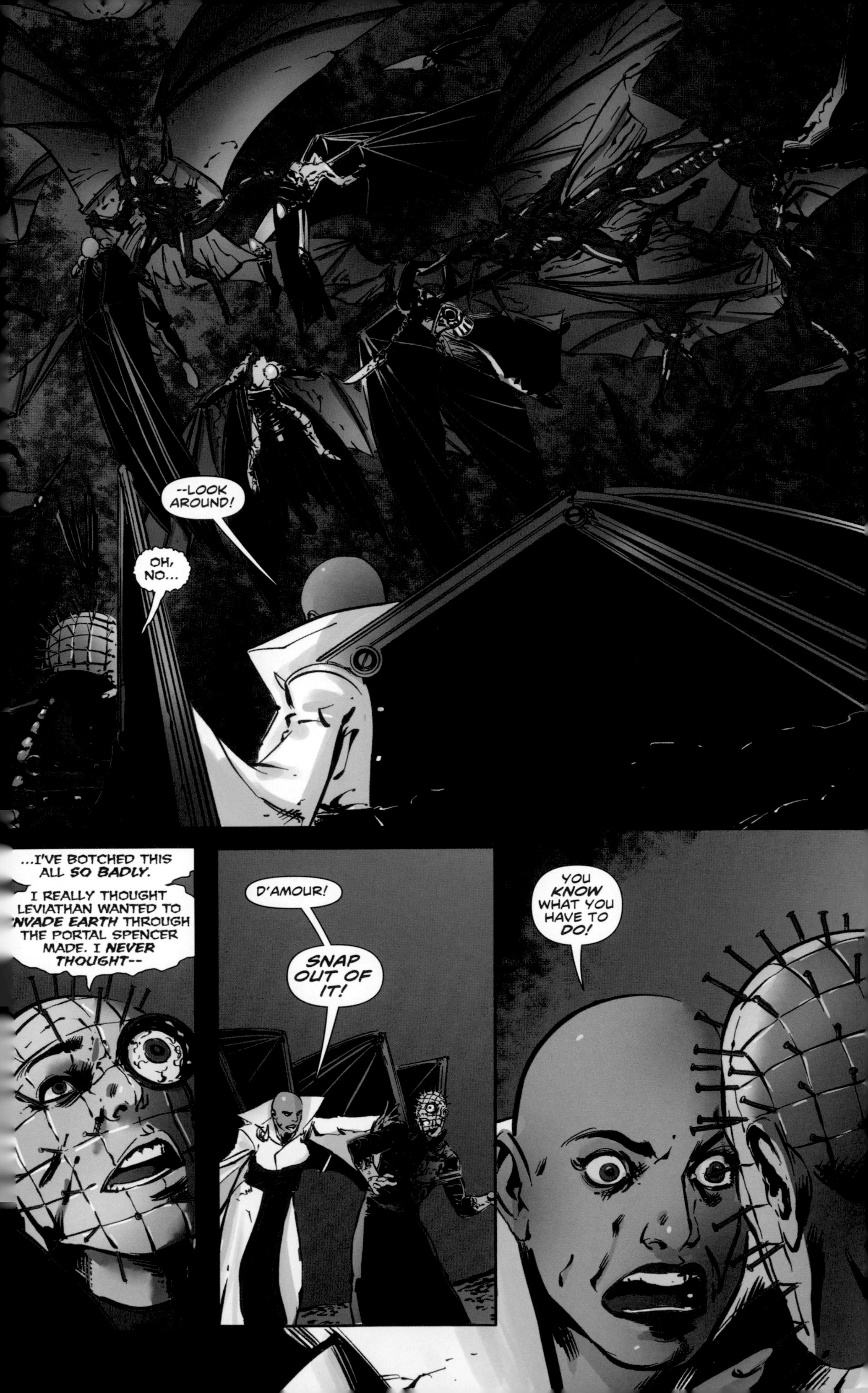
--LOOK AROUND!
OH, NO...
...I'VE BOTCHED THIS ALL SO BADLY.
I REALLY THOUGHT LEVIATHAN WANTED TO INVADE EARTH THROUGH THE PORTAL SPENCER MADE. I NEVER THOUGHT--
D'AMOUR!
SNAP OUT OF IT!
YOU KNOW WHAT YOU HAVE TO DO!

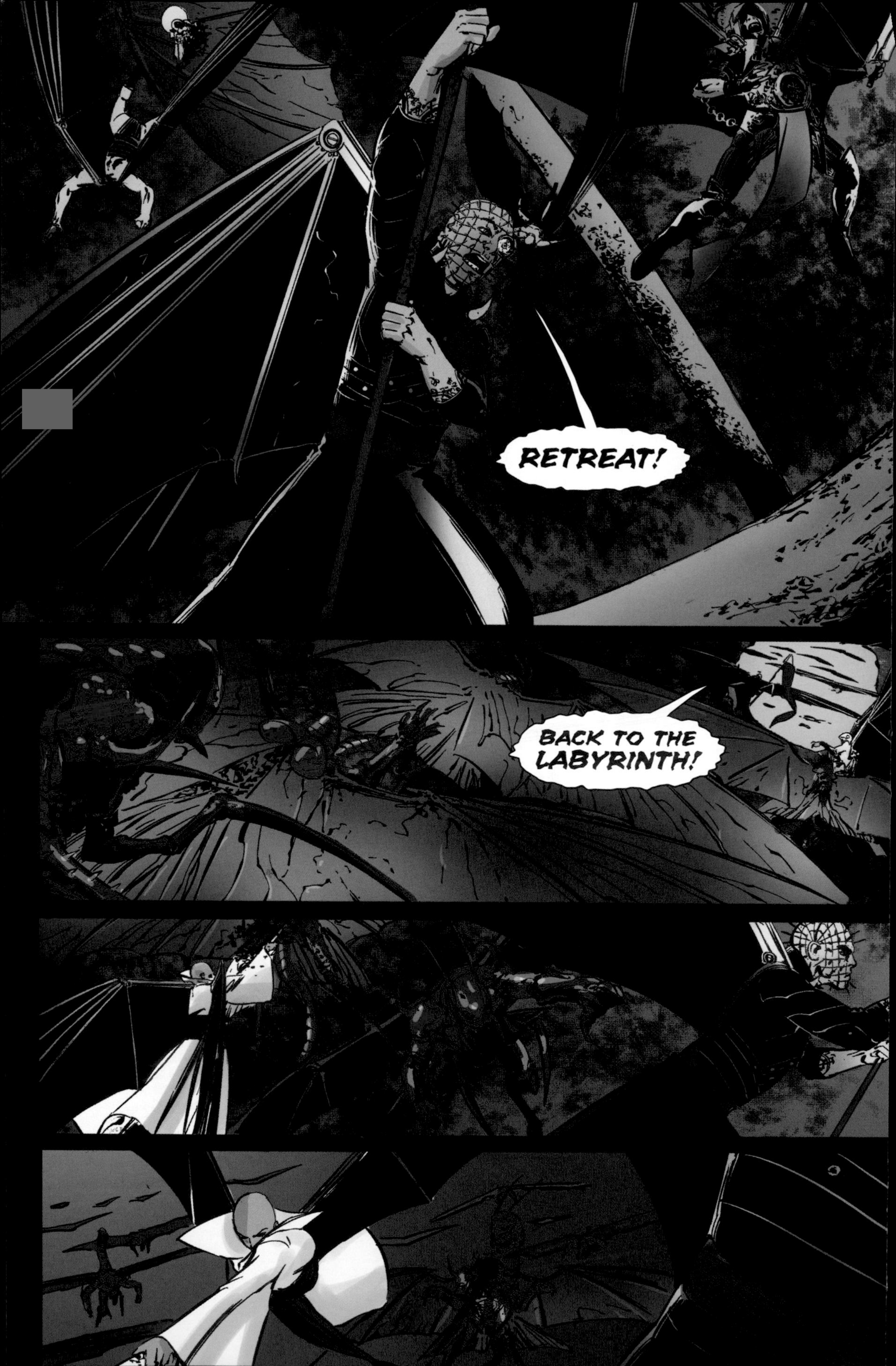
RETREAT!
BACK TO THE LABYRINTH!

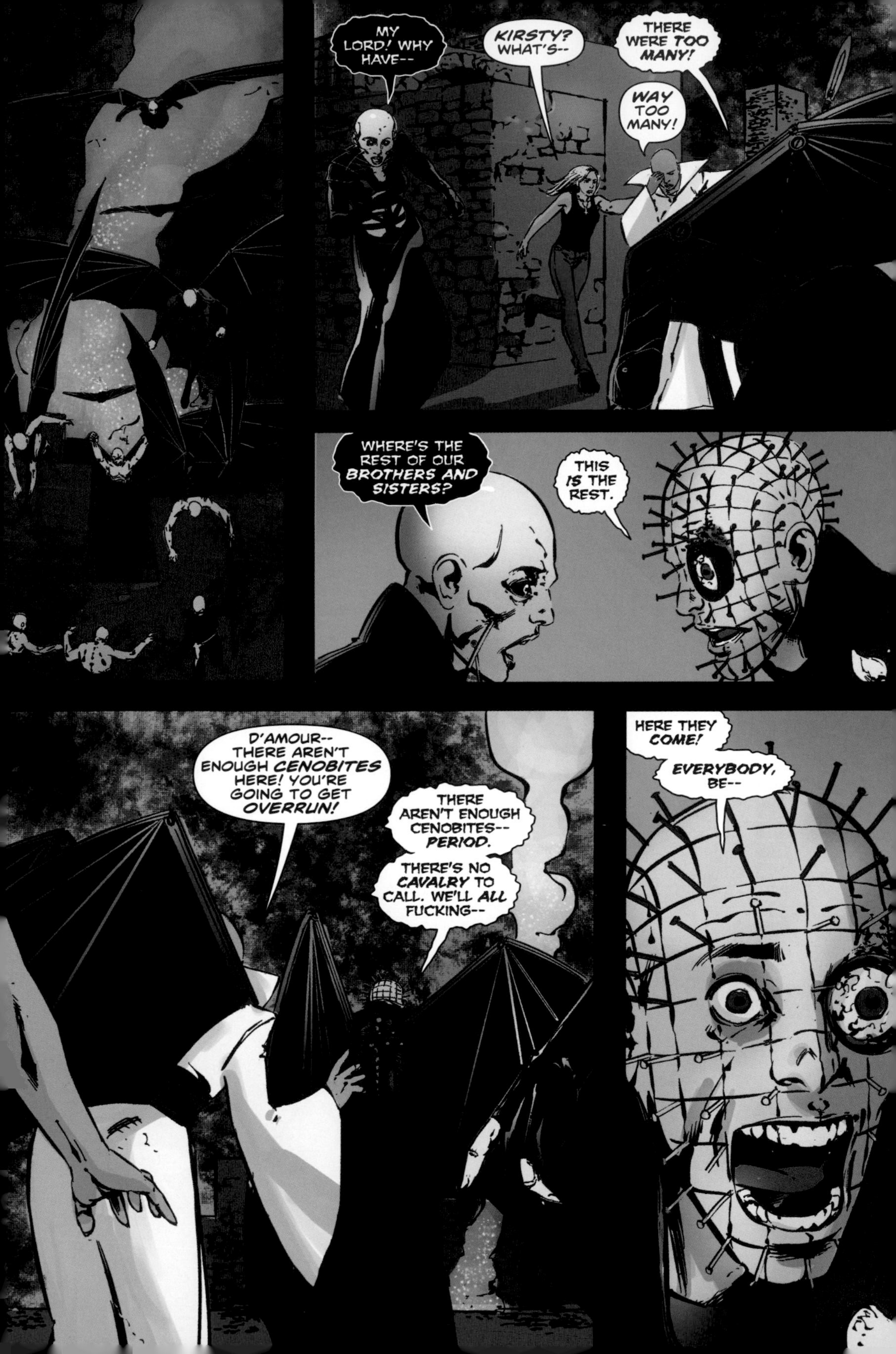
MY LORD! WHY HAVE--
KIRSTY? WHAT'S--
THERE WERE TOO MANY!
WAY TOO MANY!
WHERE'S THE REST OF OUR BROTHERS AND SISTERS?
THIS IS THE REST.
D'AMOUR-- THERE AREN'T ENOUGH CENOBITES HERE! YOU'RE GOING TO GET OVERRUN!
THERE AREN'T ENOUGH CENOBITES-- PERIOD.
THERE'S NO CAVALRY TO CALL. WE'LL ALL FUCKING--
HERE THEY COME!
EVERYBODY, BE--

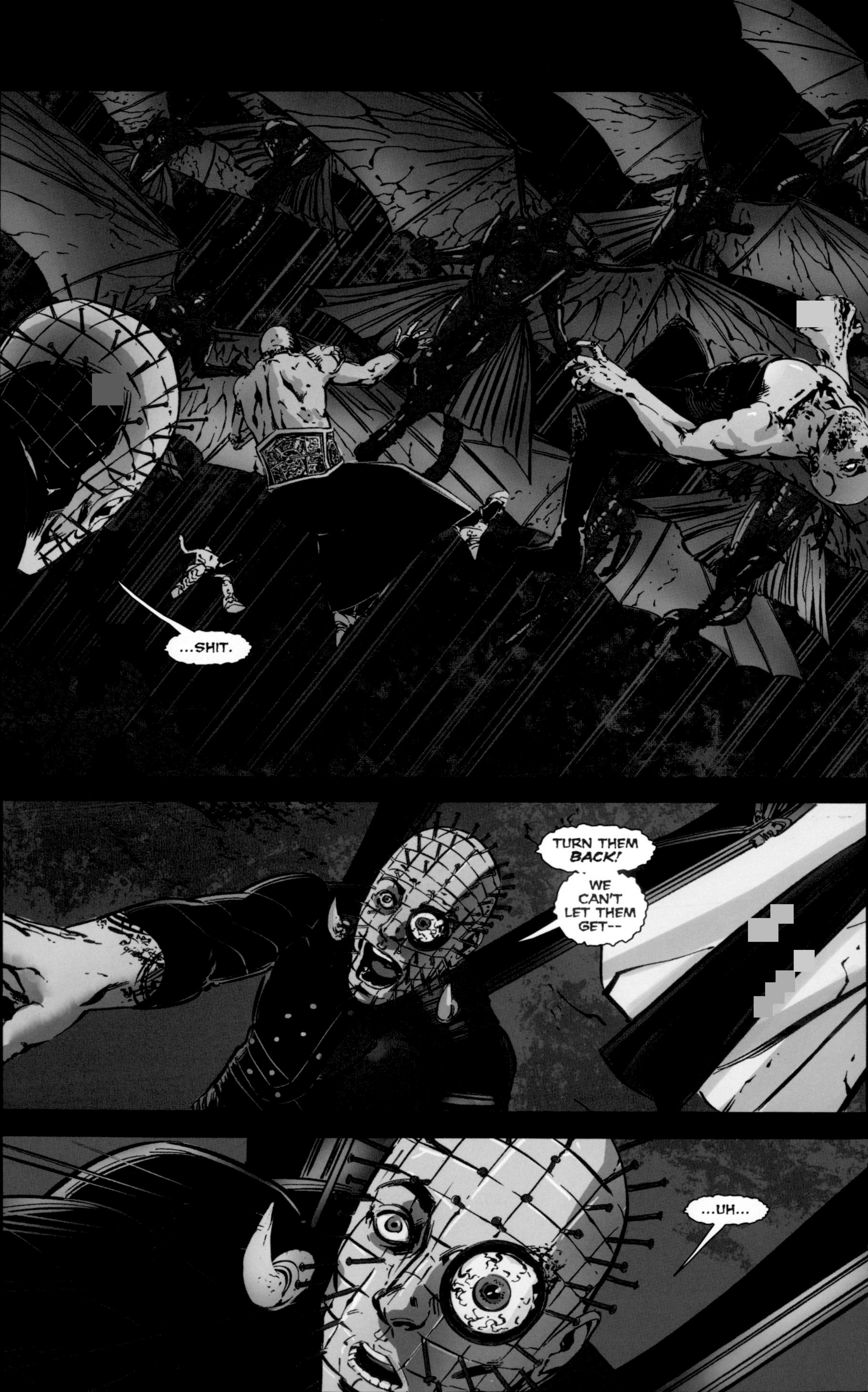
...SHIT.
TURN THEM BACK!
WE CAN'T LET THEM GET--
...UH...

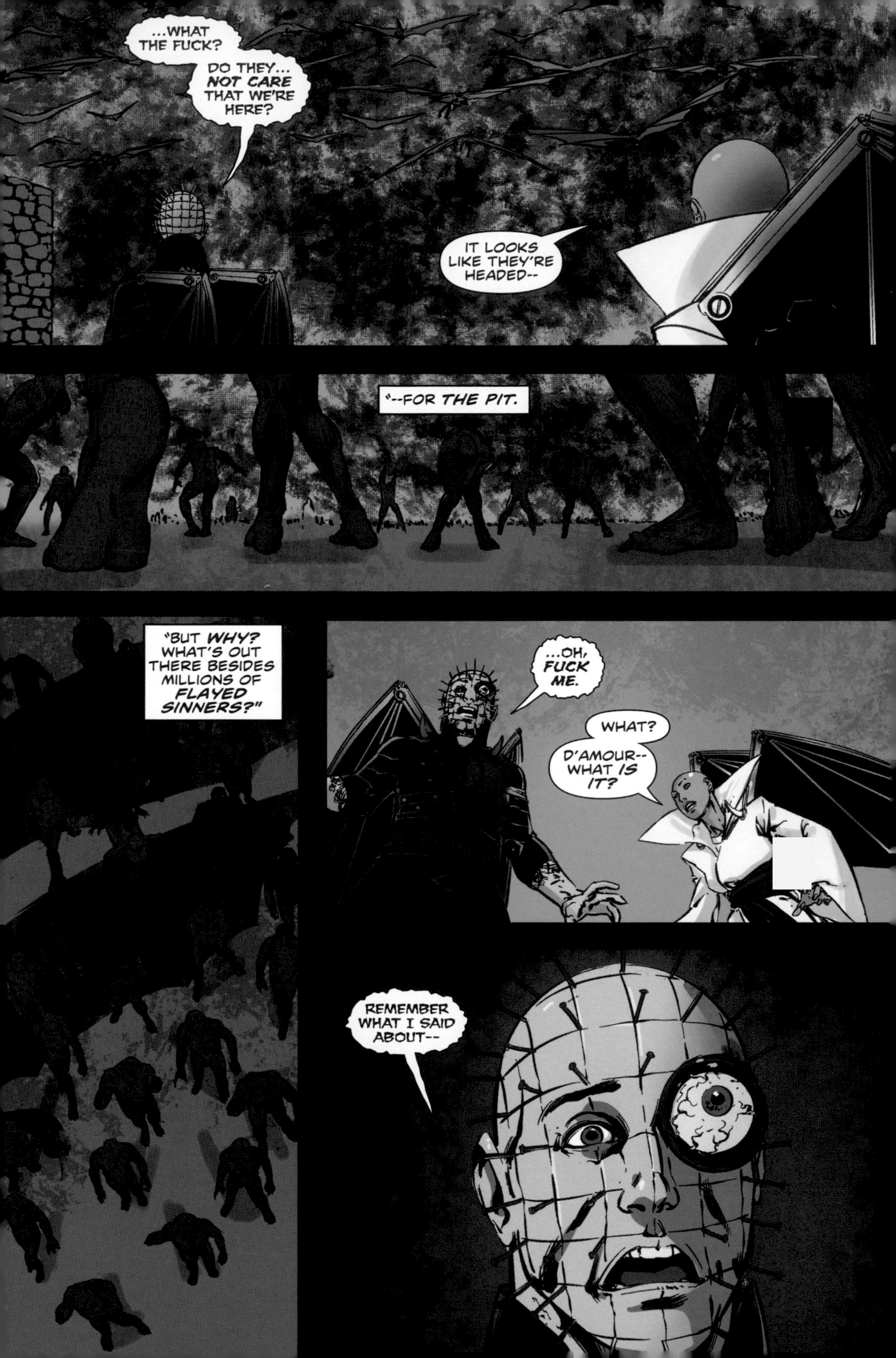
...WHAT THE FUCK?
DO THEY... NOT CARE THAT WE'RE HERE?
IT LOOKS LIKE THEY'RE HEADED--
"--FOR THE PIT.
"BUT WHY? WHAT'S OUT THERE BESIDES MILLIONS OF FLAYED SINNERS?"
...OH, FUCK ME.
WHAT?
D'AMOUR-- WHAT IS IT?
REMEMBER WHAT I SAID ABOUT--

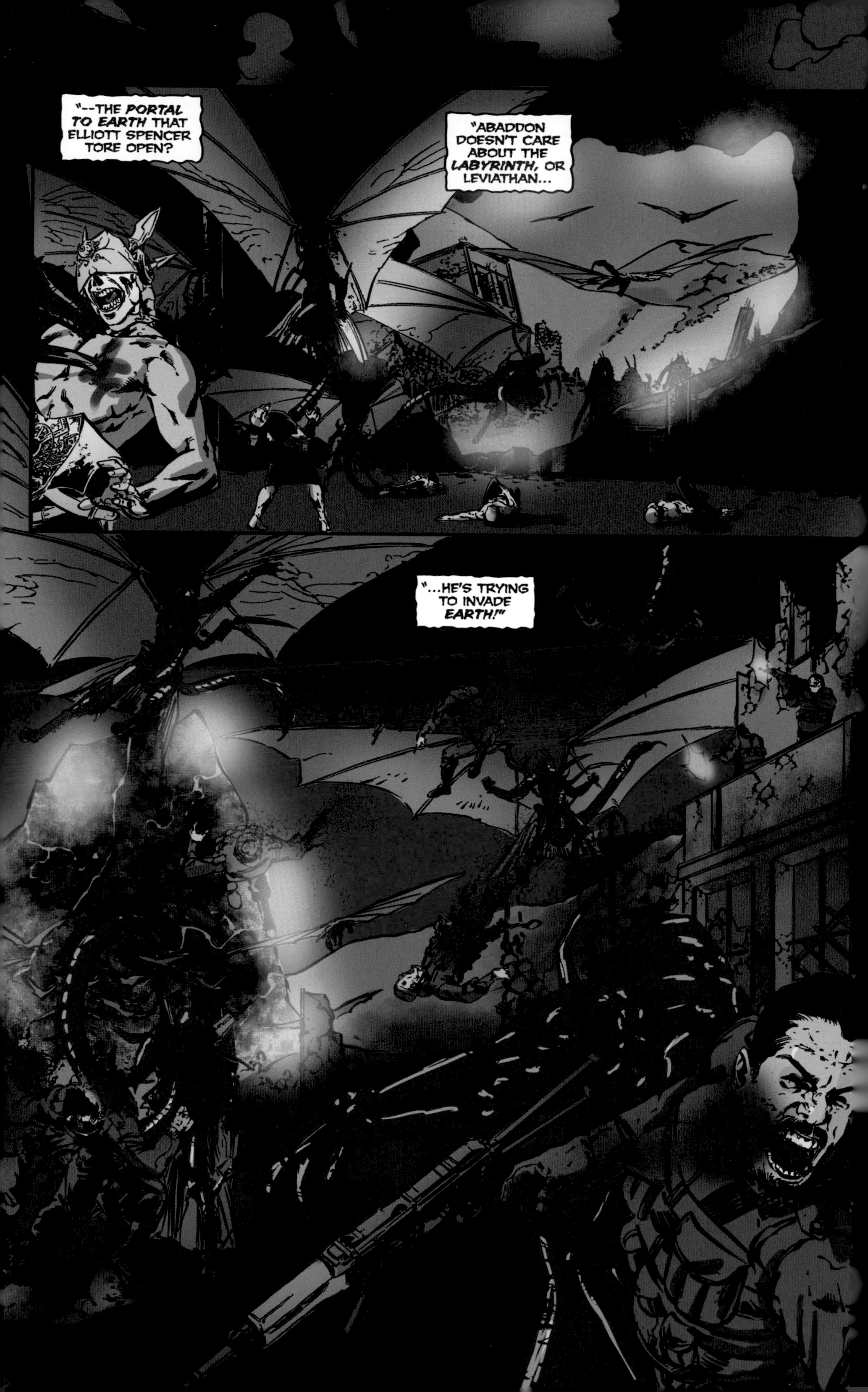
"--THE PORTAL TO EARTH THAT ELLIOTT SPENCER TORE OPEN?
"ABADDON DOESN'T CARE ABOUT THE LABYRINTH, OR LEVIATHAN...
"...HE'S TRYING TO INVADE EARTH!"

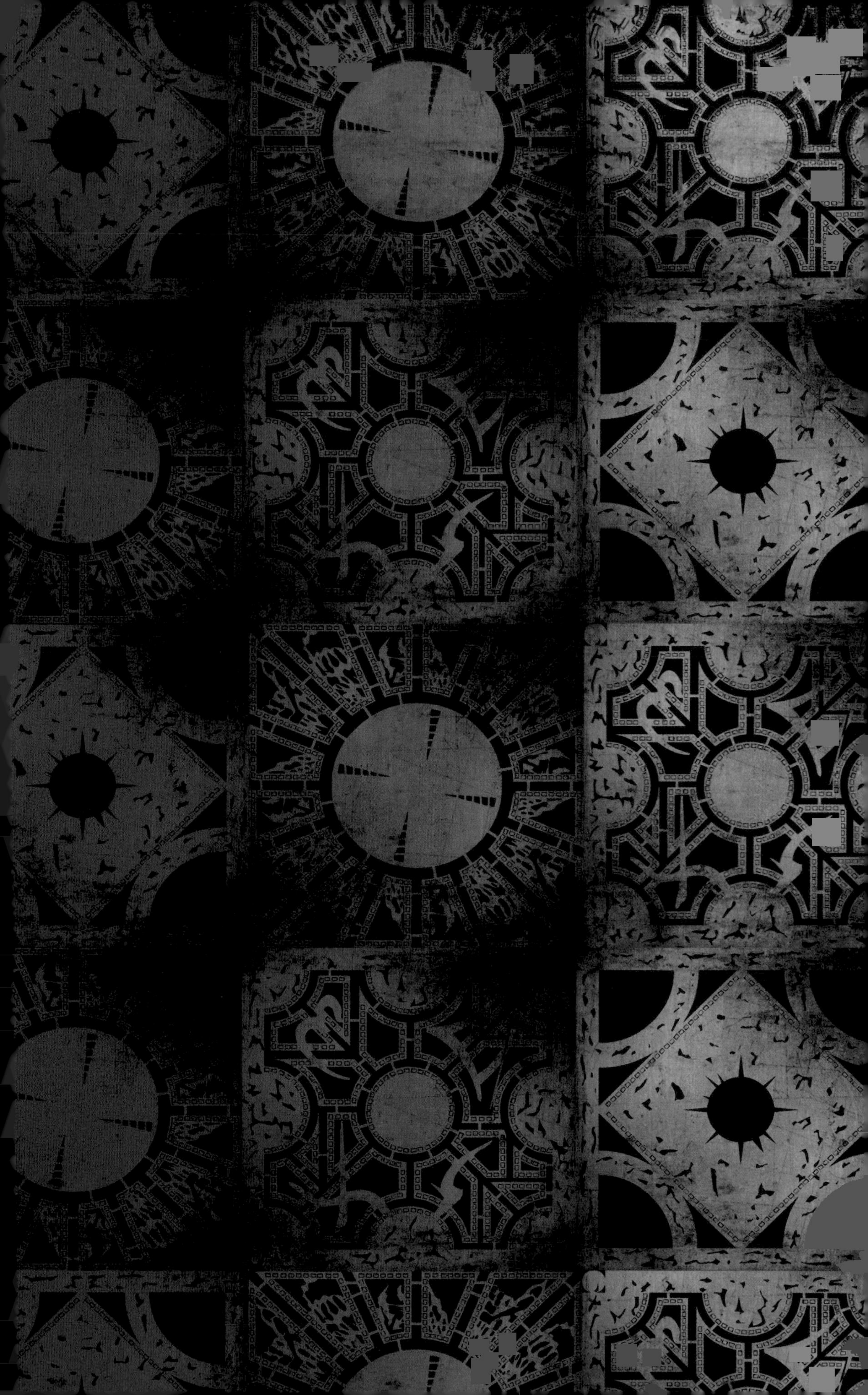

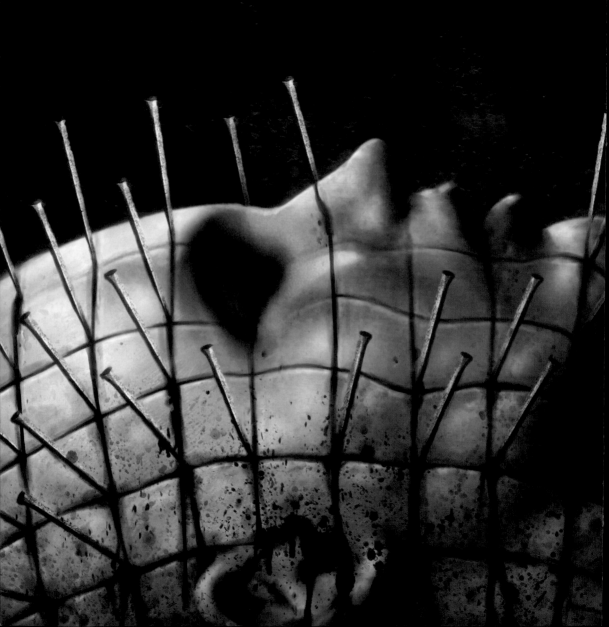

CHAPTER ELEVEN

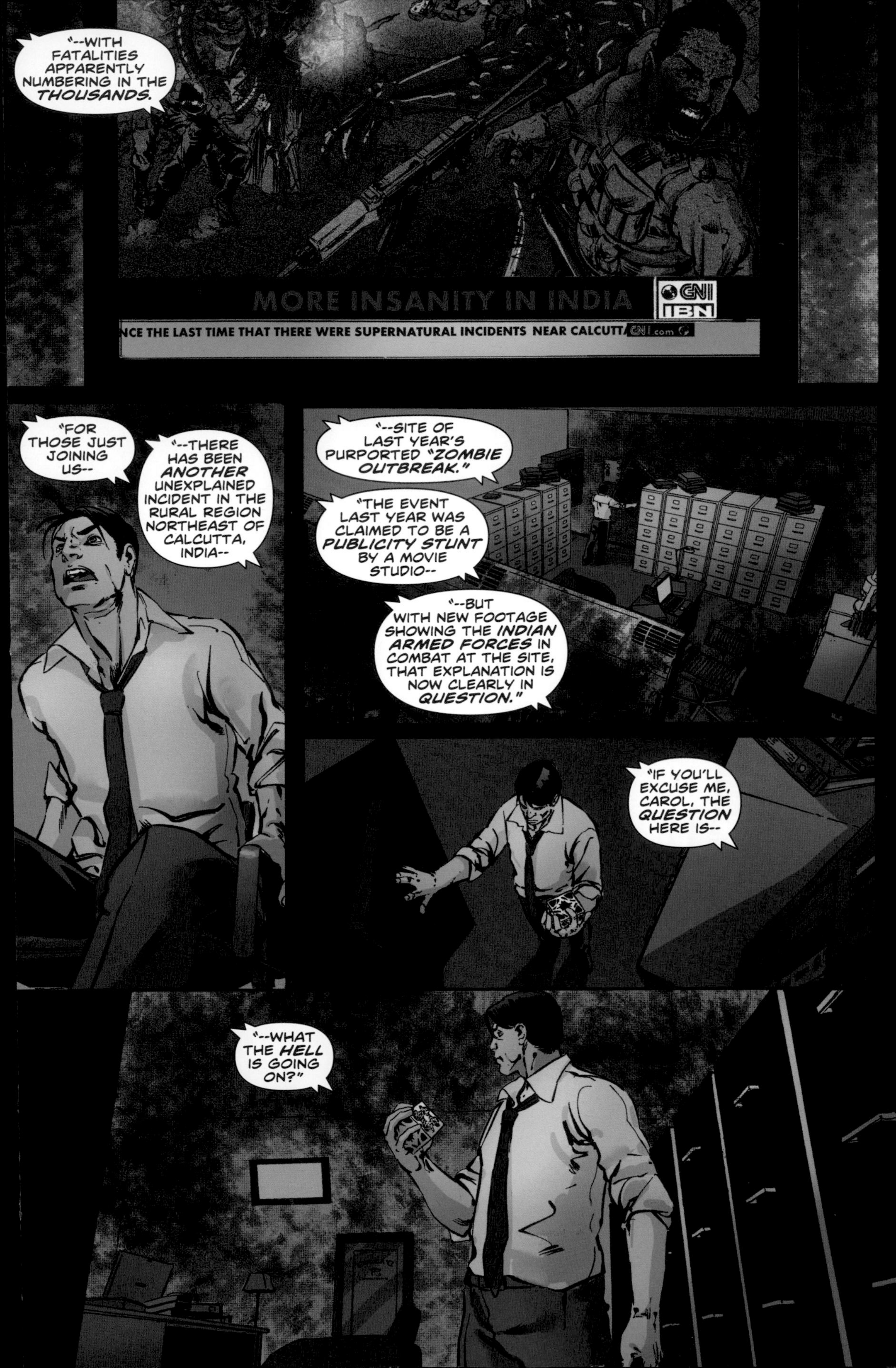
"--WITH FATALITIES APPARENTLY NUMBERING IN THE THOUSANDS.
MORE INSANITY IN INDIA
CNI IBN
NCE THE LAST TIME THAT THERE WERE SUPERNATURAL INCIDENTS NEAR CALCUTT CNI.com
"FOR THOSE JUST JOINING US--
"--THERE HAS BEEN ANOTHER UNEXPLAINED INCIDENT IN THE RURAL REGION NORTHEAST OF CALCUTTA, INDIA--
"--SITE OF LAST YEAR'S PURPORTED "ZOMBIE OUTBREAK."
"THE EVENT LAST YEAR WAS CLAIMED TO BE A PUBLICITY STUNT BY A MOVIE STUDIO--
"--BUT WITH NEW FOOTAGE SHOWING THE INDIAN ARMED FORCES IN COMBAT AT THE SITE, THAT EXPLANATION IS NOW CLEARLY IN QUESTION."
"IF YOU'LL EXCUSE ME, CAROL, THE QUESTION HERE IS--
"--WHAT THE HELL IS GOING ON?"

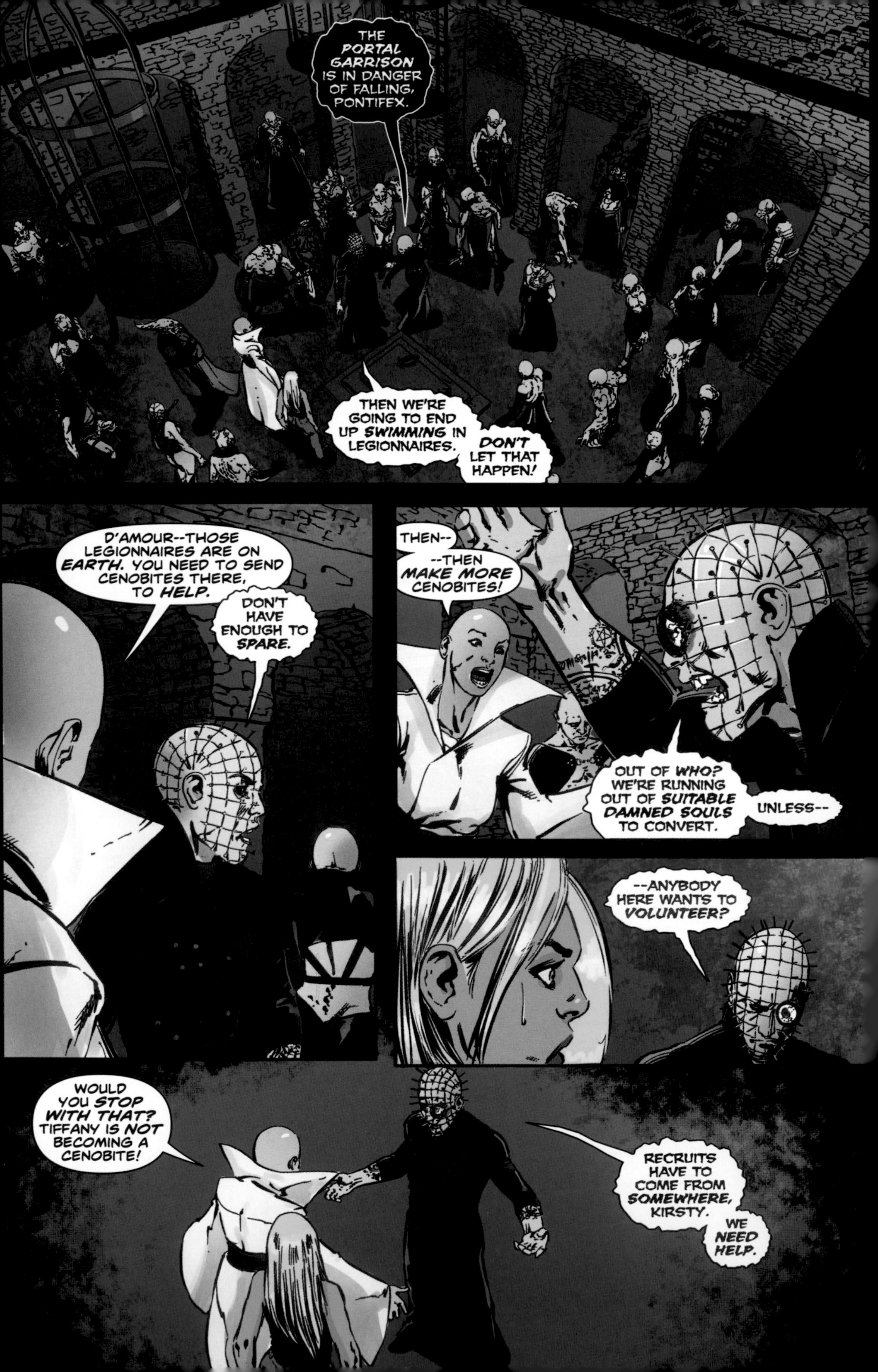
THE PORTAL GARRISON IS IN DANGER OF FALLING, PONTIFEX.
THEN WE'RE GOING TO END UP SWIMMING IN LEGIONNAIRES.
DON'T LET THAT HAPPEN!
D'AMOUR--THOSE LEGIONNAIRES ARE ON EARTH. YOU NEED TO SEND CENOBITES THERE, TO HELP.
DON'T HAVE ENOUGH TO SPARE.
THEN--
--THEN MAKE MORE CENOBITES!
OUT OF WHO? WE'RE RUNNING OUT OF SUITABLE DAMNED SOULS TO CONVERT.
UNLESS--
--ANYBODY HERE WANTS TO VOLUNTEER?
WOULD YOU STOP WITH THAT? TIFFANY IS NOT BECOMING A CENOBITE!
RECRUITS HAVE TO COME FROM SOMEWHERE, KIRSTY.
WE NEED HELP.

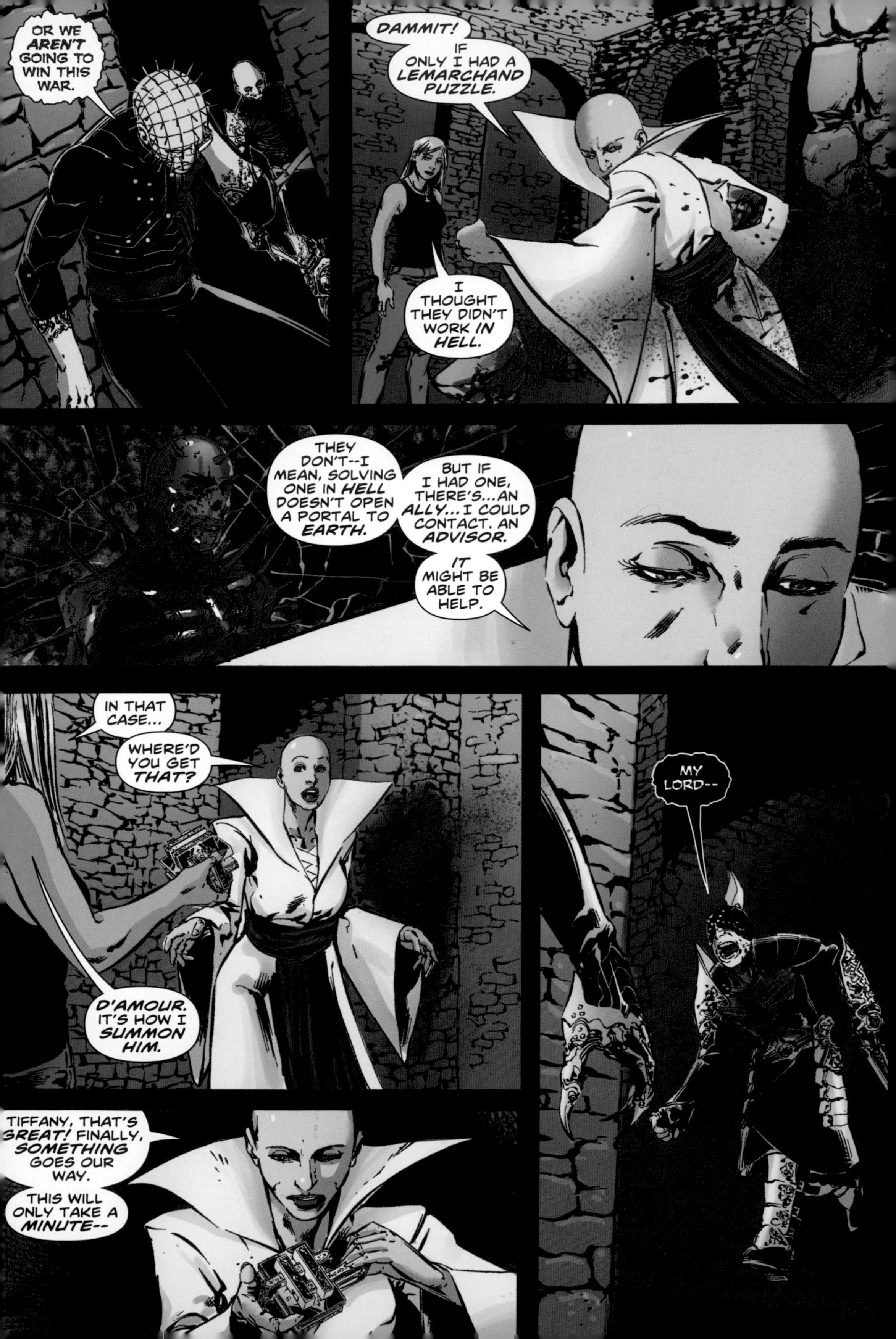
OR WE AREN'T GOING TO WIN THIS WAR.
DAMMIT!
IF ONLY I HAD A LEMARCHAND PUZZLE.
I THOUGHT THEY DIDN'T WORK IN HELL.
THEY DON'T--I MEAN, SOLVING ONE IN HELL DOESN'T OPEN A PORTAL TO EARTH.
BUT IF I HAD ONE, THERE'S...AN ALLY...I COULD CONTACT. AN ADVISOR.
IT MIGHT BE ABLE TO HELP.
IN THAT CASE...
WHERE'D YOU GET THAT?
D'AMOUR. IT'S HOW I SUMMON HIM.
TIFFANY, THAT'S GREAT! FINALLY, SOMETHING GOES OUR WAY.
THIS WILL ONLY TAKE A MINUTE--
MY LORD--

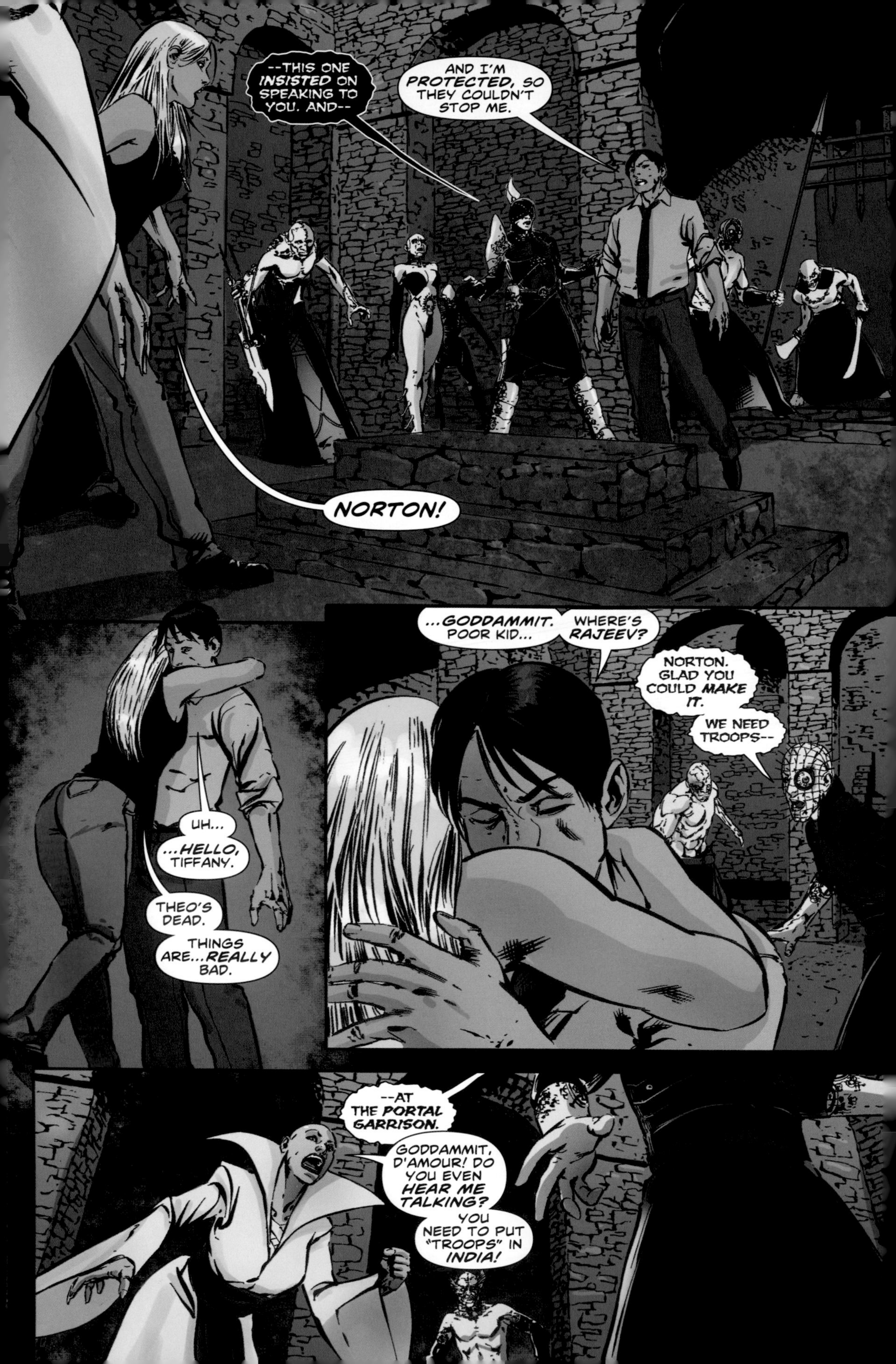
--THIS ONE INSISTED ON SPEAKING TO YOU. AND--
AND I'M PROTECTED, SO THEY COULDN'T STOP ME.
NORTON!
UH...
...HELLO, TIFFANY.
THEO'S DEAD.
THINGS ARE...REALLY BAD.
...GODDAMMIT. POOR KID...
WHERE'S RAJEEV?
NORTON. GLAD YOU COULD MAKE IT.
WE NEED TROOPS--
--AT THE PORTAL GARRISON.
GODDAMMIT, D'AMOUR! DO YOU EVEN HEAR ME TALKING?
YOU NEED TO PUT "TROOPS" IN INDIA!

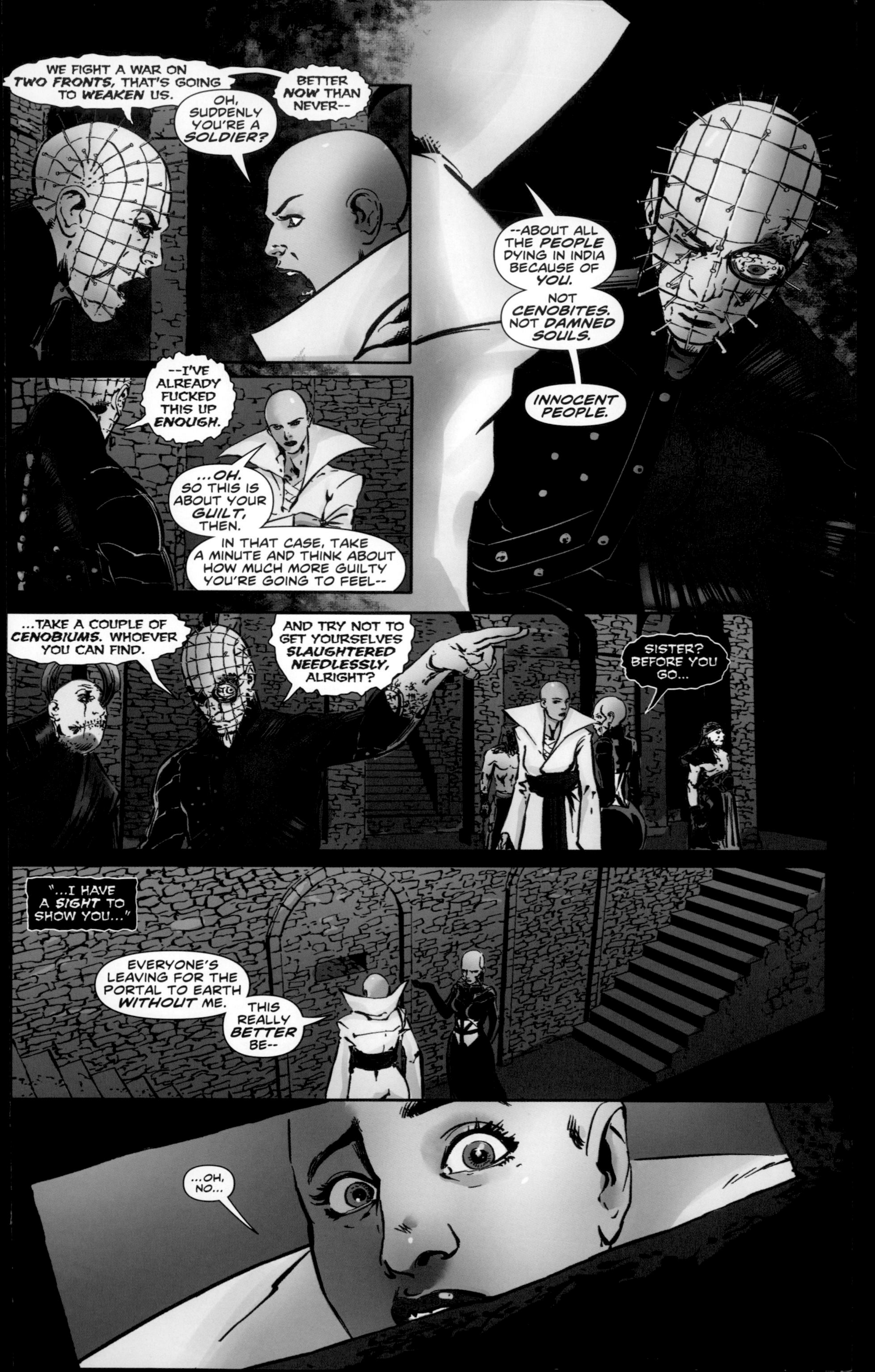

WE FIGHT A WAR ON *TWO FRONTS*, THAT'S GOING TO *WEAKEN* US.
BETTER *NOW* THAN NEVER--
OH, SUDDENLY YOU'RE A *SOLDIER*?
--ABOUT ALL THE *PEOPLE* DYING IN INDIA BECAUSE OF *YOU*.
NOT *CENOBITES*. NOT *DAMNED SOULS*.
INNOCENT PEOPLE.
--I'VE ALREADY FUCKED THIS UP *ENOUGH*.
...OH. SO THIS IS ABOUT YOUR *GUILT*, THEN.
IN THAT CASE, TAKE A MINUTE AND THINK ABOUT HOW MUCH MORE GUILTY YOU'RE GOING TO FEEL--
...TAKE A COUPLE OF *CENOBIUMS*. WHOEVER YOU CAN FIND.
AND TRY NOT TO GET YOURSELVES *SLAUGHTERED NEEDLESSLY*, ALRIGHT?
SISTER? BEFORE YOU GO...
"...I HAVE A *SIGHT* TO SHOW YOU..."
EVERYONE'S LEAVING FOR THE PORTAL TO EARTH *WITHOUT* ME.
THIS REALLY *BETTER* BE--
...OH, NO...

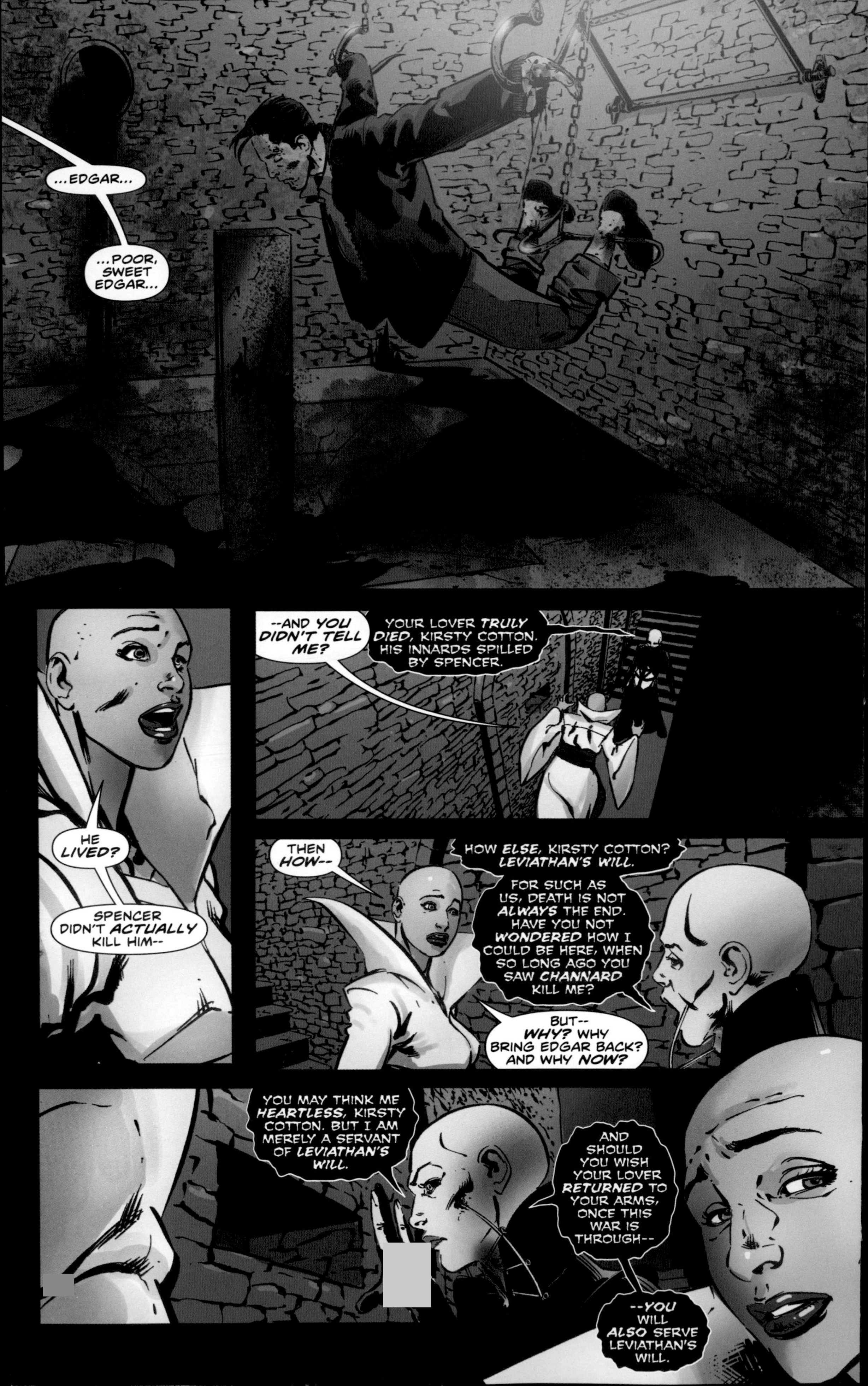
...EDGAR...
...POOR, SWEET EDGAR...
HE LIVED?
SPENCER DIDN'T ACTUALLY KILL HIM--
--AND YOU DIDN'T TELL ME?
YOUR LOVER TRULY DIED, KIRSTY COTTON. HIS INNARDS SPILLED BY SPENCER.
THEN HOW--
HOW ELSE, KIRSTY COTTON? LEVIATHAN'S WILL.
FOR SUCH AS US, DEATH IS NOT ALWAYS THE END. HAVE YOU NOT WONDERED HOW I COULD BE HERE, WHEN SO LONG AGO YOU SAW CHANNARD KILL ME?
BUT-- WHY? WHY BRING EDGAR BACK? AND WHY NOW?
YOU MAY THINK ME HEARTLESS, KIRSTY COTTON. BUT I AM MERELY A SERVANT OF LEVIATHAN'S WILL.
AND SHOULD YOU WISH YOUR LOVER RETURNED TO YOUR ARMS, ONCE THIS WAR IS THROUGH--
--YOU WILL ALSO SERVE LEVIATHAN'S WILL.

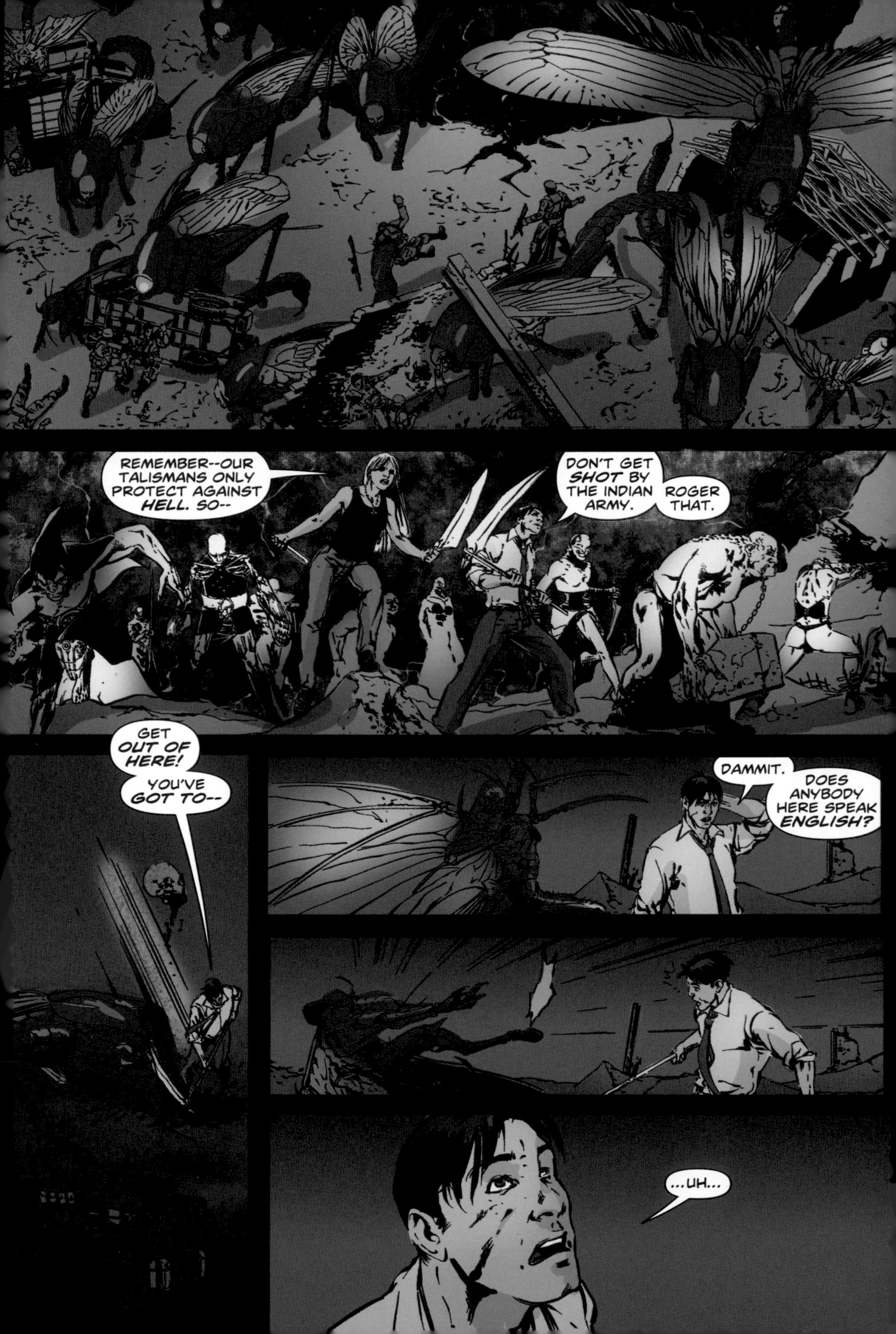
REMEMBER--OUR TALISMANS ONLY PROTECT AGAINST HELL. SO--
DON'T GET SHOT BY THE INDIAN ARMY.
ROGER THAT.
GET OUT OF HERE!
YOU'VE GOT TO--
DAMMIT.
DOES ANYBODY HERE SPEAK ENGLISH?
...UH...

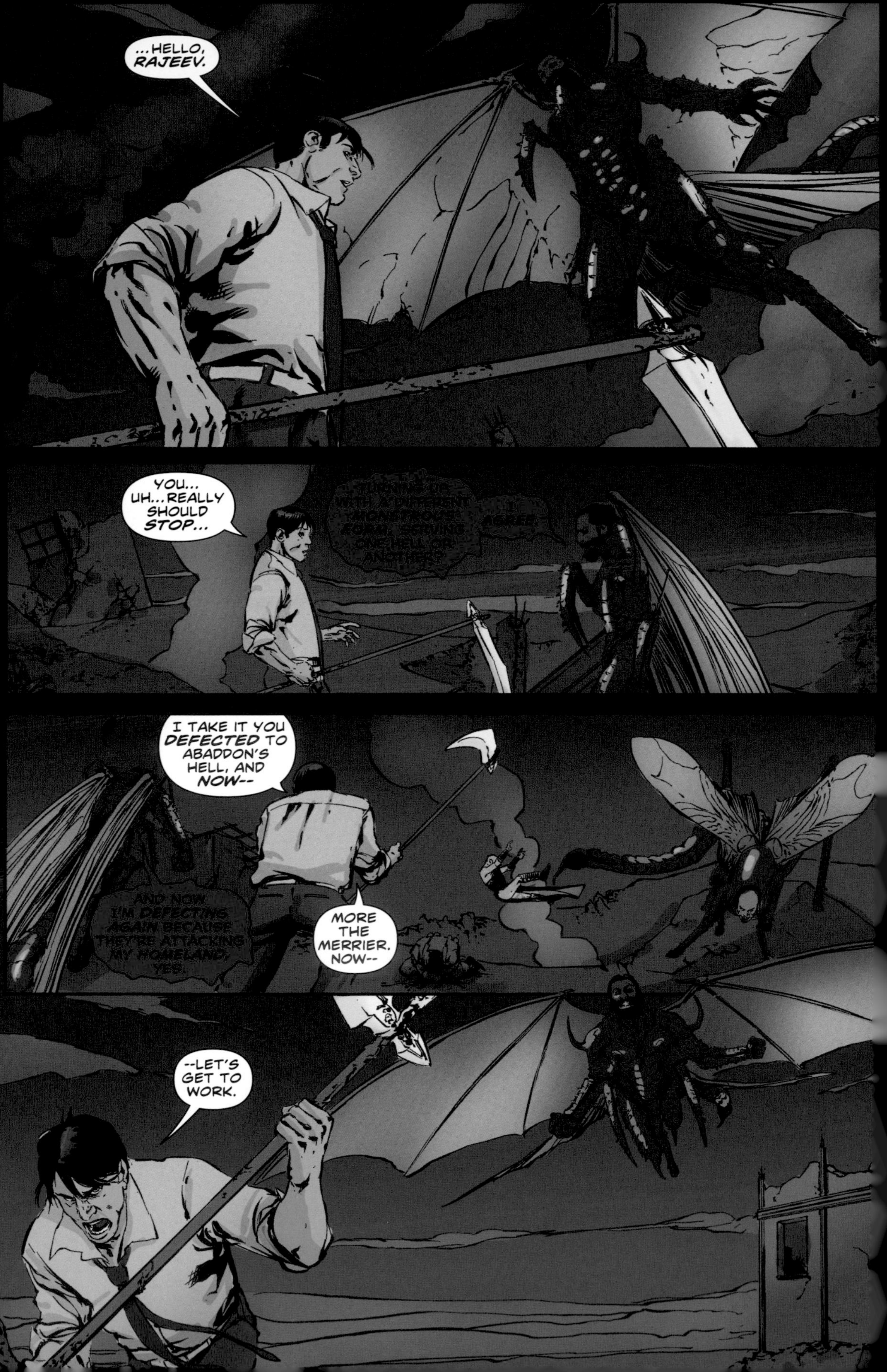
...HELLO, RAJEEV.
YOU... UH...REALLY SHOULD STOP...
...TURNING UP WITH A DIFFERENT MONSTROUS FORM, SERVING ONE HELL OR ANOTHER?
...I AGREE.
I TAKE IT YOU DEFECTED TO ABADDON'S HELL, AND NOW--
AND NOW I'M DEFECTING AGAIN BECAUSE THEY'RE ATTACKING MY HOMELAND, YES.
MORE THE MERRIER. NOW--
--LET'S GET TO WORK.

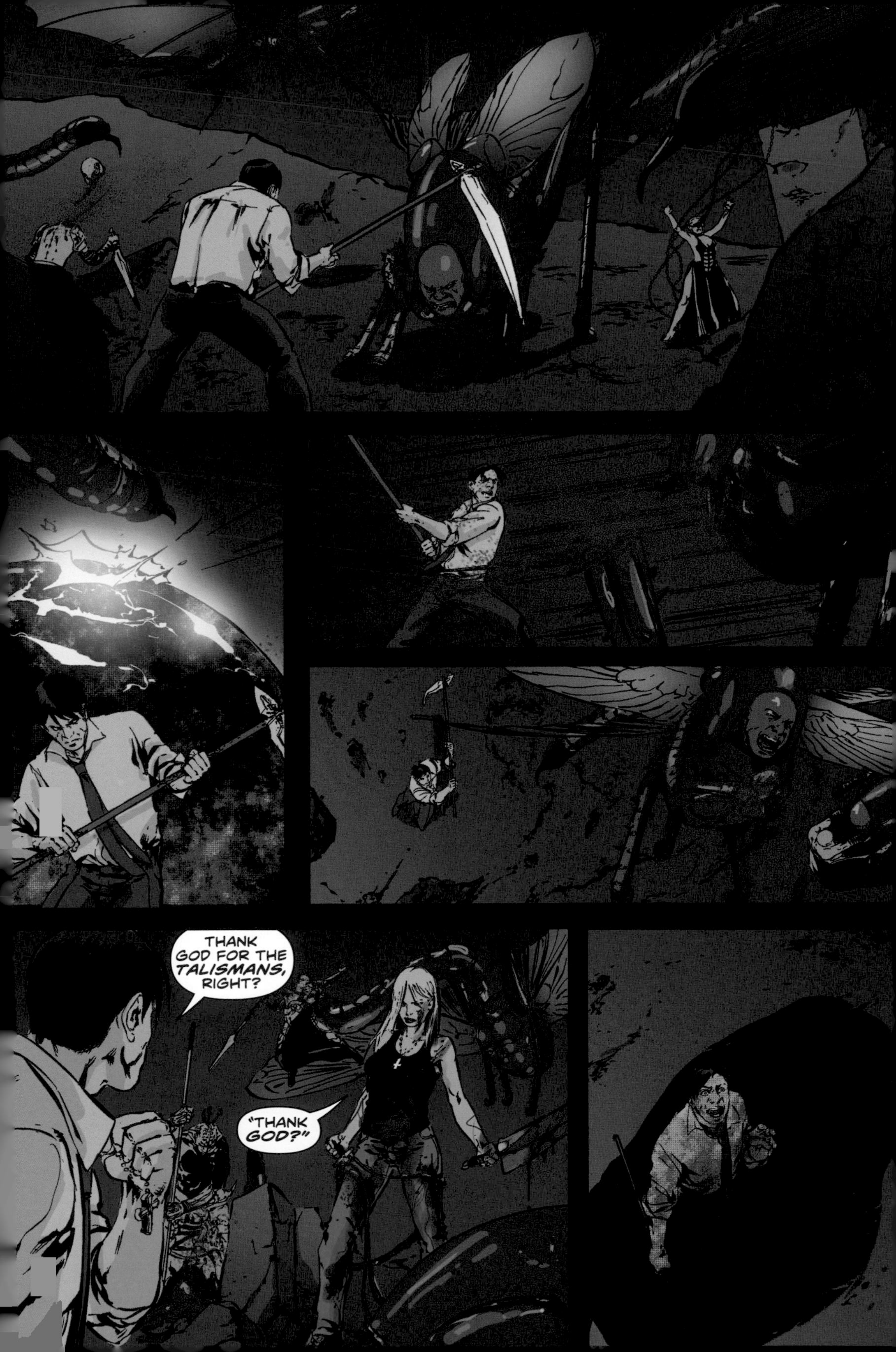
THANK GOD FOR THE *TALISMANS,* RIGHT?
"THANK *GOD?*"

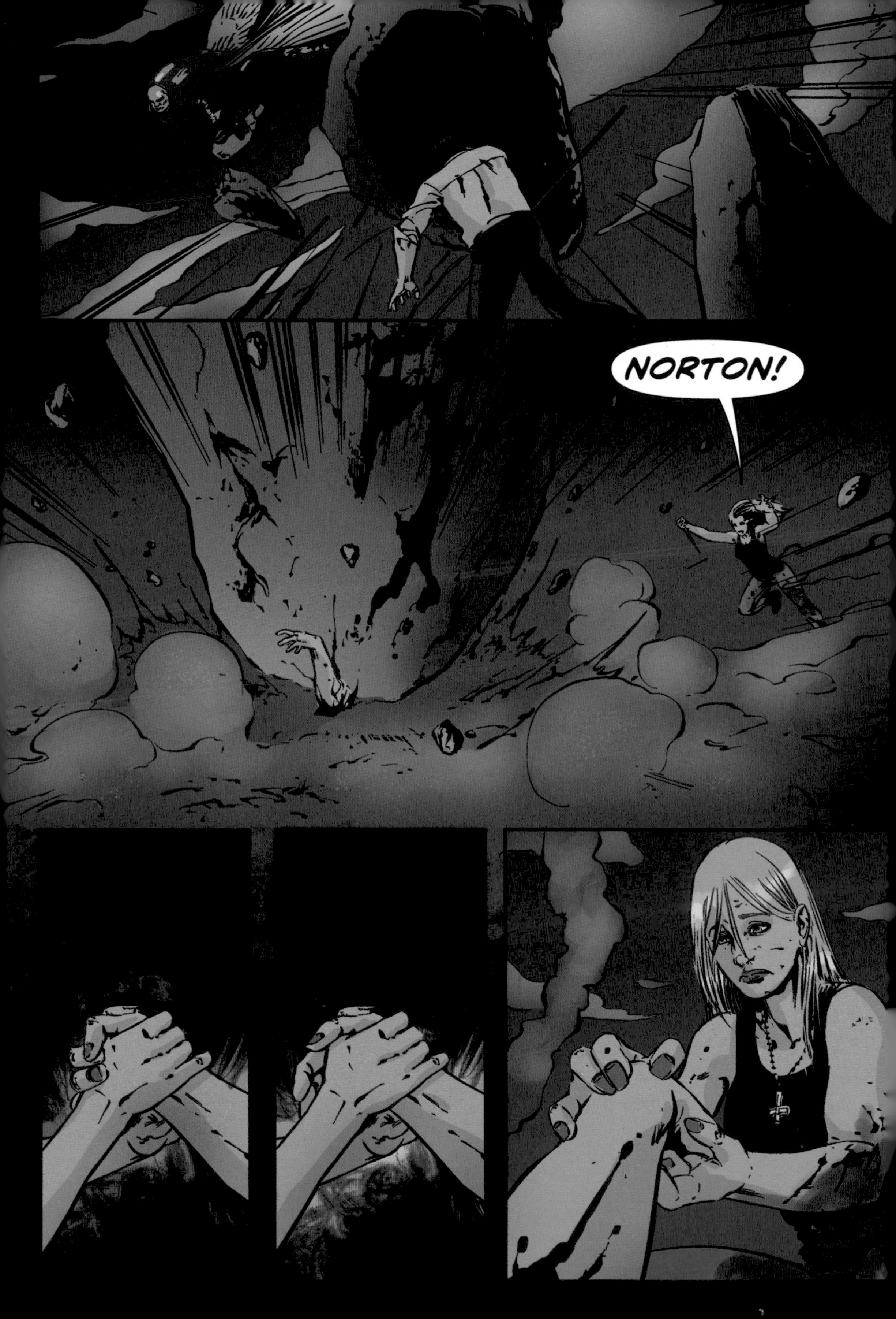
NORTON!

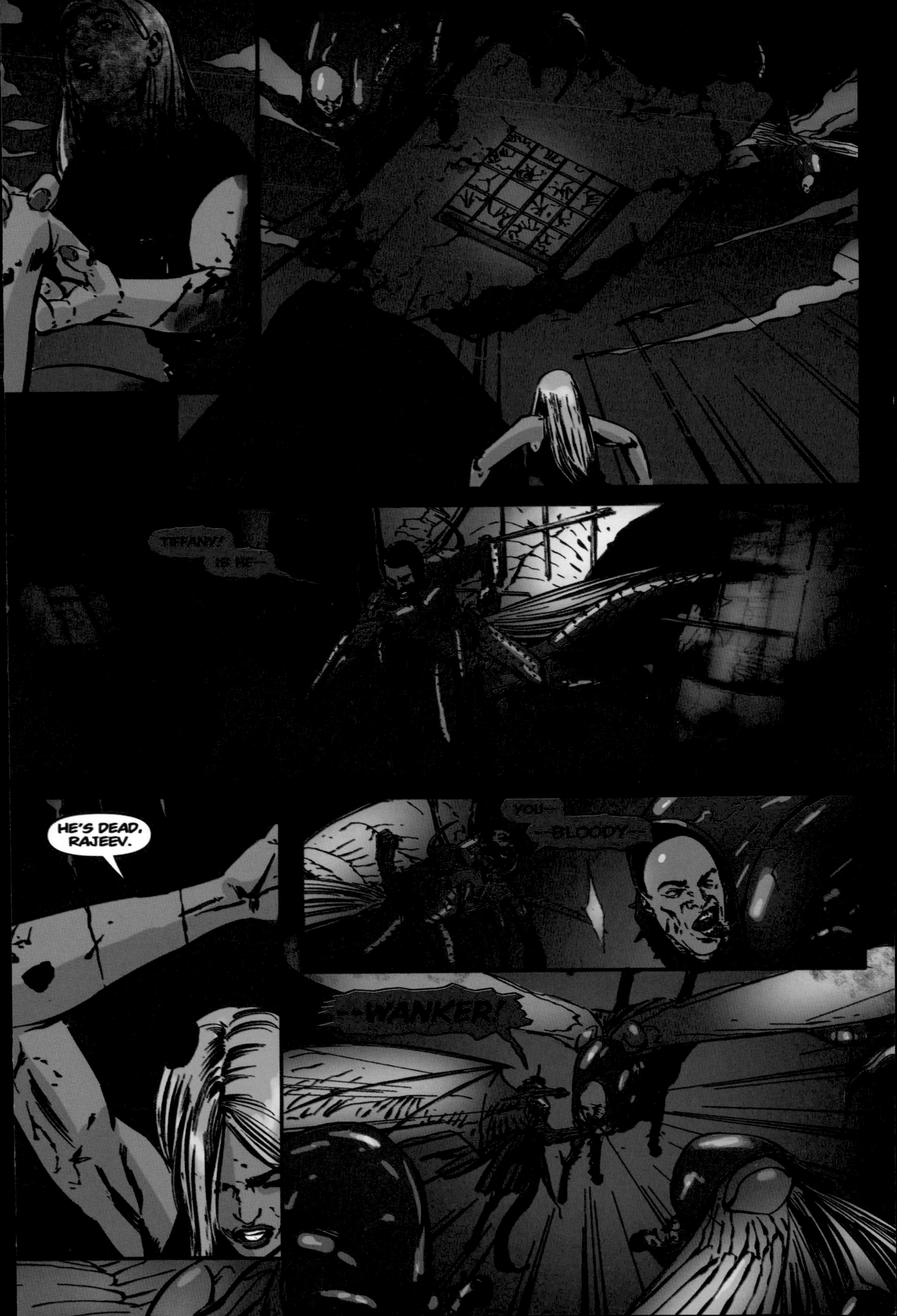
TIFFANY!
IS HE--
HE'S DEAD, RAJEEV.
YOU--
--BLOODY--
--WANKER!

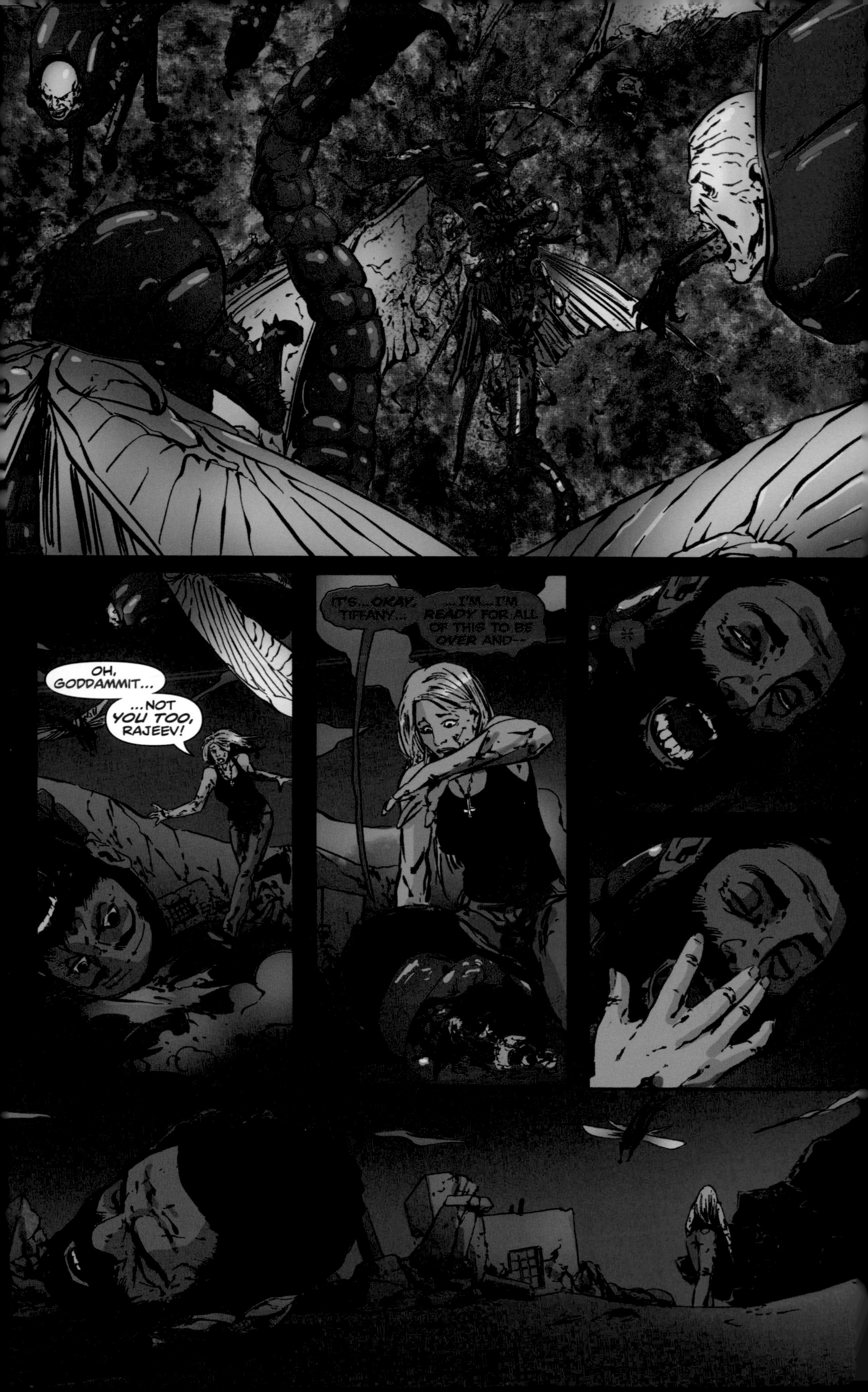
OH, GODDAMMIT...
...NOT YOU TOO, RAJEEV!
IT'S...OKAY, TIFFANY...
...I'M...I'M READY FOR ALL OF THIS TO BE OVER AND--
*

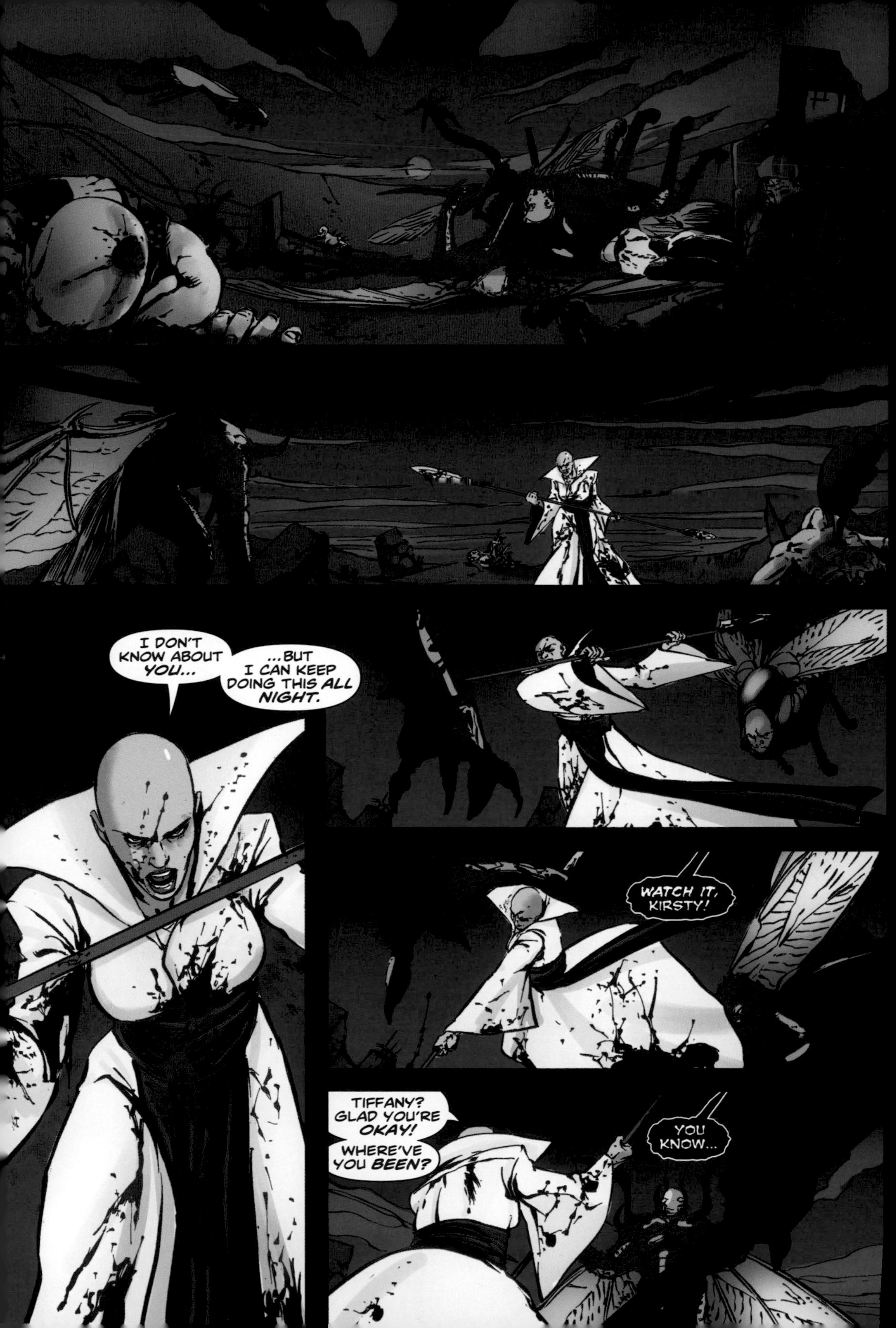
I DON'T KNOW ABOUT YOU...
...BUT I CAN KEEP DOING THIS ALL NIGHT.
WATCH IT, KIRSTY!
TIFFANY? GLAD YOU'RE OKAY! WHERE'VE YOU BEEN?
YOU KNOW...

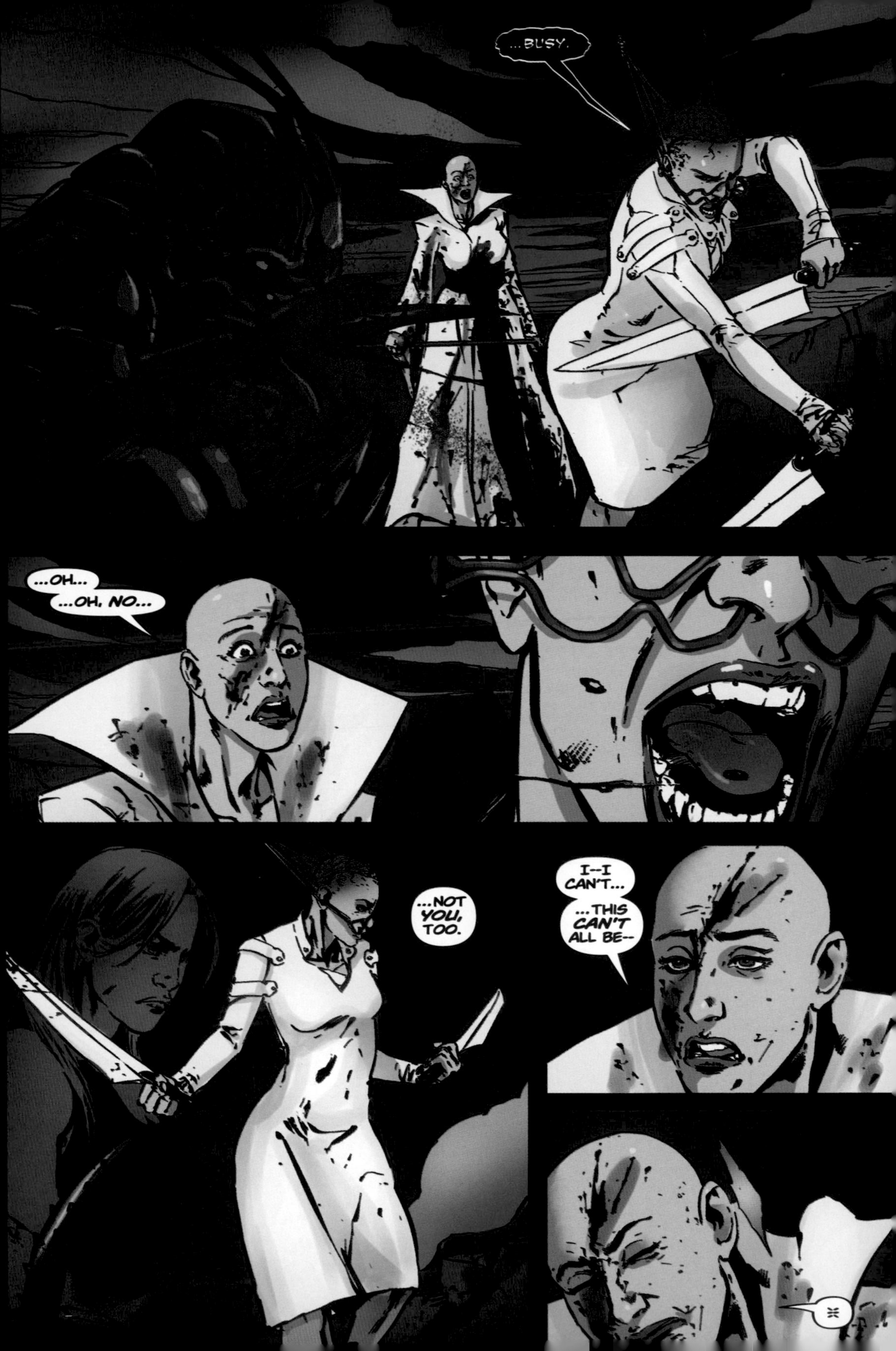
...BUSY.
...OH...
...OH, NO...
...NOT YOU, TOO.
I--I CAN'T...
...THIS CAN'T ALL BE--

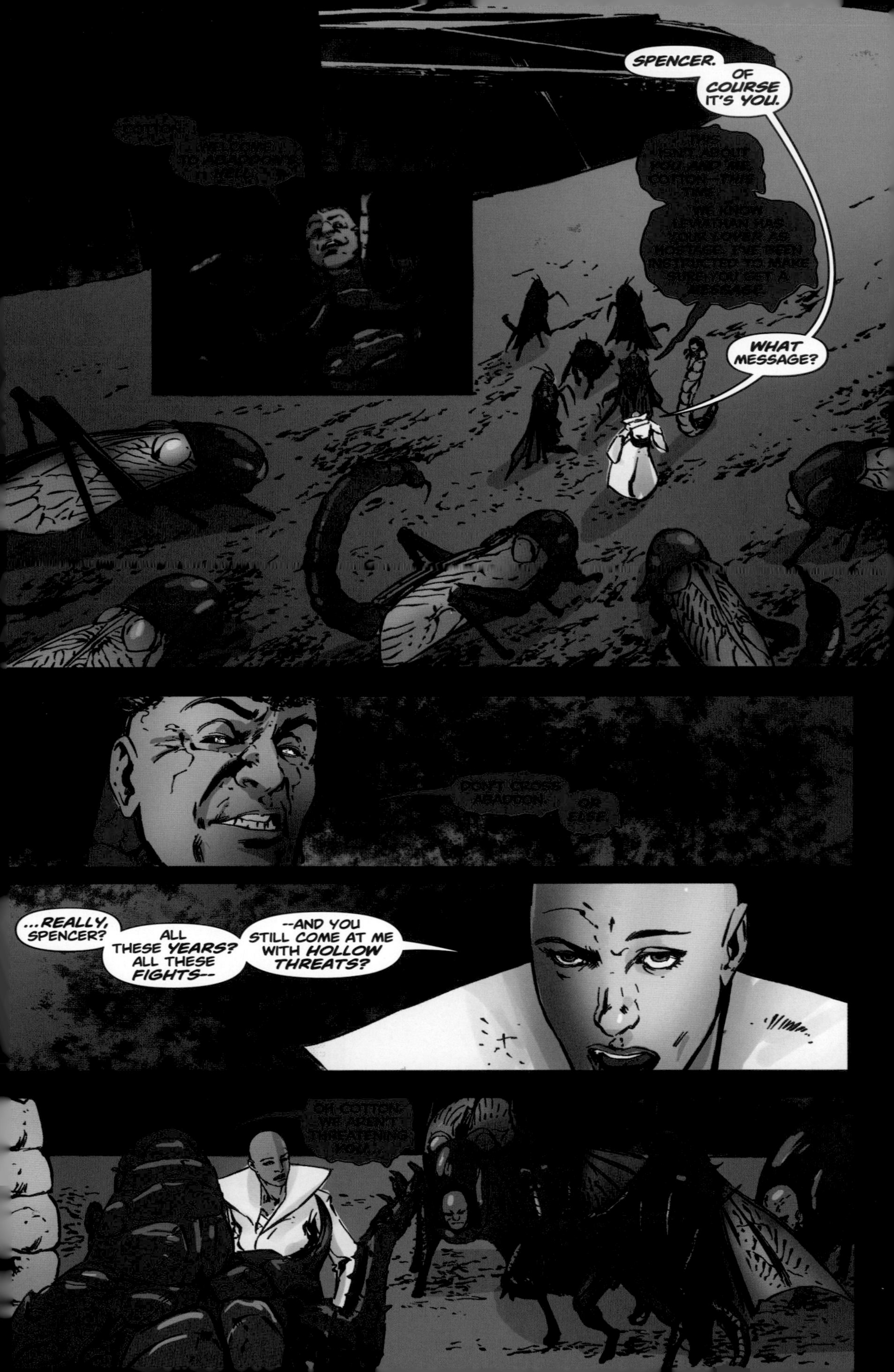
SPENCER.
OF COURSE IT'S YOU.
WHAT MESSAGE?
...REALLY, SPENCER?
ALL THESE YEARS? ALL THESE FIGHTS--
--AND YOU STILL COME AT ME WITH HOLLOW THREATS?

...WE'RE THREATENING YOUR *FAMILY*

...KIRSTY?

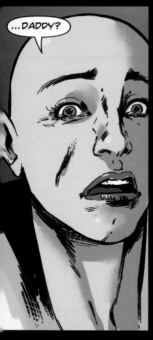

...DADDY?

JESUS, KIRSTY--

--WHAT'D THESE MONSTERS DO TO YOU?

THEY DIDN'T--

--IT WASN'T--

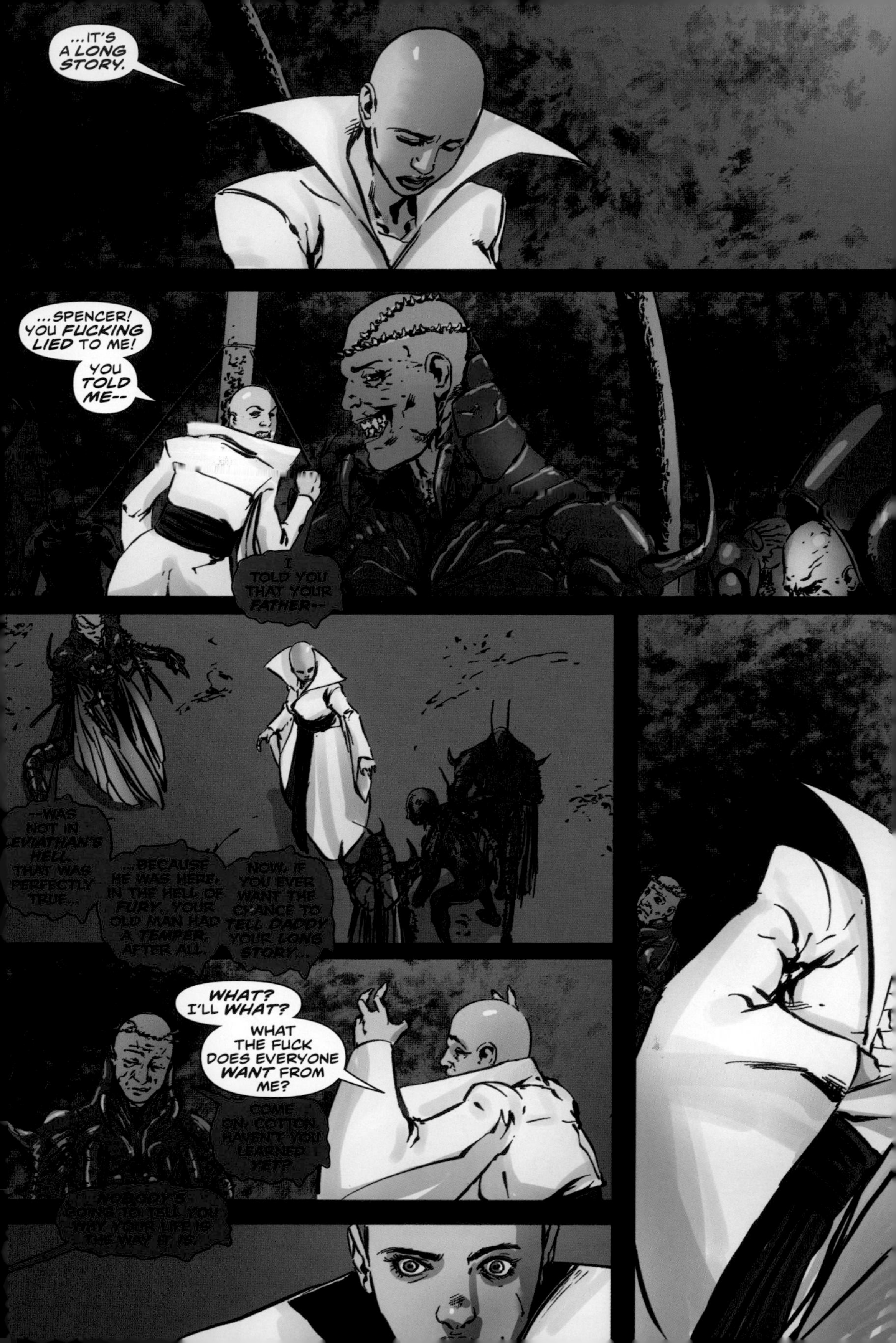
...IT'S A LONG STORY.
...SPENCER! YOU FUCKING LIED TO ME!
YOU TOLD ME--
I TOLD YOU THAT YOUR FATHER--
--WAS NOT IN LEVIATHAN'S HELL. THAT WAS PERFECTLY TRUE...
...BECAUSE HE WAS HERE, IN THE HELL OF FURY. YOUR OLD MAN HAD A TEMPER, AFTER ALL.
NOW, IF YOU EVER WANT THE CHANCE TO TELL DADDY YOUR LONG STORY...
WHAT? I'LL WHAT?
WHAT THE FUCK DOES EVERYONE WANT FROM ME?
COME ON, COTTON. HAVEN'T YOU LEARNED YET?
NOBODY'S GOING TO TELL YOU WHY YOUR LIFE IS THE WAY IT IS.

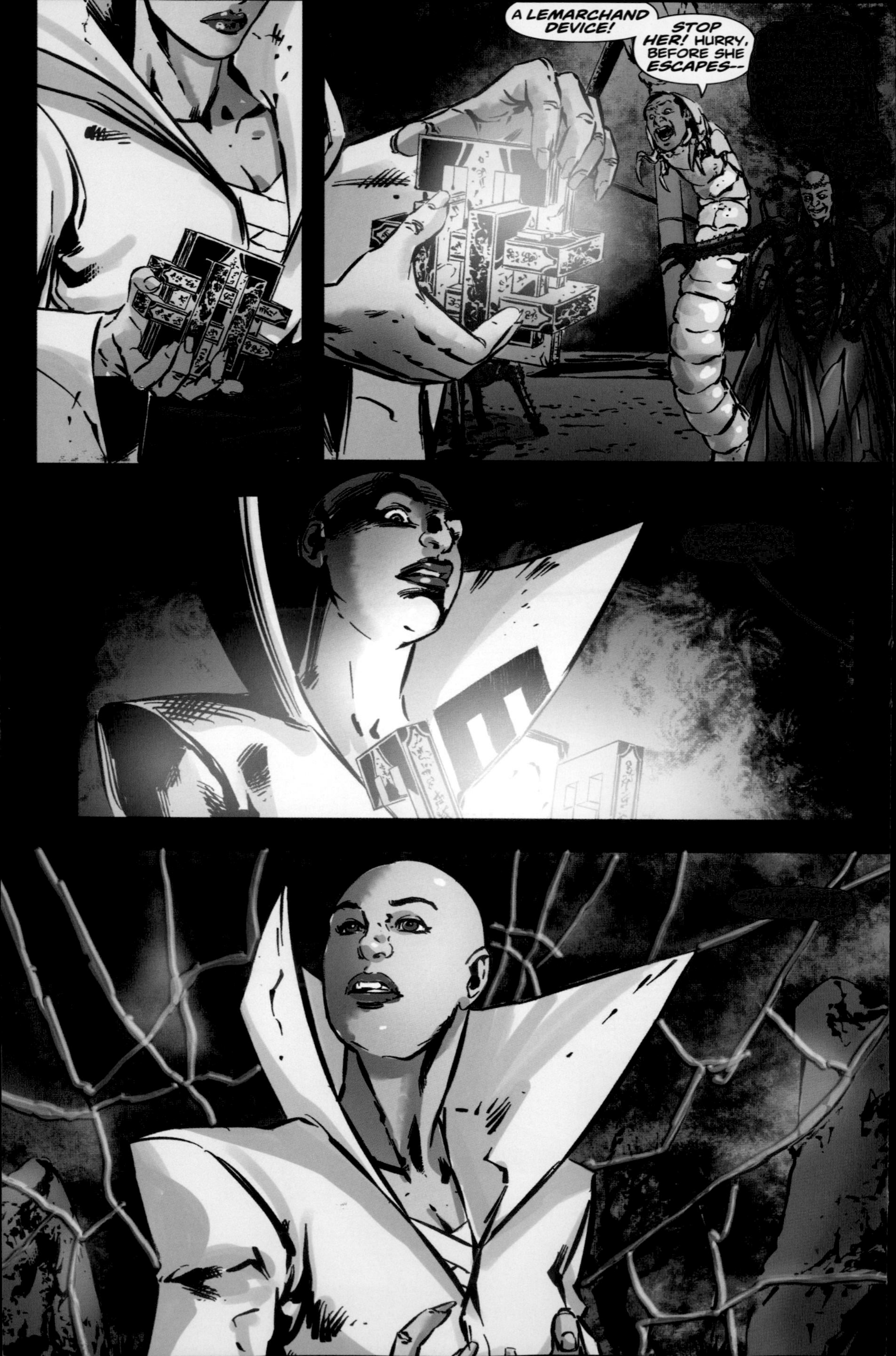
A LEMARCHAND DEVICE!
STOP HER! HURRY, BEFORE SHE ESCAPES--

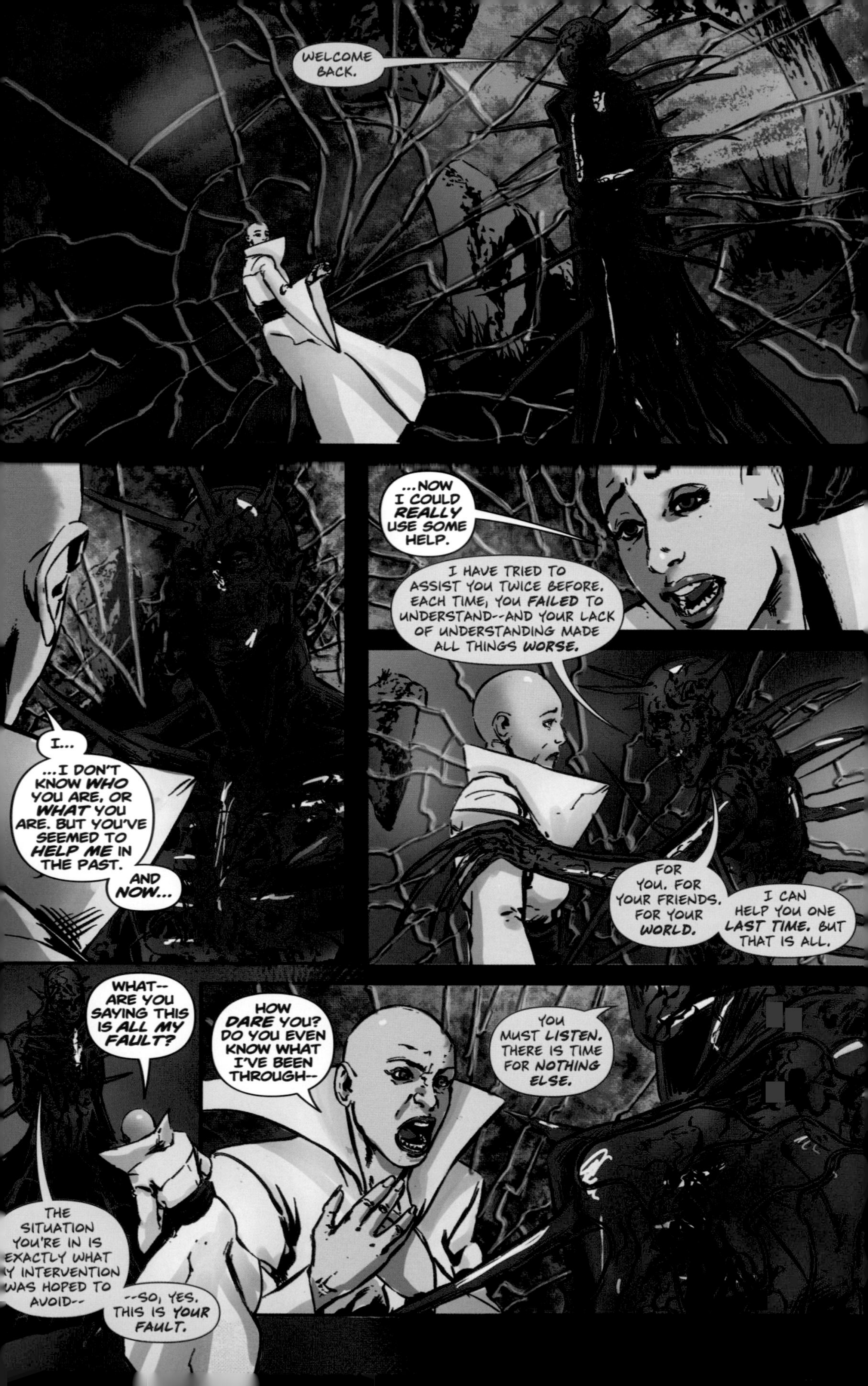
WELCOME BACK.
I...
...I DON'T KNOW WHO YOU ARE, OR WHAT YOU ARE. BUT YOU'VE SEEMED TO HELP ME IN THE PAST.
AND NOW...
...NOW I COULD REALLY USE SOME HELP.
I HAVE TRIED TO ASSIST YOU TWICE BEFORE. EACH TIME, YOU FAILED TO UNDERSTAND--AND YOUR LACK OF UNDERSTANDING MADE ALL THINGS WORSE.
FOR YOU. FOR YOUR FRIENDS. FOR YOUR WORLD.
I CAN HELP YOU ONE LAST TIME. BUT THAT IS ALL.
WHAT--ARE YOU SAYING THIS IS ALL MY FAULT?
THE SITUATION YOU'RE IN IS EXACTLY WHAT Y INTERVENTION WAS HOPED TO AVOID--
--SO, YES. THIS IS YOUR FAULT.
HOW DARE YOU? DO YOU EVEN KNOW WHAT I'VE BEEN THROUGH--
YOU MUST LISTEN. THERE IS TIME FOR NOTHING ELSE.

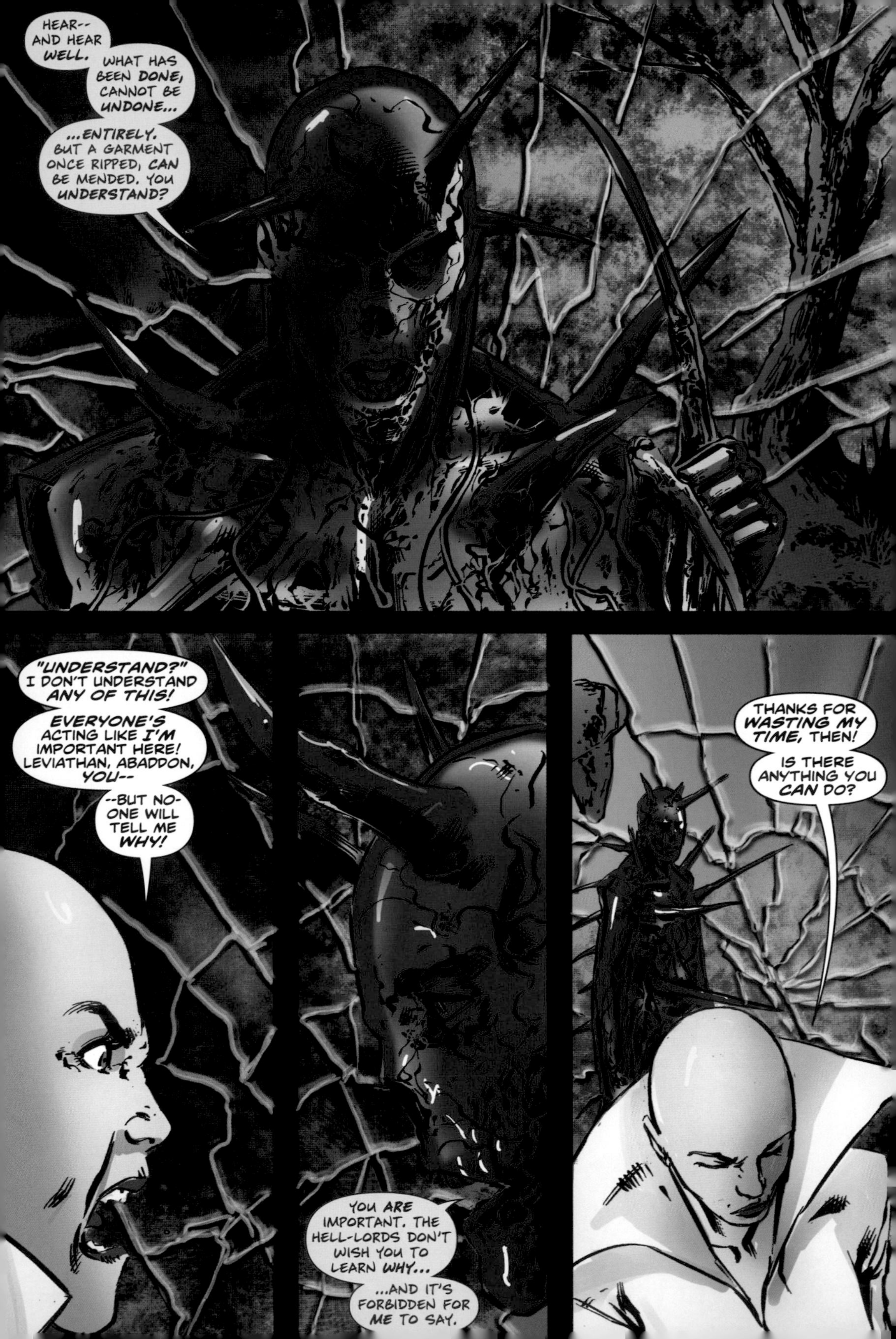
HEAR--
AND HEAR WELL.
WHAT HAS BEEN DONE, CANNOT BE UNDONE...
...ENTIRELY. BUT A GARMENT ONCE RIPPED, CAN BE MENDED. YOU UNDERSTAND?
"UNDERSTAND?" I DON'T UNDERSTAND ANY OF THIS!
EVERYONE'S ACTING LIKE I'M IMPORTANT HERE! LEVIATHAN, ABADDON, YOU--
--BUT NO-ONE WILL TELL ME WHY!
YOU ARE IMPORTANT. THE HELL-LORDS DON'T WISH YOU TO LEARN WHY...
...AND IT'S FORBIDDEN FOR ME TO SAY.
THANKS FOR WASTING MY TIME, THEN!
IS THERE ANYTHING YOU CAN DO?

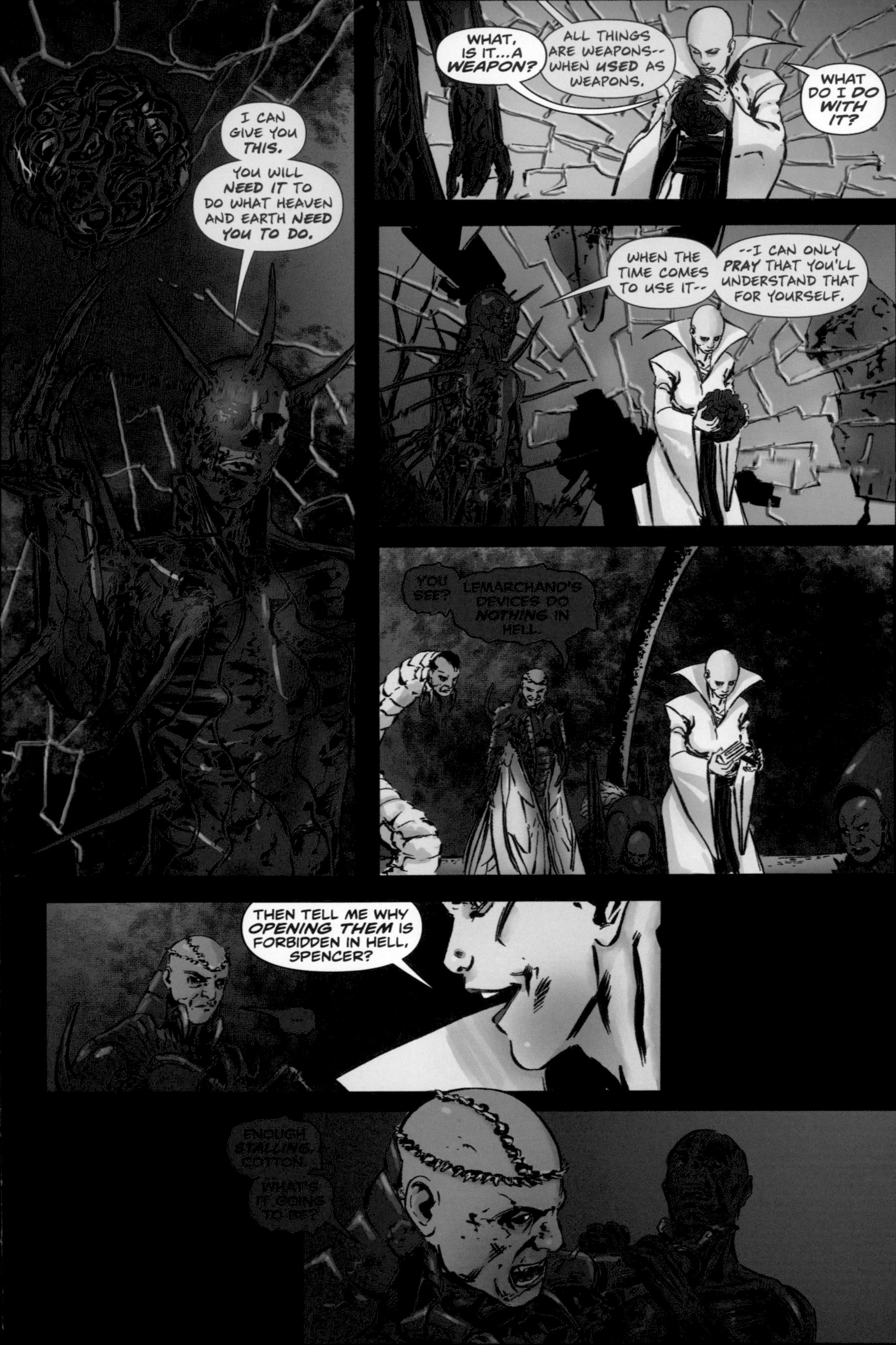
I CAN GIVE YOU THIS.
YOU WILL NEED IT TO DO WHAT HEAVEN AND EARTH NEED YOU TO DO.
WHAT, IS IT...A WEAPON?
ALL THINGS ARE WEAPONS-- WHEN USED AS WEAPONS.
WHAT DO I DO WITH IT?
WHEN THE TIME COMES TO USE IT--
--I CAN ONLY PRAY THAT YOU'LL UNDERSTAND THAT FOR YOURSELF.
YOU SEE?
LEMARCHAND'S DEVICES DO NOTHING IN HELL.
THEN TELL ME WHY OPENING THEM IS FORBIDDEN IN HELL, SPENCER?
ENOUGH STALLING, COTTON.
WHAT'S IT GOING TO BE?

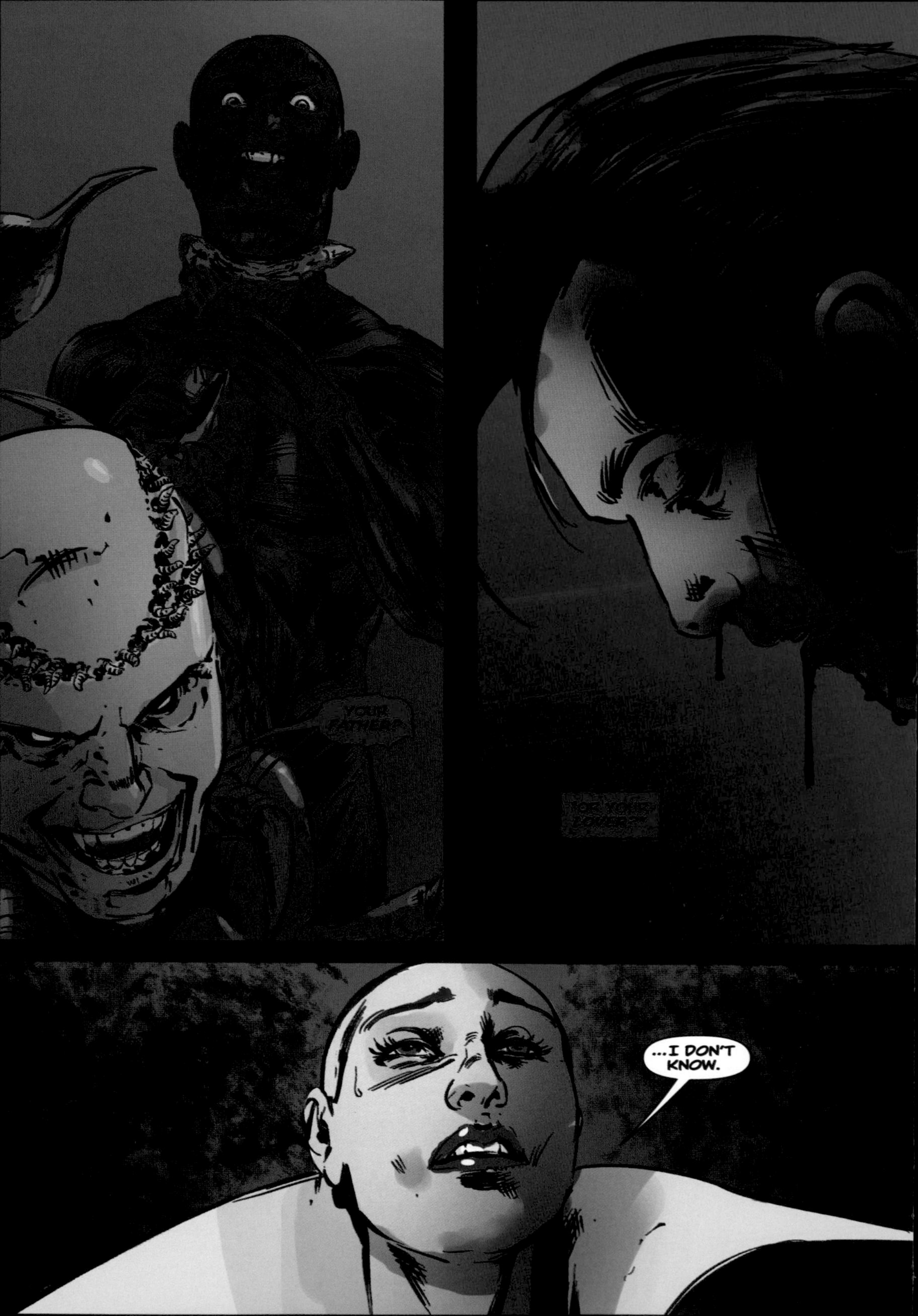
YOUR FATHER?
OR YOUR LOVER?
...I DON'T KNOW.

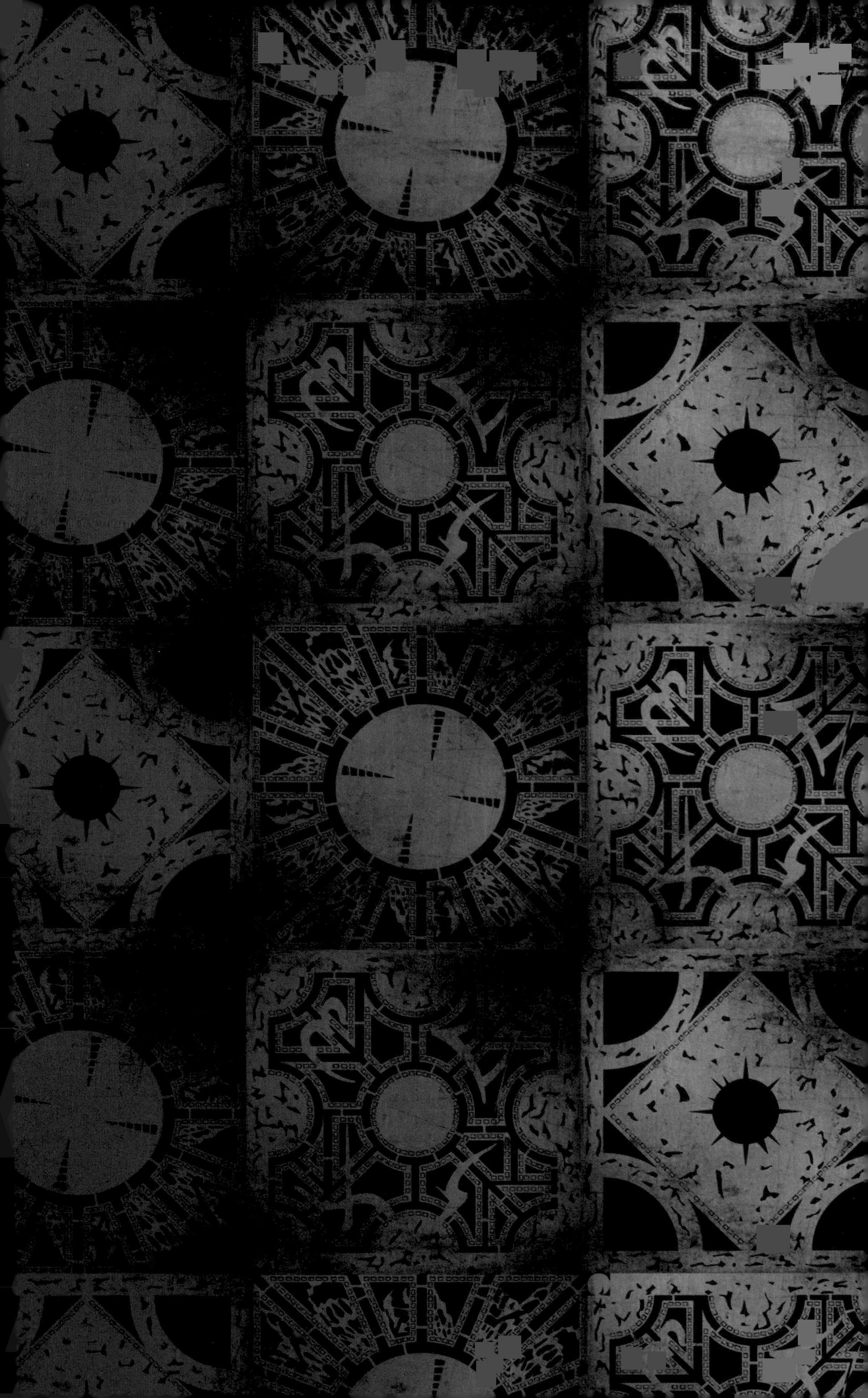

CHAPTER TWELVE

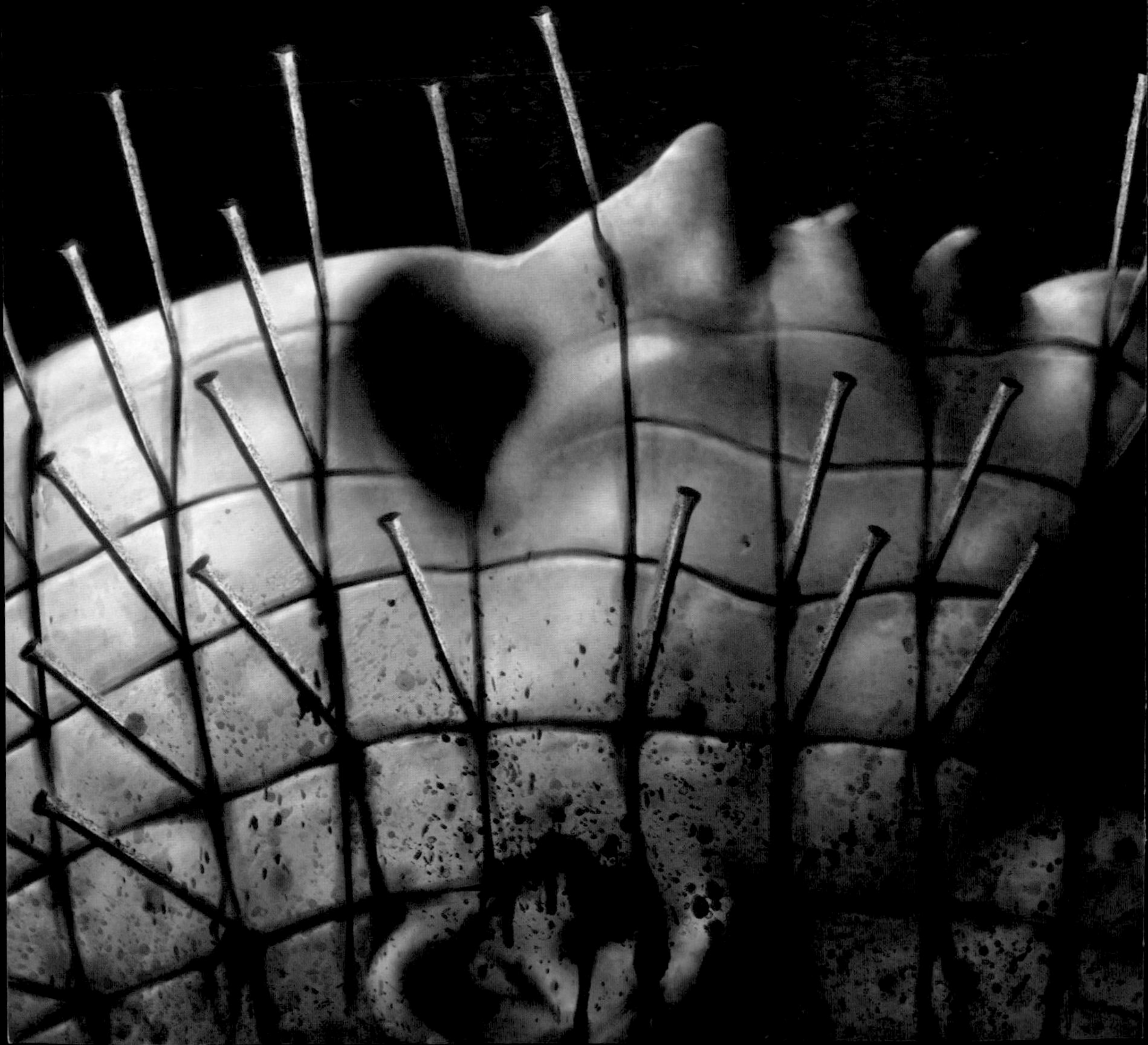

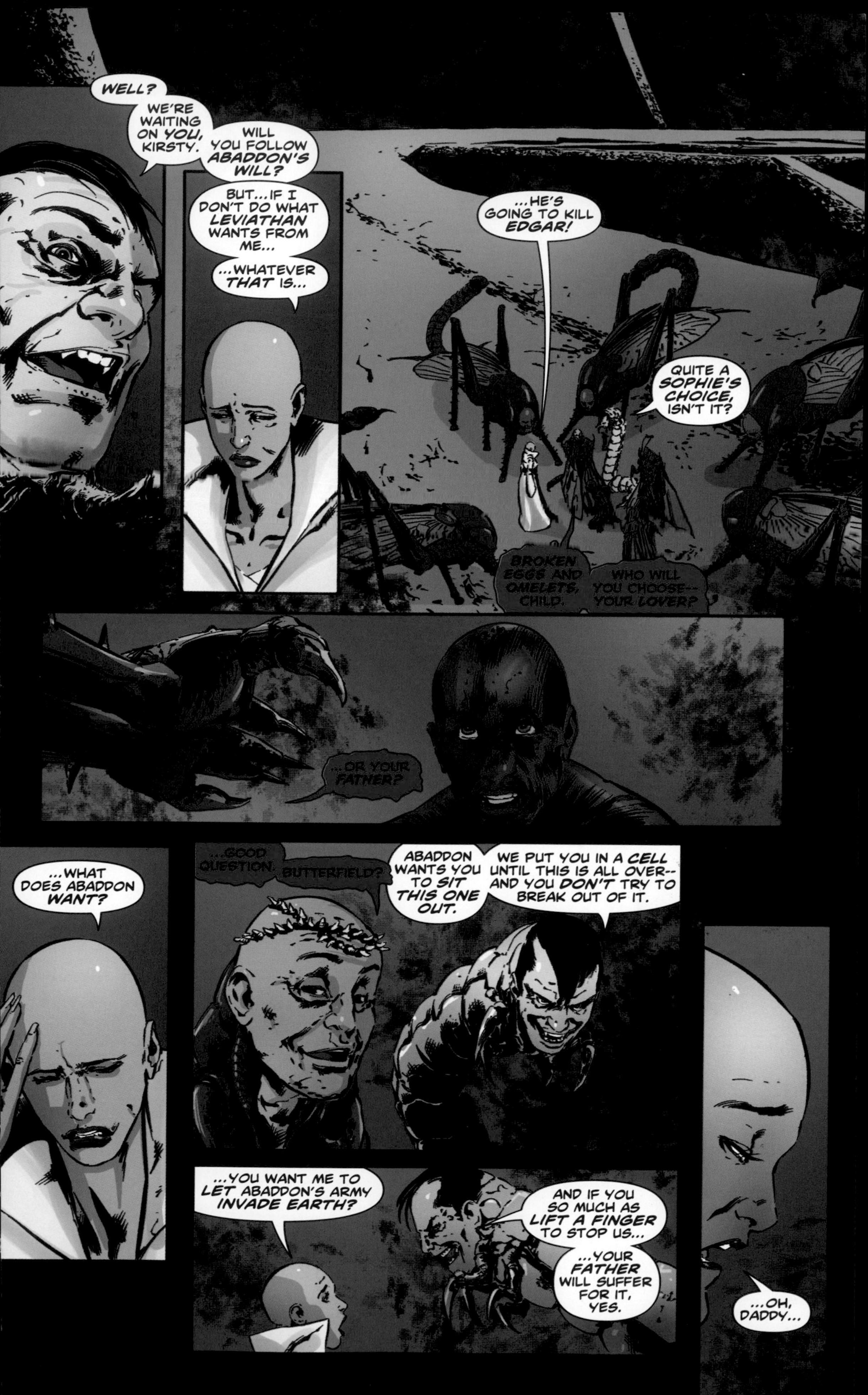
WELL?
WE'RE WAITING ON YOU, KIRSTY.
WILL YOU FOLLOW ABADDON'S WILL?
BUT... IF I DON'T DO WHAT LEVIATHAN WANTS FROM ME...
...WHATEVER THAT IS...
...HE'S GOING TO KILL EDGAR!
QUITE A SOPHIE'S CHOICE, ISN'T IT?
BROKEN EGGS AND OMELETS, CHILD.
WHO WILL YOU CHOOSE-- YOUR LOVER?
...OR YOUR FATHER?
...WHAT DOES ABADDON WANT?
...GOOD QUESTION.
BUTTERFIELD?
ABADDON WANTS YOU TO SIT THIS ONE OUT.
WE PUT YOU IN A CELL UNTIL THIS IS ALL OVER-- AND YOU DON'T TRY TO BREAK OUT OF IT.
...YOU WANT ME TO LET ABADDON'S ARMY INVADE EARTH?
AND IF YOU SO MUCH AS LIFT A FINGER TO STOP US...
...YOUR FATHER WILL SUFFER FOR IT, YES.
...OH, DADDY...

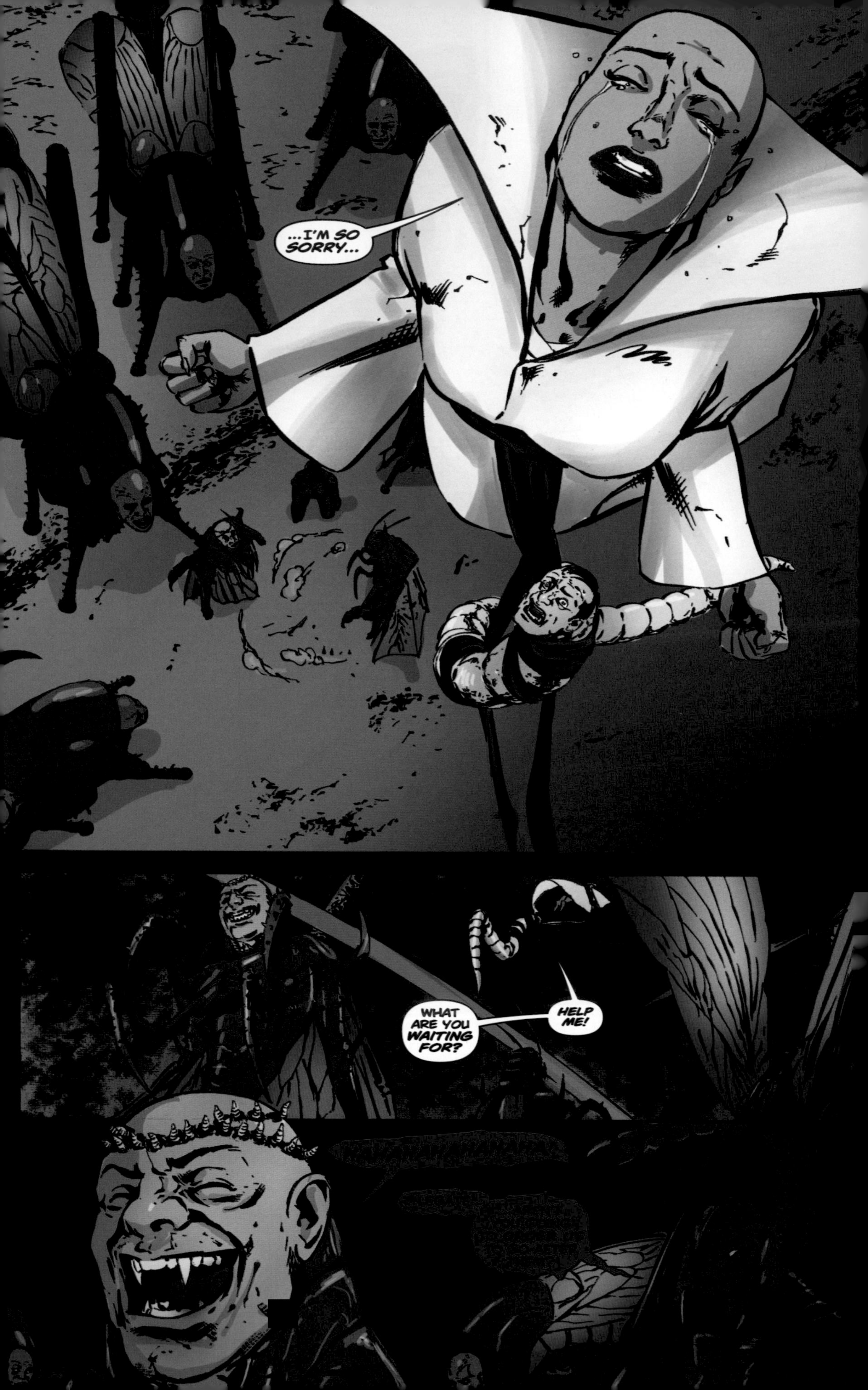
...I'M SO SORRY...
WHAT ARE YOU WAITING FOR?
HELP ME!

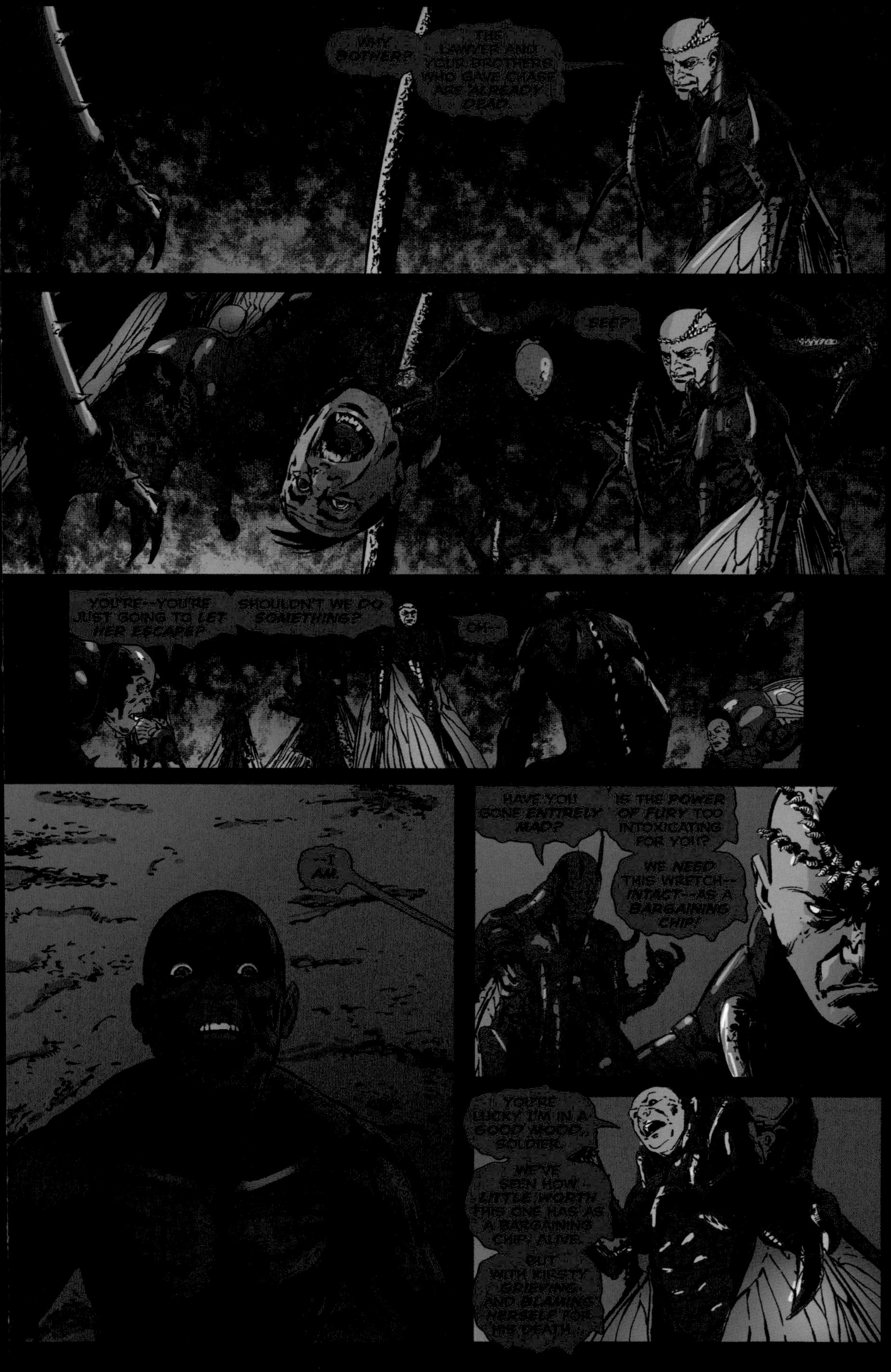
WHY BOTHER?
THE LAWYER AND YOUR BROTHERS WHO GAVE CHASE ARE ALREADY DEAD.
SEE?
YOU'RE--YOU'RE JUST GOING TO LET HER ESCAPE?
SHOULDN'T WE DO SOMETHING?
OH--
--I AM.
HAVE YOU GONE ENTIRELY MAD?
IS THE POWER OF FURY TOO INTOXICATING FOR YOU?
WE NEED THIS WRETCH--INTACT--AS A BARGAINING CHIP!
YOU'RE LUCKY I'M IN A GOOD MOOD, SOLDIER.
WE'VE SEEN HOW LITTLE WORTH THIS ONE HAS AS A BARGAINING CHIP, ALIVE.
BUT WITH KIRSTY GRIEVING, AND BLAMING HERSELF FOR HIS DEATH...

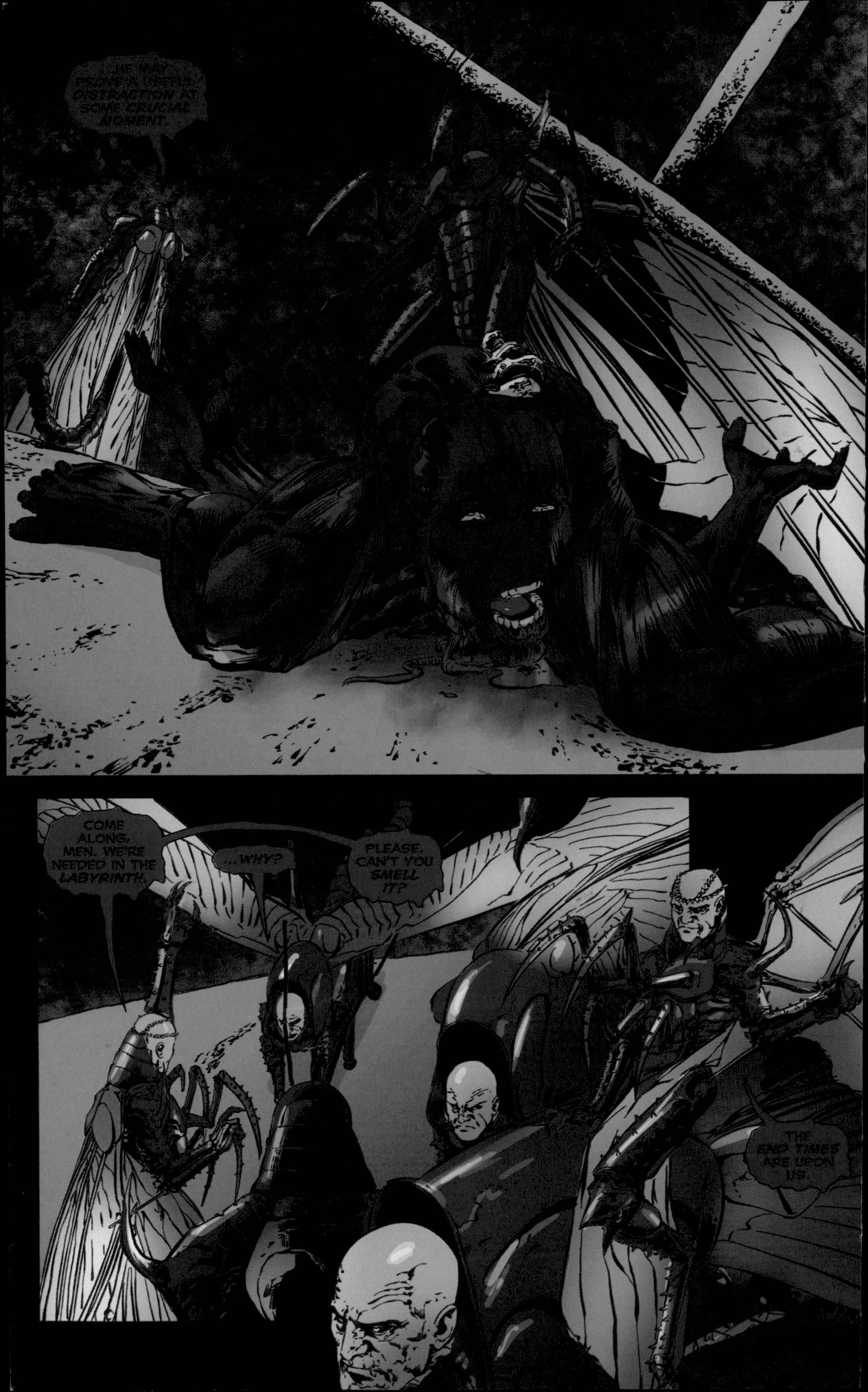
HE MAY PROVE A USEFUL DISTRACTION AT SOME CRUCIAL MOMENT.
COME ALONG, MEN. WE'RE NEEDED IN THE LABYRINTH.
...WHY?
PLEASE. CAN'T YOU SMELL IT?
THE END TIMES ARE UPON US.

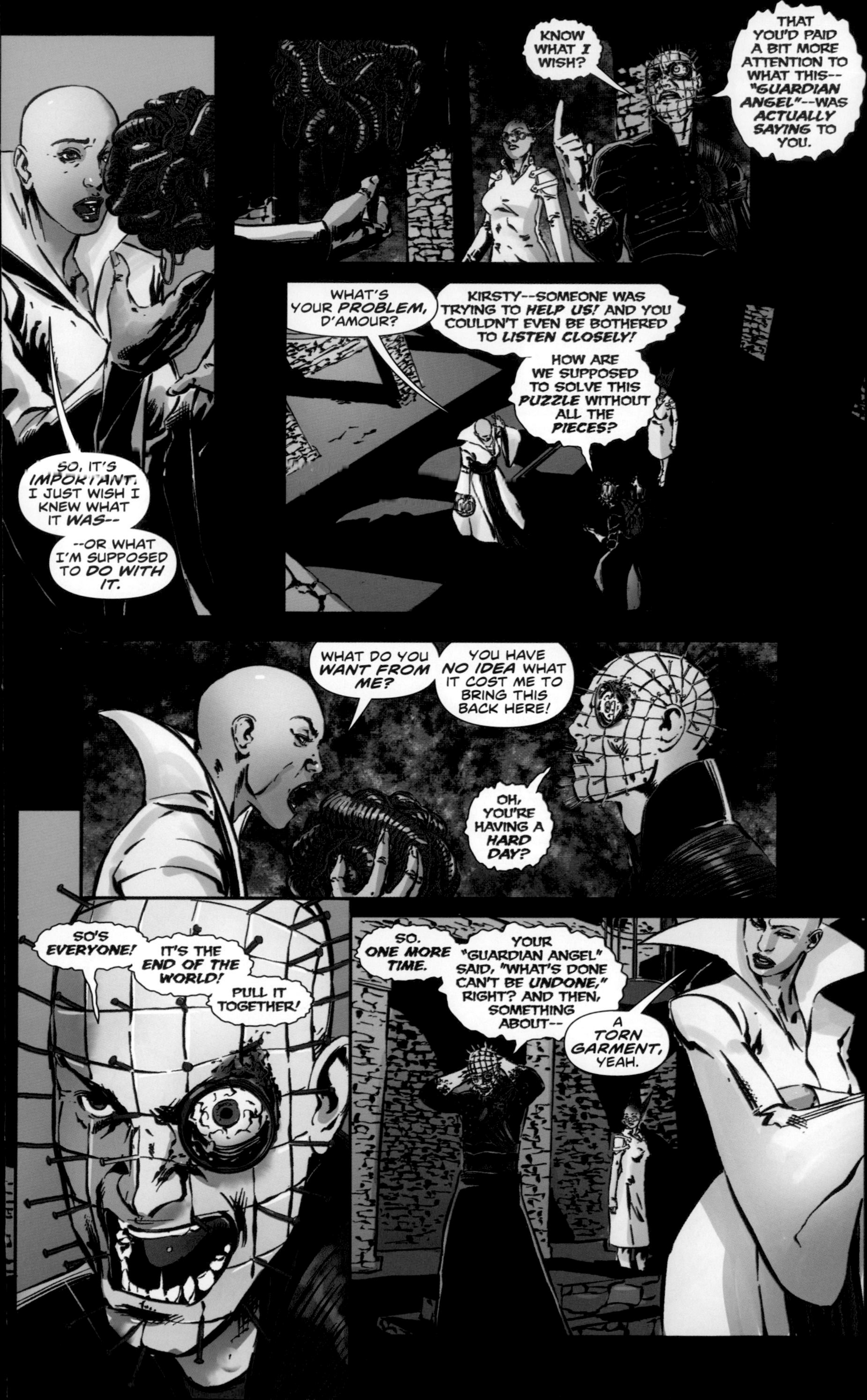
SO, IT'S IMPORTANT. I JUST WISH I KNEW WHAT IT WAS--
--OR WHAT I'M SUPPOSED TO DO WITH IT.
KNOW WHAT I WISH?
THAT YOU'D PAID A BIT MORE ATTENTION TO WHAT THIS--"GUARDIAN ANGEL"--WAS ACTUALLY SAYING TO YOU.
WHAT'S YOUR PROBLEM, D'AMOUR?
KIRSTY--SOMEONE WAS TRYING TO HELP US! AND YOU COULDN'T EVEN BE BOTHERED TO LISTEN CLOSELY!
HOW ARE WE SUPPOSED TO SOLVE THIS PUZZLE WITHOUT ALL THE PIECES?
WHAT DO YOU WANT FROM ME?
YOU HAVE NO IDEA WHAT IT COST ME TO BRING THIS BACK HERE!
OH, YOU'RE HAVING A HARD DAY?
SO'S EVERYONE!
IT'S THE END OF THE WORLD!
PULL IT TOGETHER!
SO. ONE MORE TIME.
YOUR "GUARDIAN ANGEL" SAID, "WHAT'S DONE CAN'T BE UNDONE," RIGHT? AND THEN, SOMETHING ABOUT--
A TORN GARMENT, YEAH.

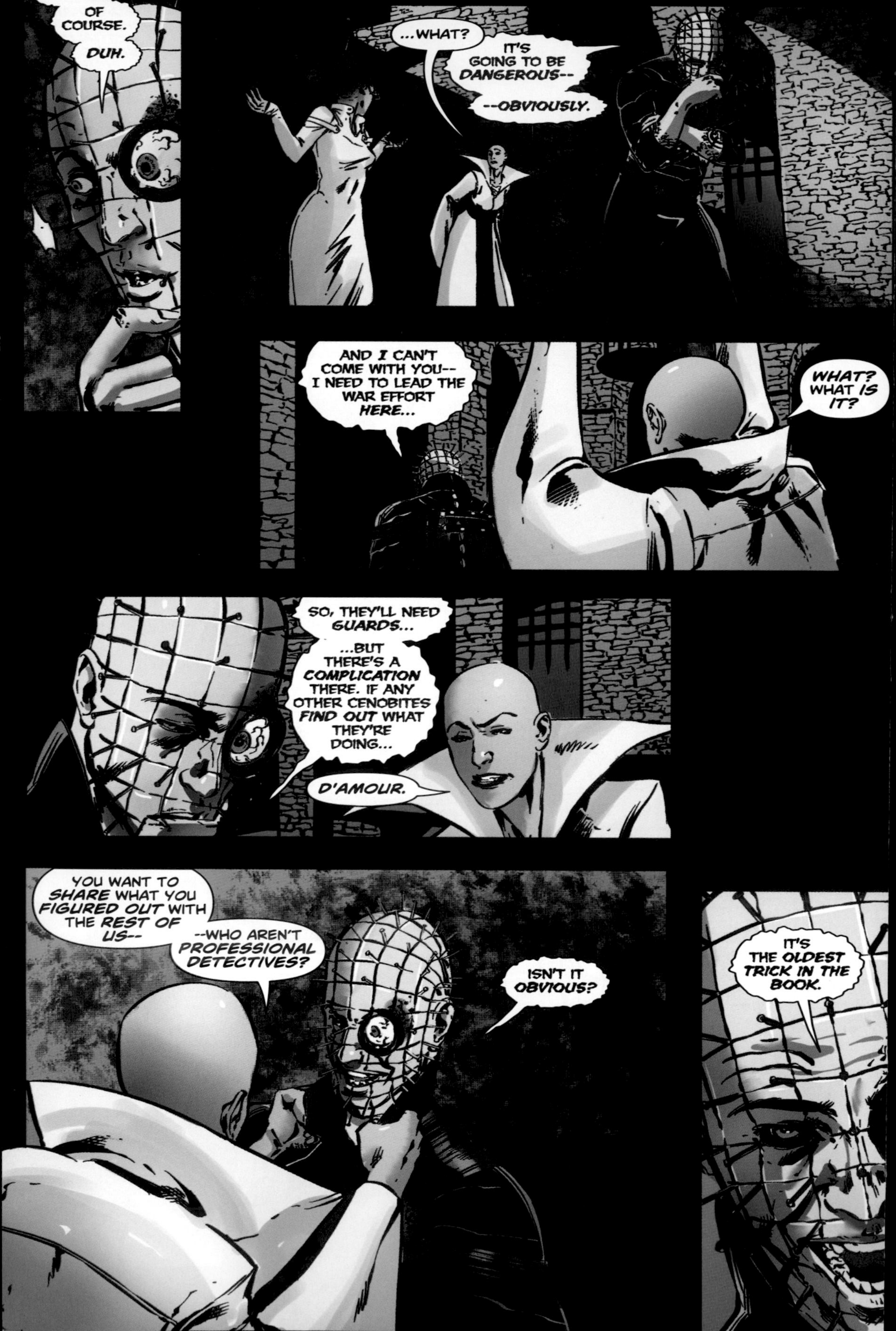
...OH.
OF COURSE.
DUH.
...WHAT?
IT'S GOING TO BE DANGEROUS--
--OBVIOUSLY.
AND I CAN'T COME WITH YOU-- I NEED TO LEAD THE WAR EFFORT HERE...
WHAT? WHAT IS IT?
SO, THEY'LL NEED GUARDS...
...BUT THERE'S A COMPLICATION THERE. IF ANY OTHER CENOBITES FIND OUT WHAT THEY'RE DOING...
D'AMOUR.
YOU WANT TO SHARE WHAT YOU FIGURED OUT WITH THE REST OF US--
--WHO AREN'T PROFESSIONAL DETECTIVES?
ISN'T IT OBVIOUS?
IT'S THE OLDEST TRICK IN THE BOOK.

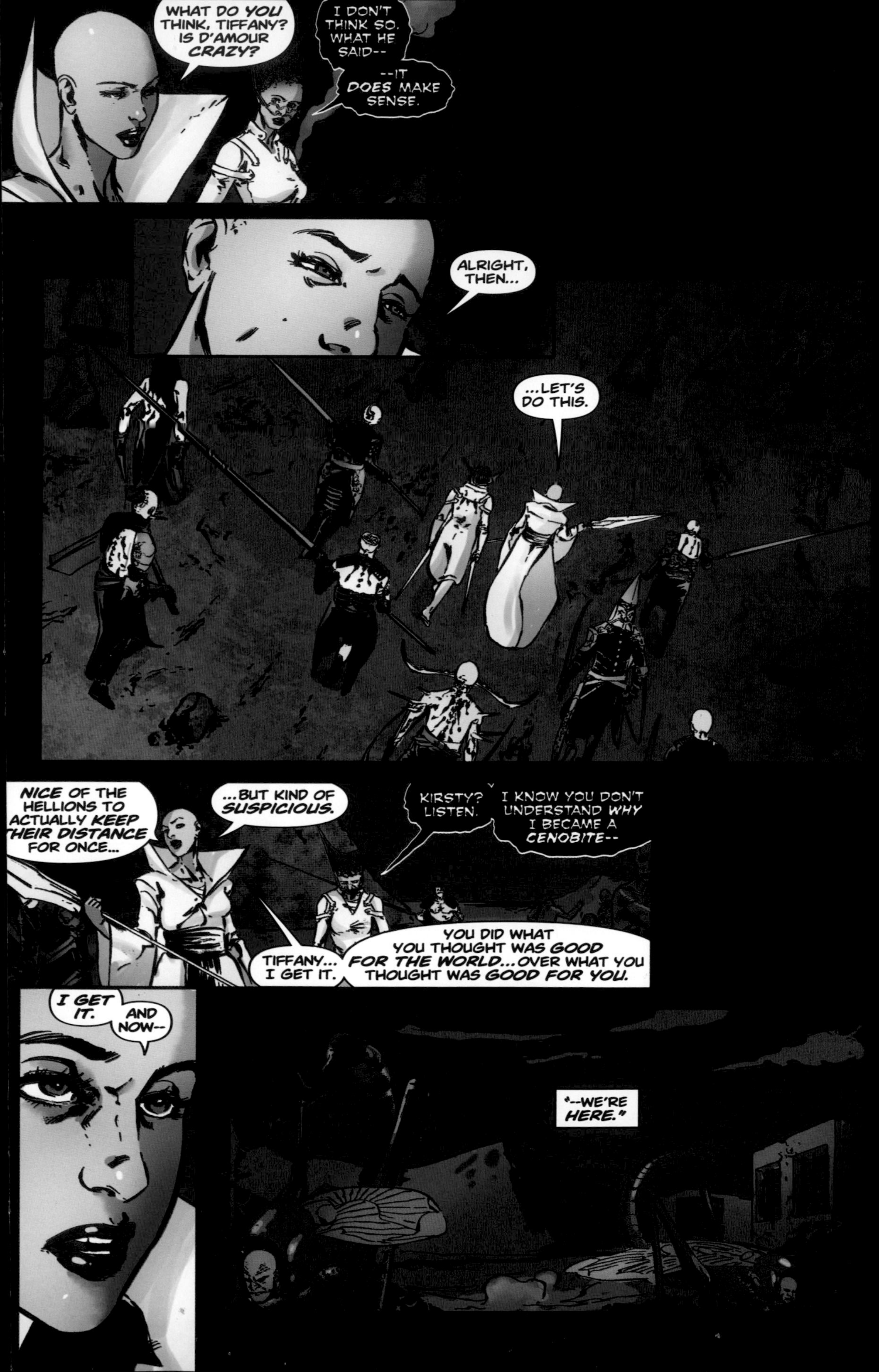
WHAT DO YOU THINK, TIFFANY? IS D'AMOUR CRAZY?
I DON'T THINK SO. WHAT HE SAID--
--IT DOES MAKE SENSE.
ALRIGHT, THEN...
...LET'S DO THIS.
NICE OF THE HELLIONS TO ACTUALLY KEEP THEIR DISTANCE FOR ONCE...
...BUT KIND OF SUSPICIOUS.
KIRSTY? LISTEN.
I KNOW YOU DON'T UNDERSTAND WHY I BECAME A CENOBITE--
TIFFANY... I GET IT.
YOU DID WHAT YOU THOUGHT WAS GOOD FOR THE WORLD...OVER WHAT YOU THOUGHT WAS GOOD FOR YOU.
I GET IT.
AND NOW--
"--WE'RE HERE."

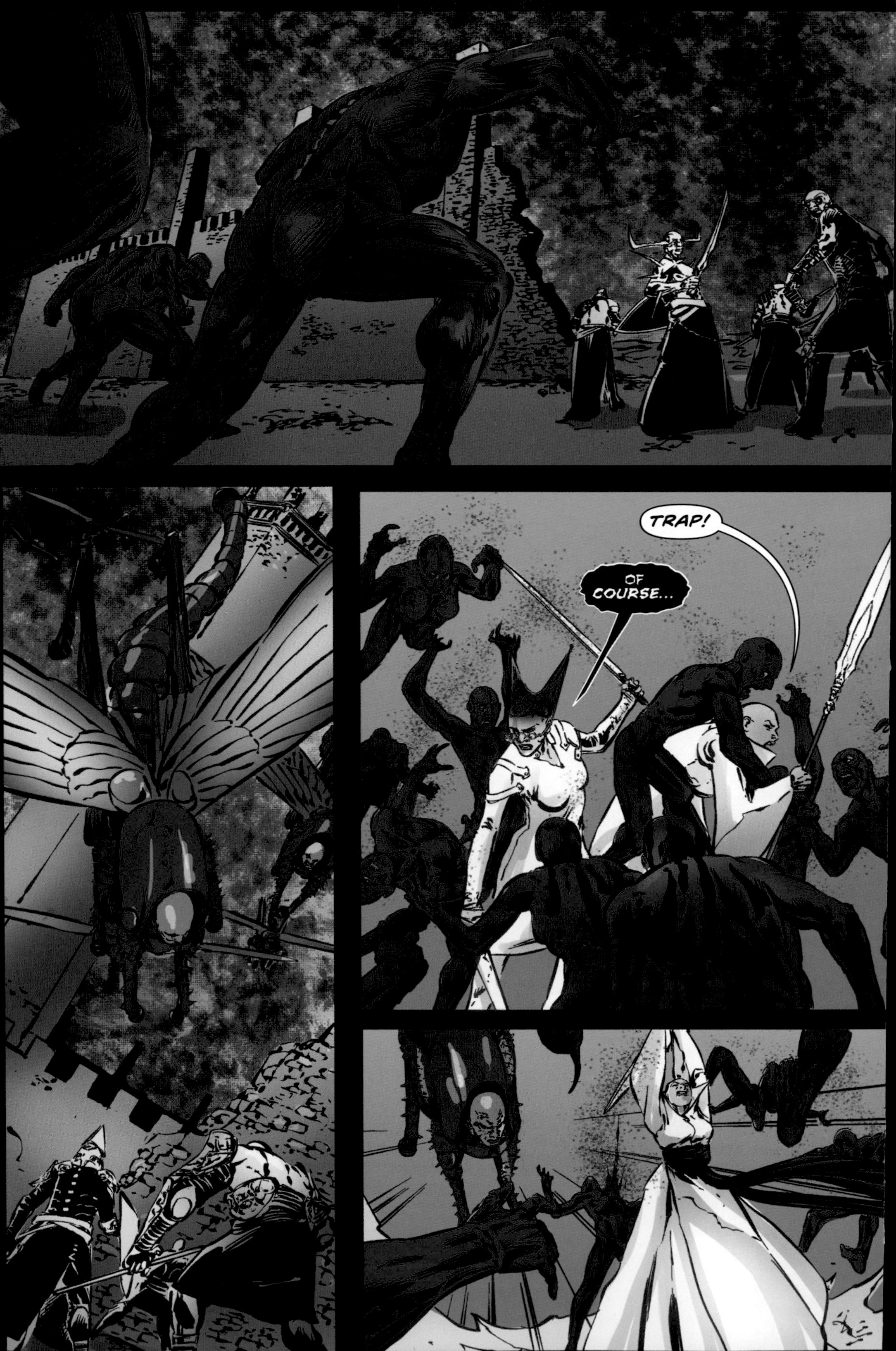
OF COURSE...
TRAP!

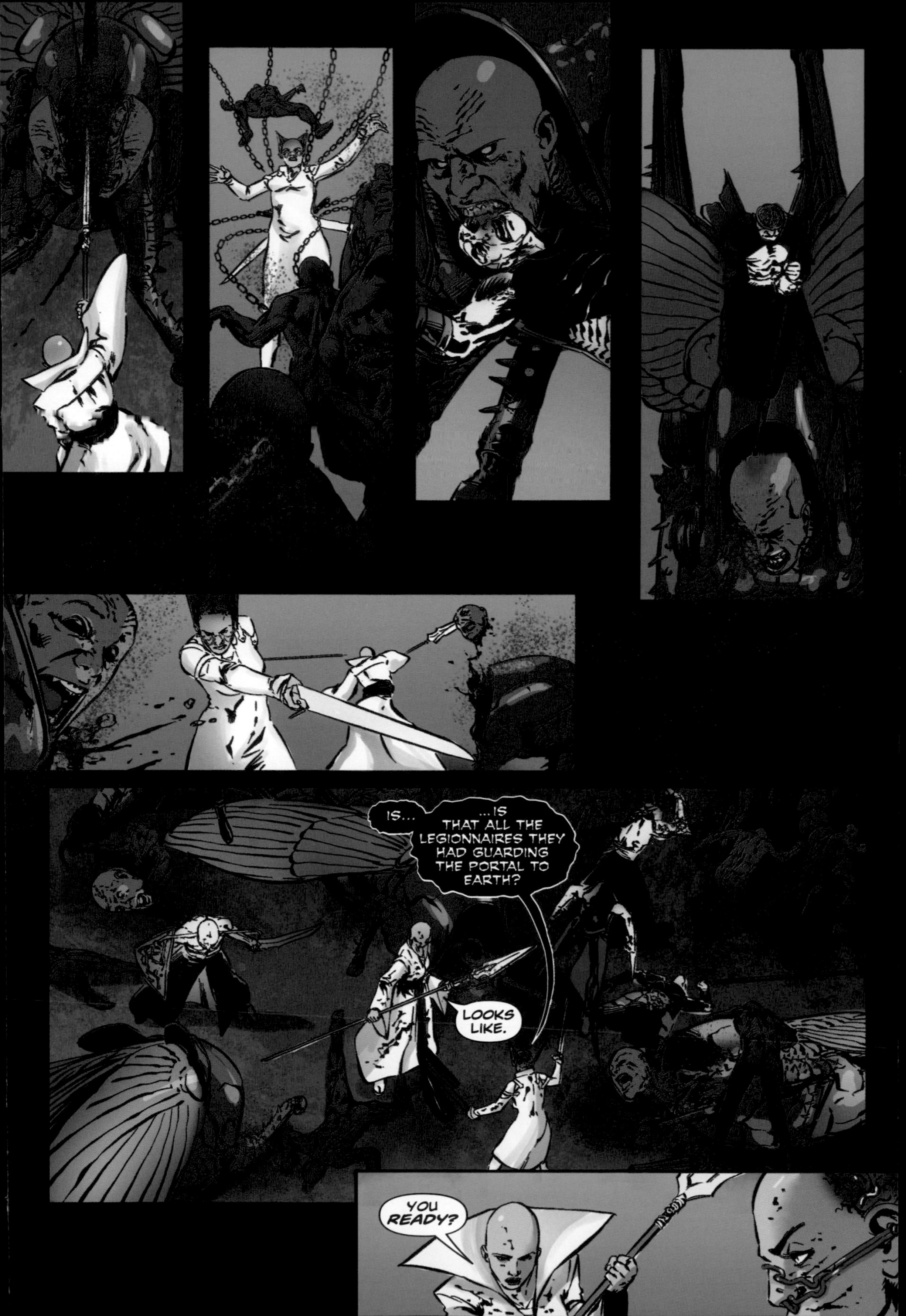
IS...
...IS THAT ALL THE LEGIONNAIRES THEY HAD GUARDING THE PORTAL TO EARTH?
LOOKS LIKE.
YOU READY?

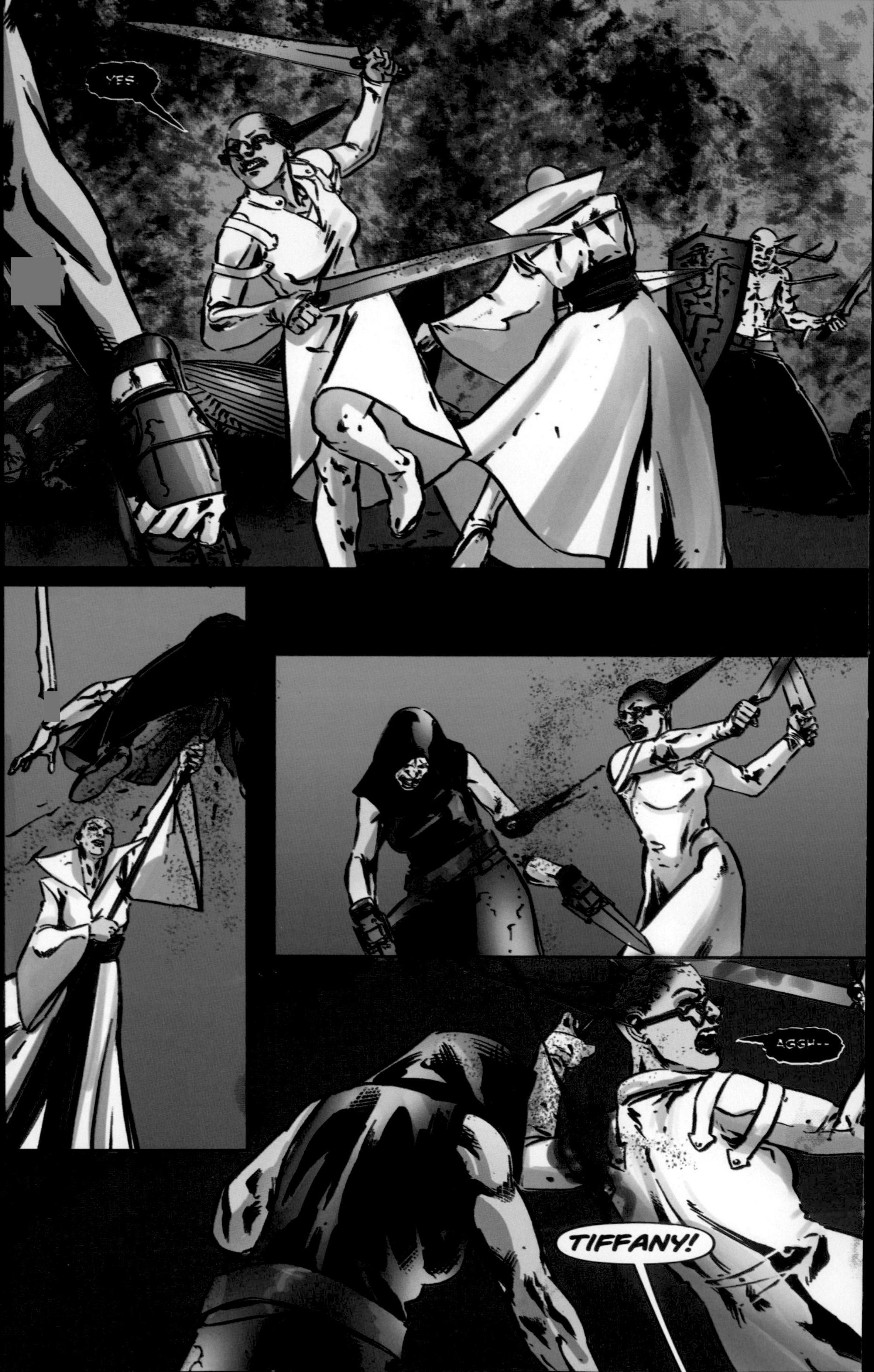
YES.
AGGH--
TIFFANY!

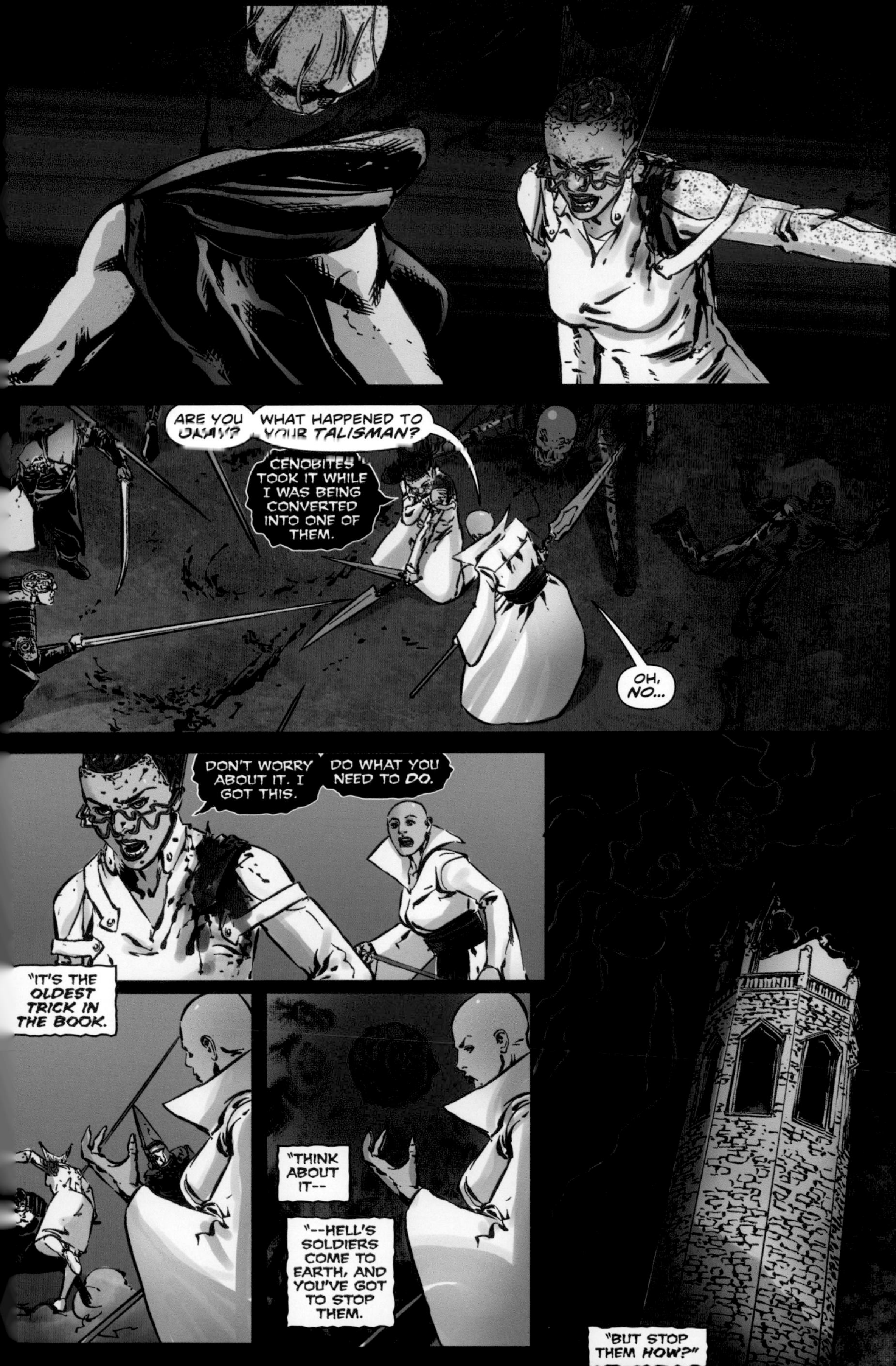
ARE YOU OKAY?
WHAT HAPPENED TO YOUR TALISMAN?
CENOBITES TOOK IT WHILE I WAS BEING CONVERTED INTO ONE OF THEM.
OH, NO...
DON'T WORRY ABOUT IT. I GOT THIS.
DO WHAT YOU NEED TO DO.
"IT'S THE OLDEST TRICK IN THE BOOK.
"THINK ABOUT IT--
"--HELL'S SOLDIERS COME TO EARTH, AND YOU'VE GOT TO STOP THEM.
"BUT STOP THEM HOW?"

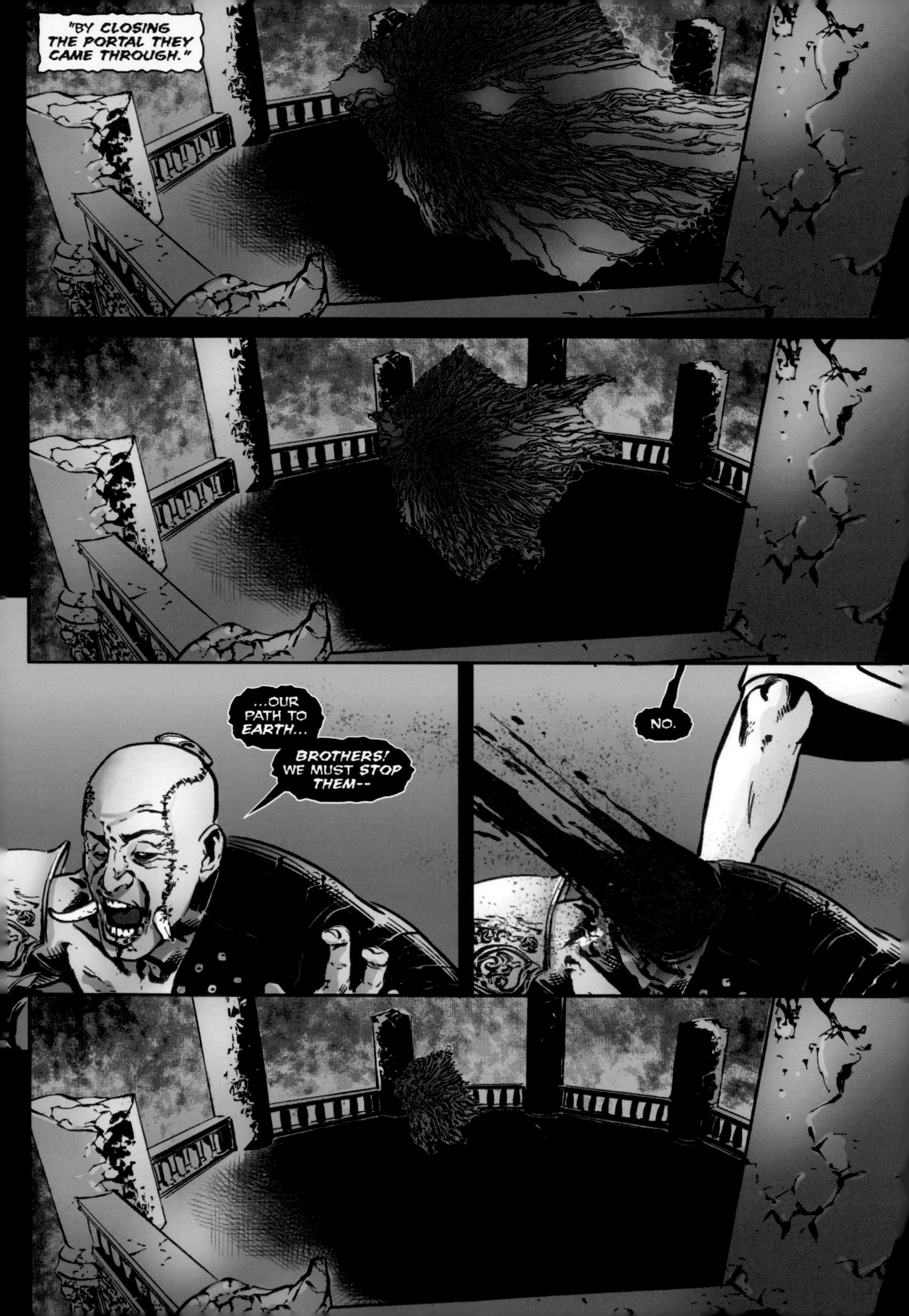
"BY CLOSING THE PORTAL THEY CAME THROUGH."
...OUR PATH TO EARTH...
BROTHERS! WE MUST STOP THEM--
NO.

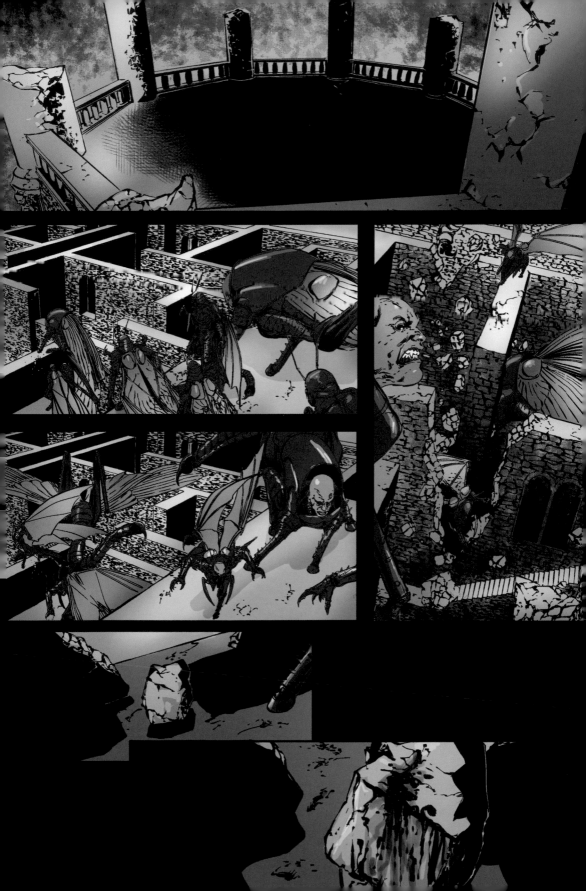

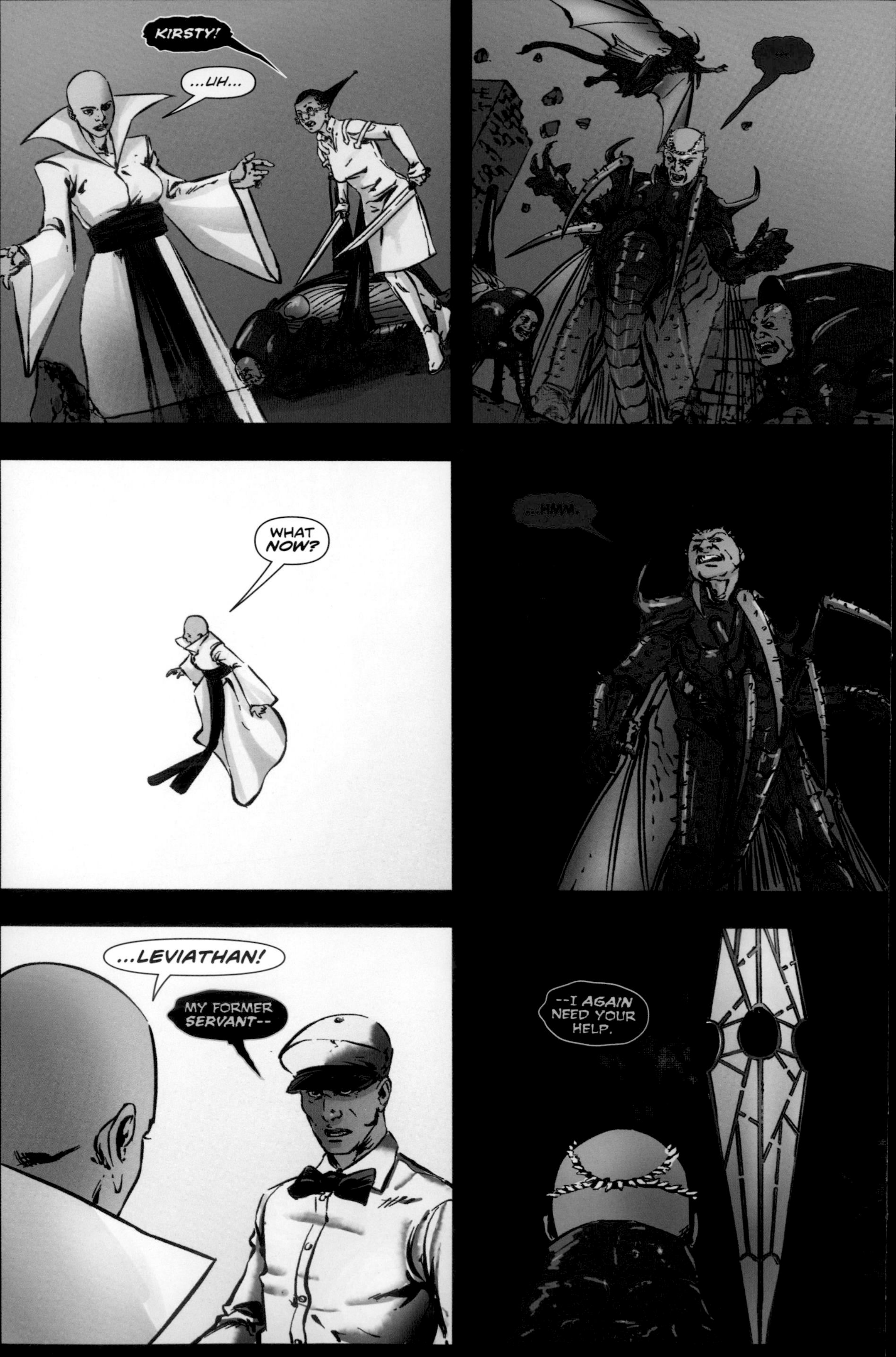
KIRSTY!
...UH...
WHAT NOW?
...HMM.
...LEVIATHAN!
MY FORMER SERVANT--
--I AGAIN NEED YOUR HELP.

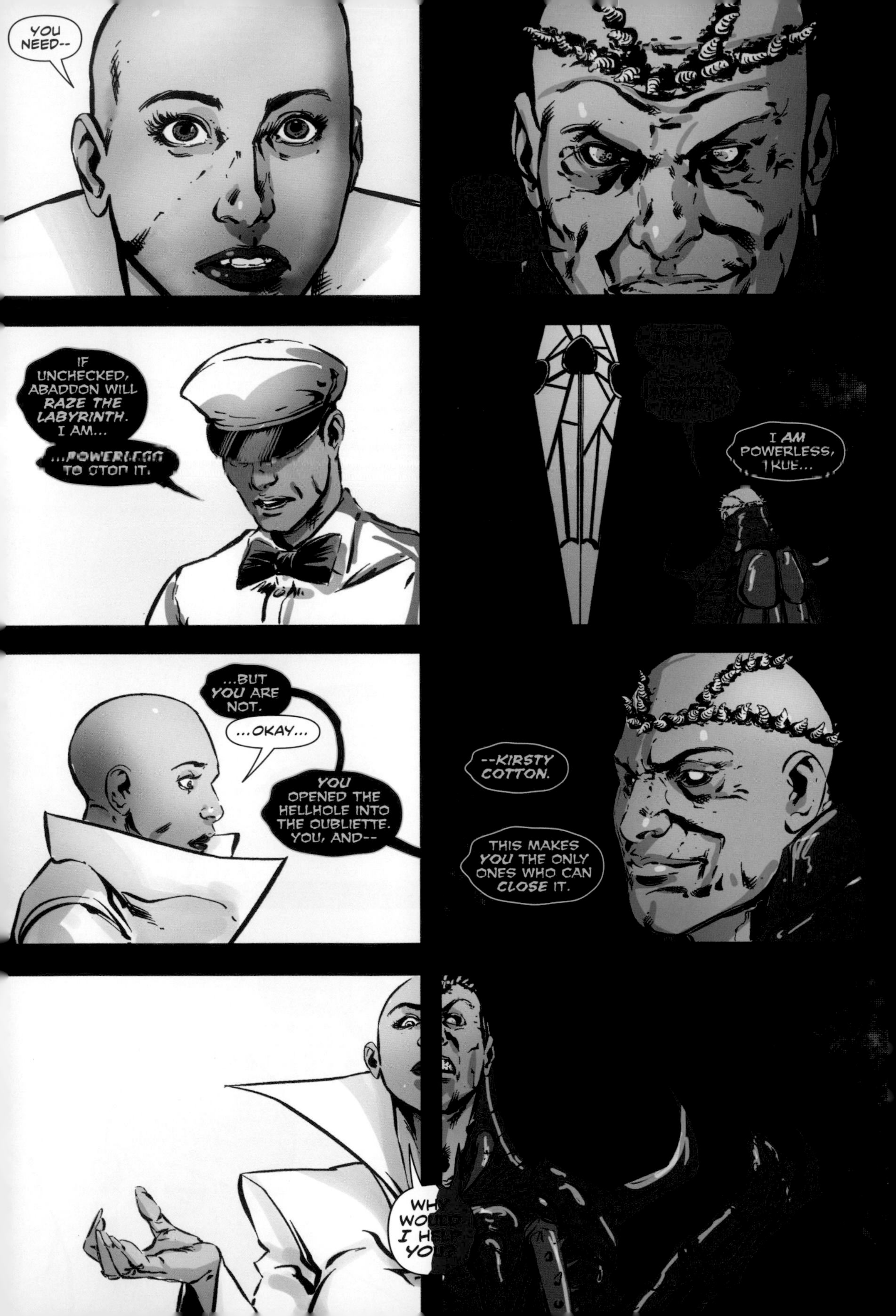
YOU NEED--
IF UNCHECKED, ABADDON WILL RAZE THE LABYRINTH. I AM...
...POWERLESS TO STOP IT.
I AM POWERLESS, TRUE...
...BUT YOU ARE NOT.
...OKAY...
YOU OPENED THE HELLHOLE INTO THE OUBLIETTE. YOU, AND--
--KIRSTY COTTON.
THIS MAKES YOU THE ONLY ONES WHO CAN CLOSE IT.
WH WOU I HE YO

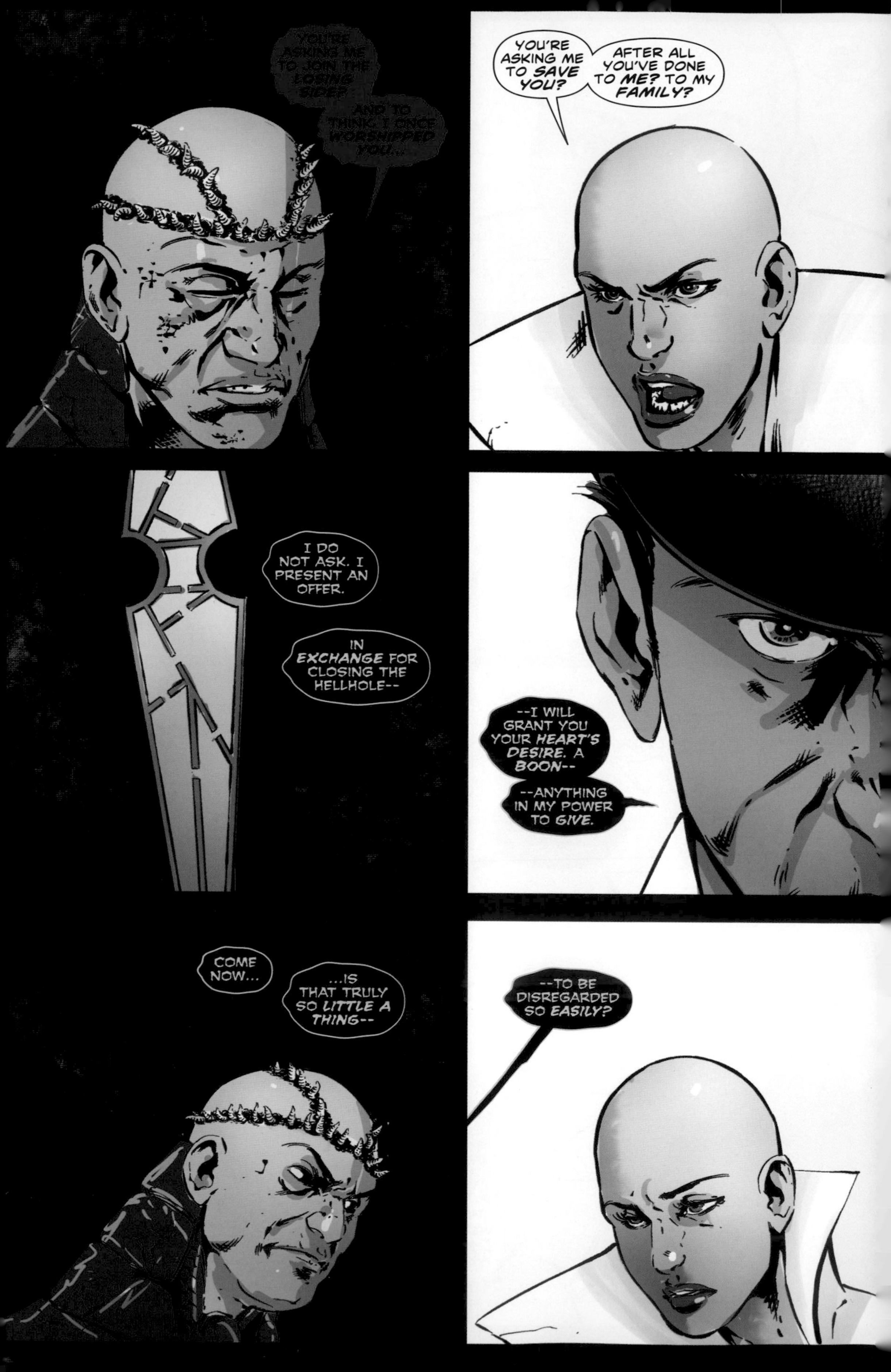
YOU'RE ASKING ME TO JOIN THE LOSING SIDE?
AND TO THINK, I ONCE WORSHIPPED YOU...
YOU'RE ASKING ME TO SAVE YOU?
AFTER ALL YOU'VE DONE TO ME? TO MY FAMILY?
I DO NOT ASK. I PRESENT AN OFFER.
IN EXCHANGE FOR CLOSING THE HELLHOLE--
--I WILL GRANT YOU YOUR HEART'S DESIRE. A BOON--
--ANYTHING IN MY POWER TO GIVE.
COME NOW...
...IS THAT TRULY SO LITTLE A THING--
--TO BE DISREGARDED SO EASILY?

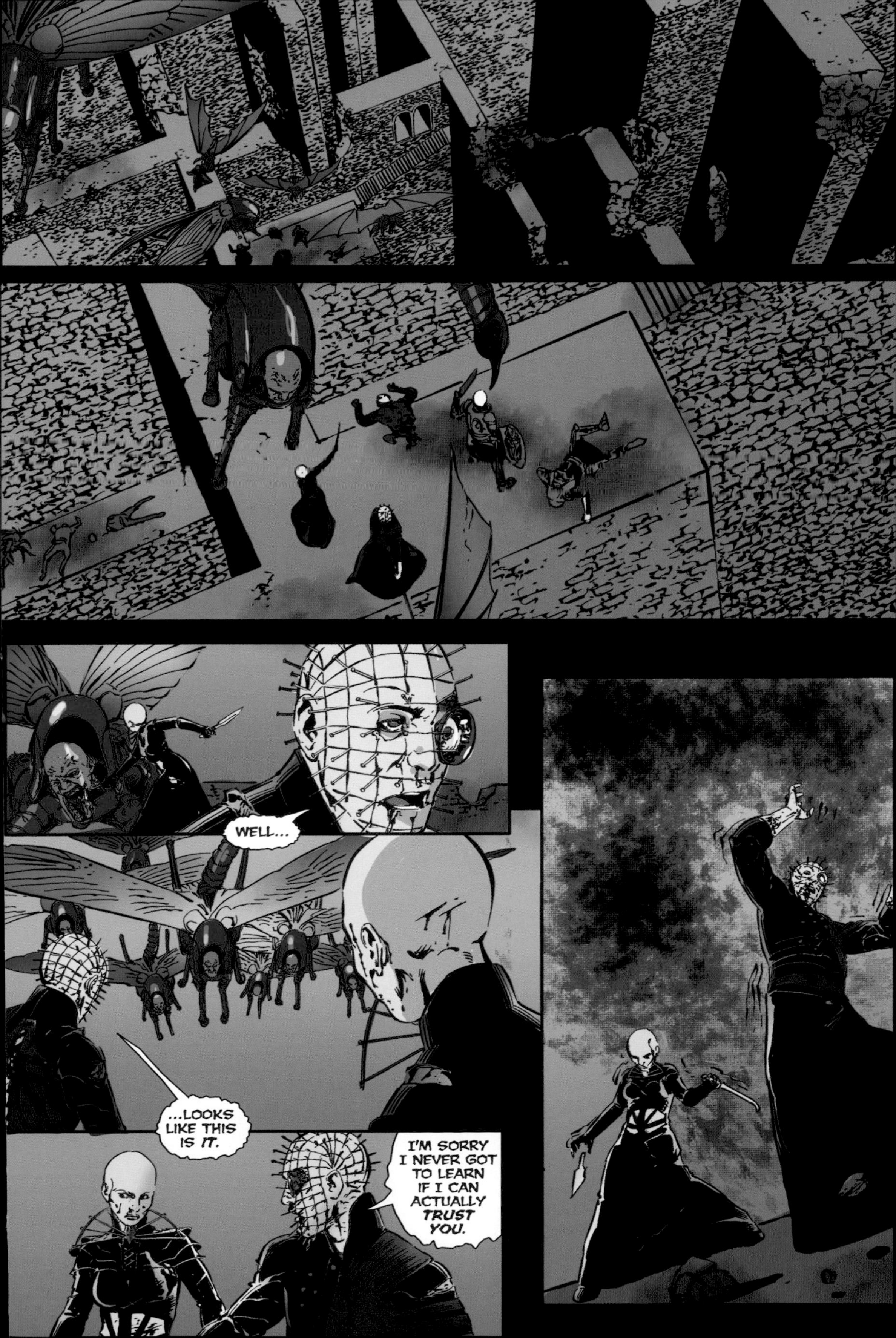
WELL...
...LOOKS LIKE THIS IS *IT*.
I'M SORRY I NEVER GOT TO LEARN IF I CAN ACTUALLY *TRUST YOU*.

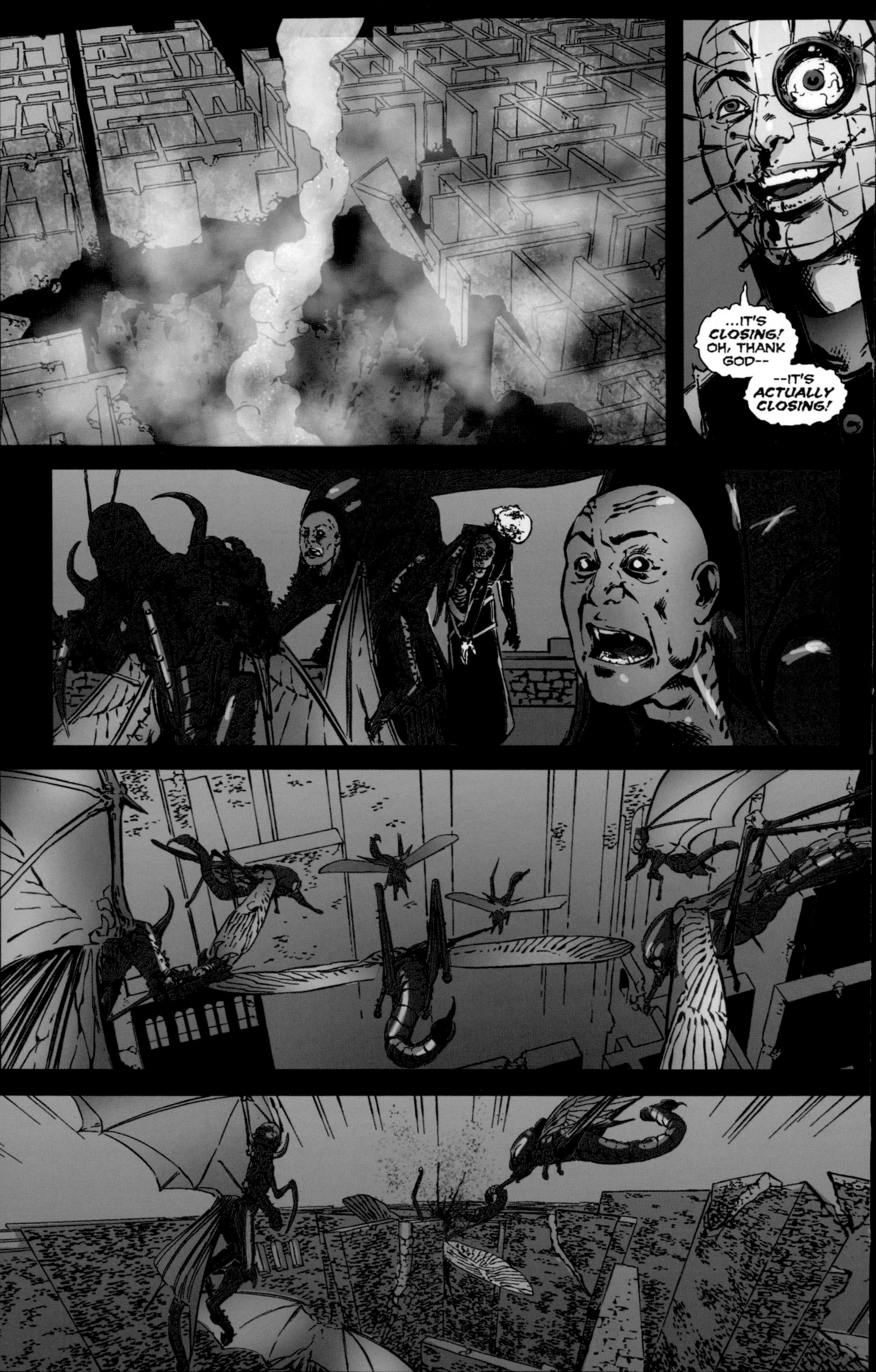

...IT'S CLOSING! OH, THANK GOD--
--IT'S ACTUALLY CLOSING!

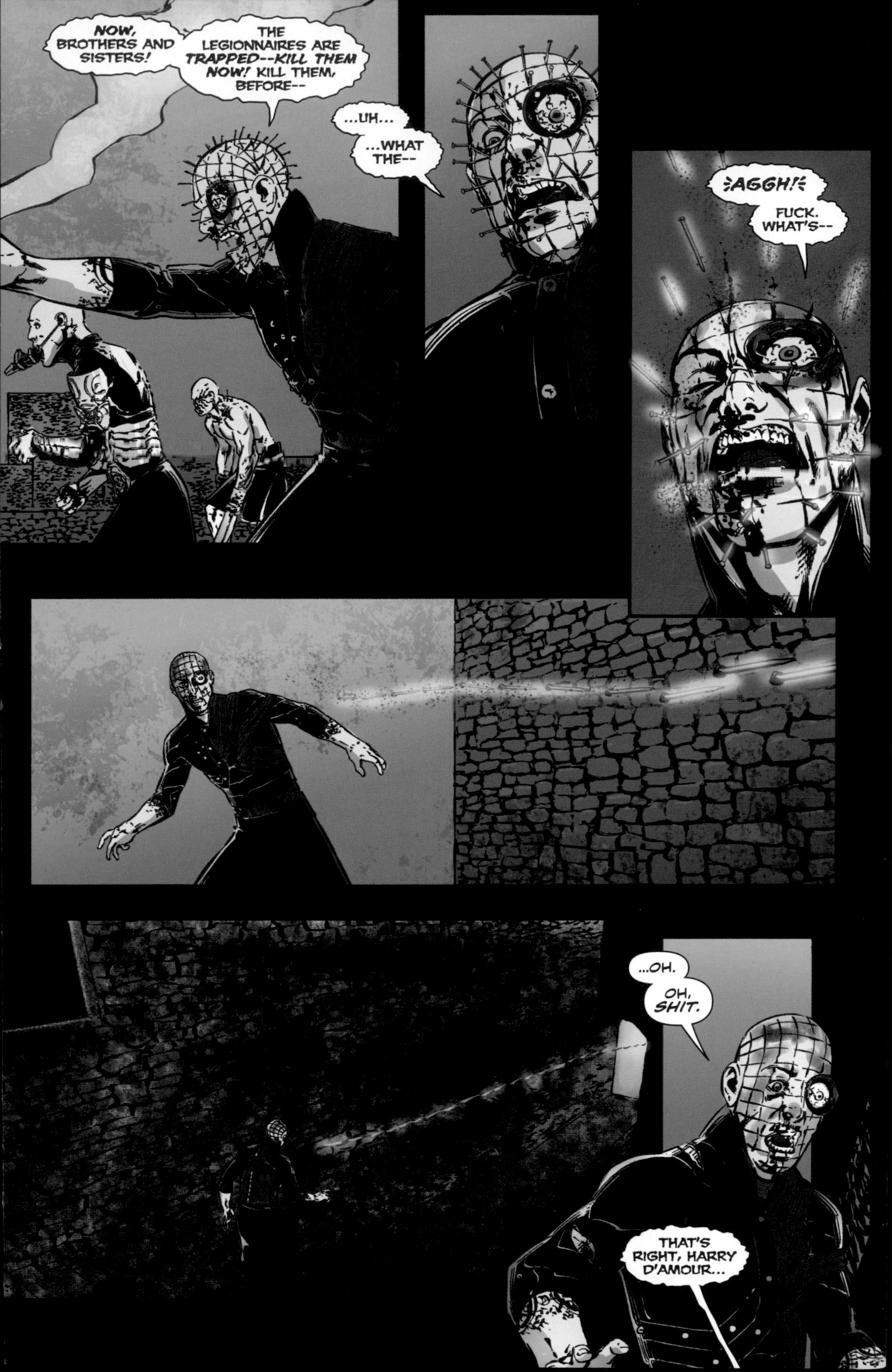
NOW, BROTHERS AND SISTERS!
THE LEGIONNAIRES ARE TRAPPED--KILL THEM NOW! KILL THEM, BEFORE--
...UH...
...WHAT THE--
AGGH!
FUCK. WHAT'S--
...OH.
OH, SHIT.
THAT'S RIGHT, HARRY D'AMOUR...

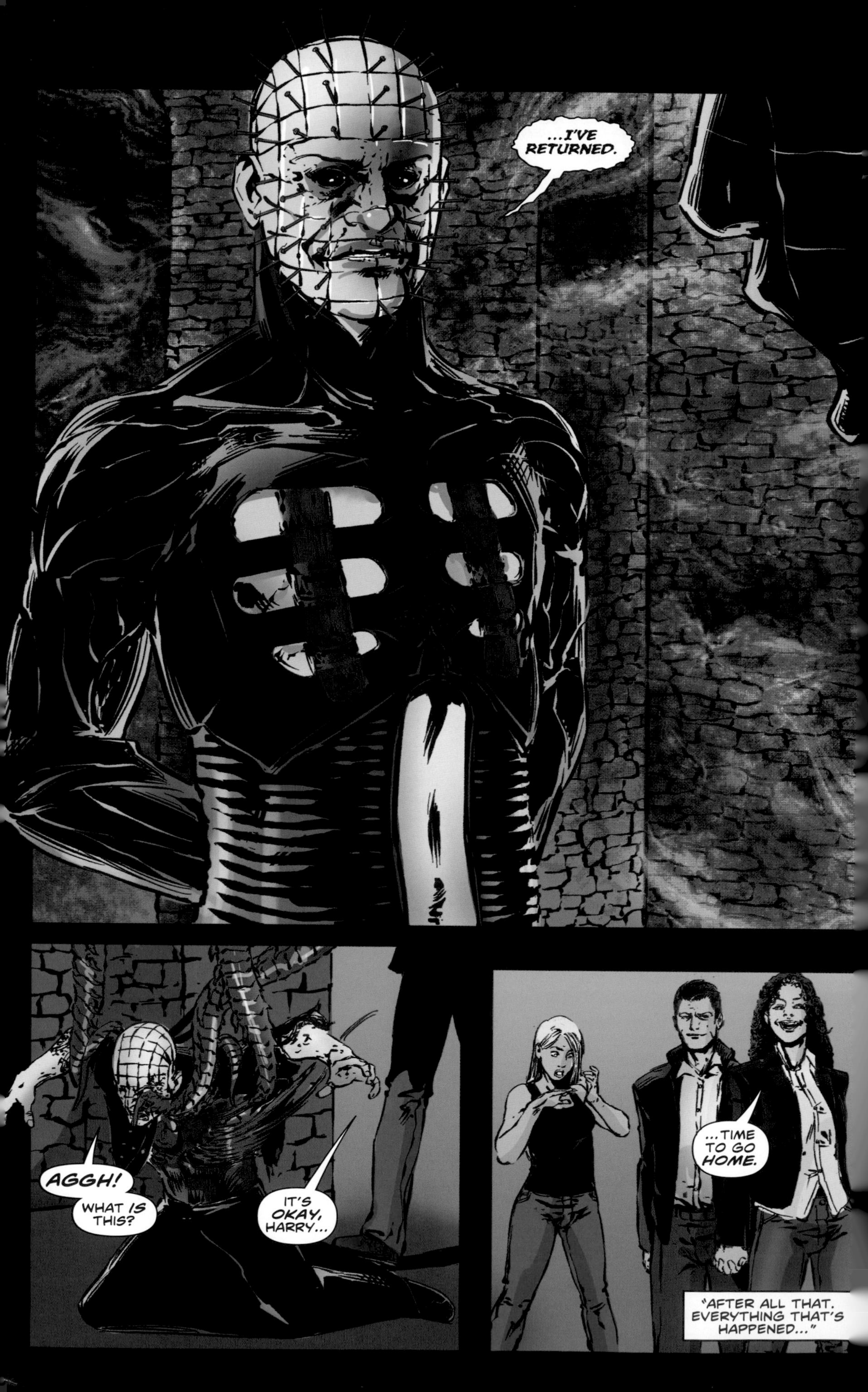
...I'VE RETURNED.
AGGH! WHAT IS THIS?
IT'S OKAY, HARRY...
...TIME TO GO HOME.
"AFTER ALL THAT. EVERYTHING THAT'S HAPPENED..."

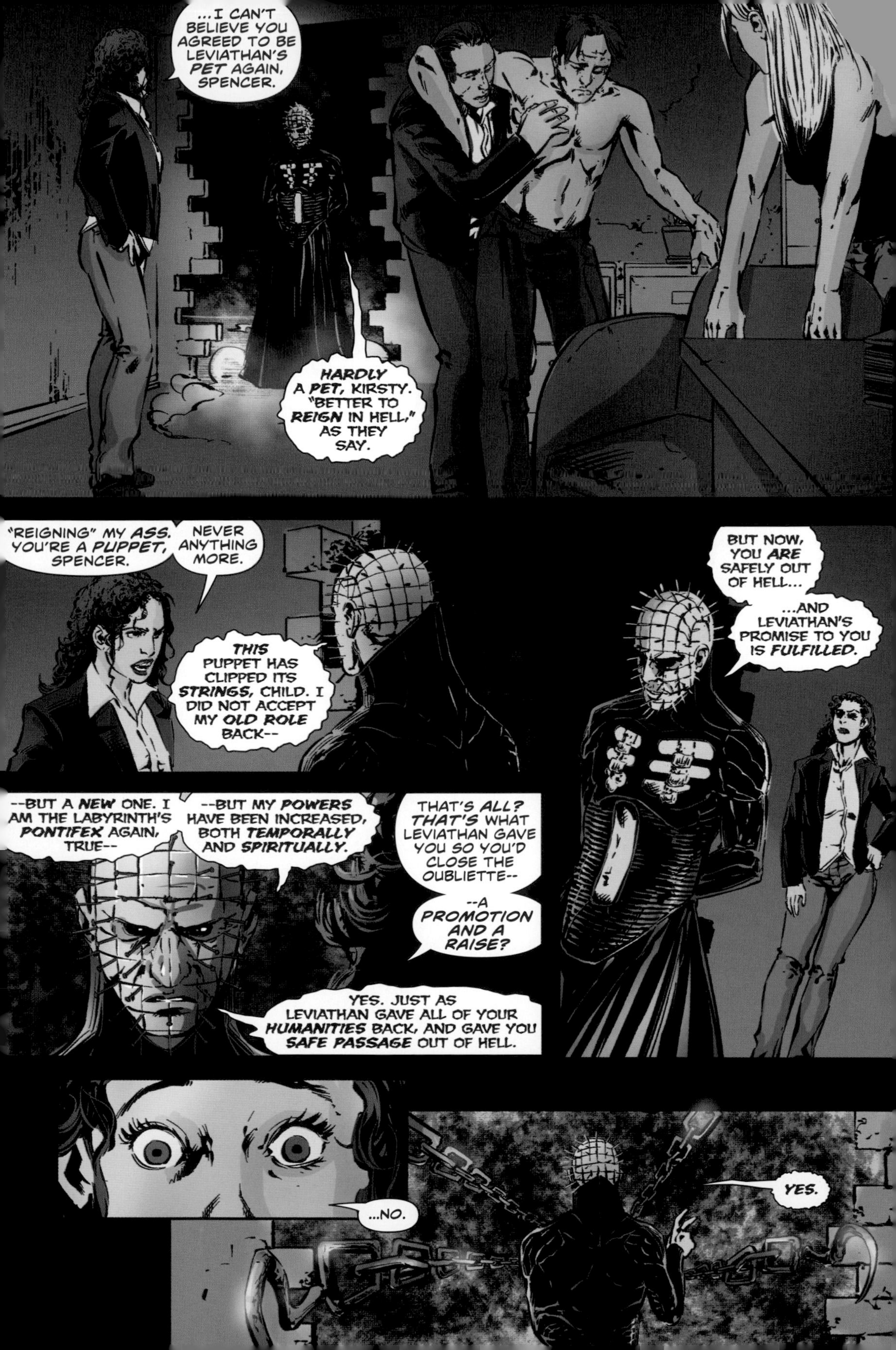
...I CAN'T BELIEVE YOU AGREED TO BE LEVIATHAN'S PET AGAIN, SPENCER.
HARDLY A PET, KIRSTY. "BETTER TO REIGN IN HELL," AS THEY SAY.
"REIGNING" MY ASS. YOU'RE A PUPPET, SPENCER.
NEVER ANYTHING MORE.
THIS PUPPET HAS CLIPPED ITS STRINGS, CHILD. I DID NOT ACCEPT MY OLD ROLE BACK--
BUT NOW, YOU ARE SAFELY OUT OF HELL...
...AND LEVIATHAN'S PROMISE TO YOU IS FULFILLED.
--BUT A NEW ONE. I AM THE LABYRINTH'S PONTIFEX AGAIN, TRUE--
--BUT MY POWERS HAVE BEEN INCREASED, BOTH TEMPORALLY AND SPIRITUALLY.
THAT'S ALL? THAT'S WHAT LEVIATHAN GAVE YOU SO YOU'D CLOSE THE OUBLIETTE--
--A PROMOTION AND A RAISE?
YES. JUST AS LEVIATHAN GAVE ALL OF YOUR HUMANITIES BACK, AND GAVE YOU SAFE PASSAGE OUT OF HELL.
...NO.
YES.

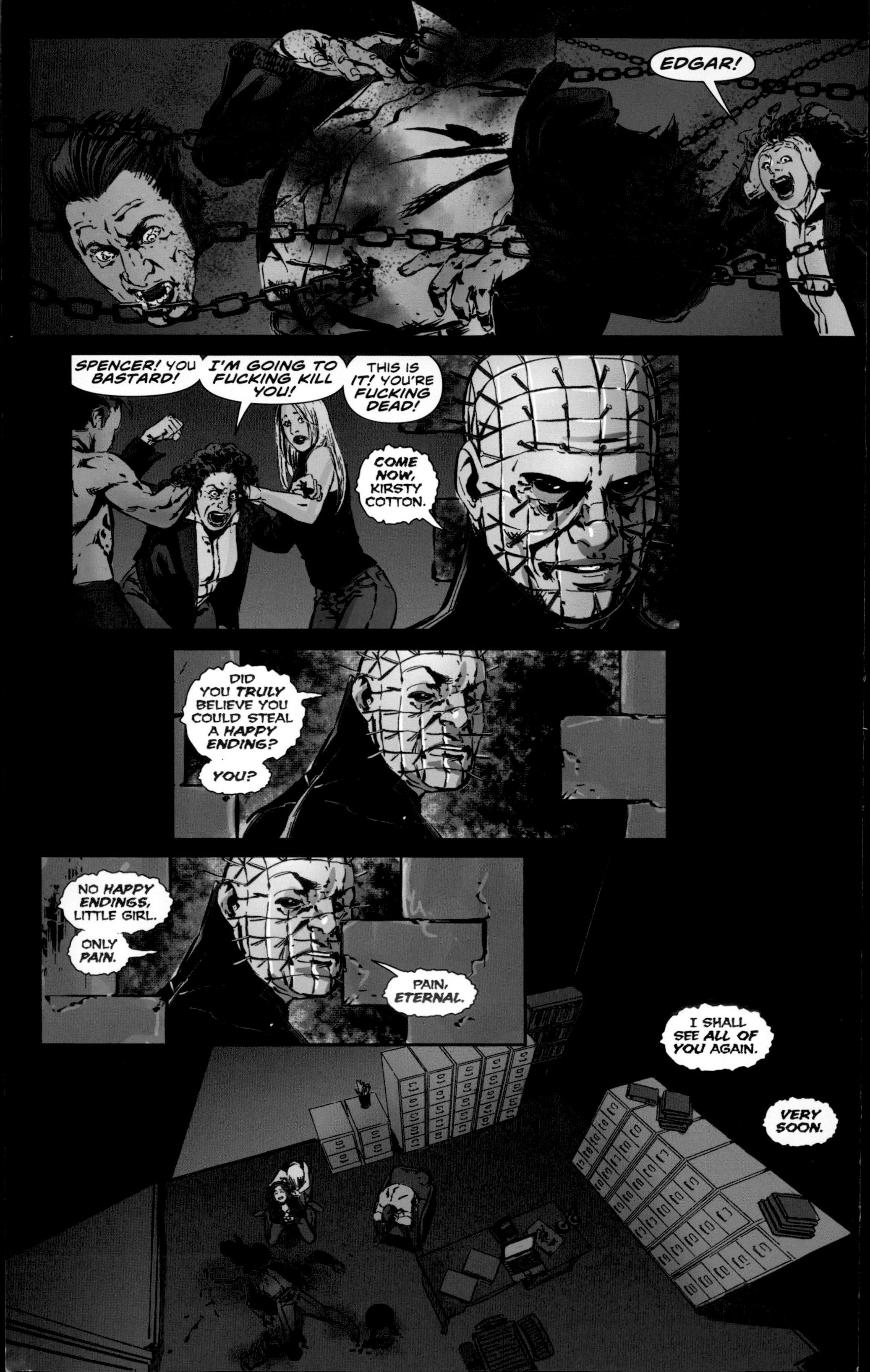
EDGAR!
SPENCER! YOU BASTARD!
I'M GOING TO FUCKING KILL YOU!
THIS IS IT! YOU'RE FUCKING DEAD!
COME NOW, KIRSTY COTTON.
DID YOU TRULY BELIEVE YOU COULD STEAL A HAPPY ENDING?
YOU?
NO HAPPY ENDINGS, LITTLE GIRL.
ONLY PAIN.
PAIN, ETERNAL.
I SHALL SEE ALL OF YOU AGAIN.
VERY SOON.

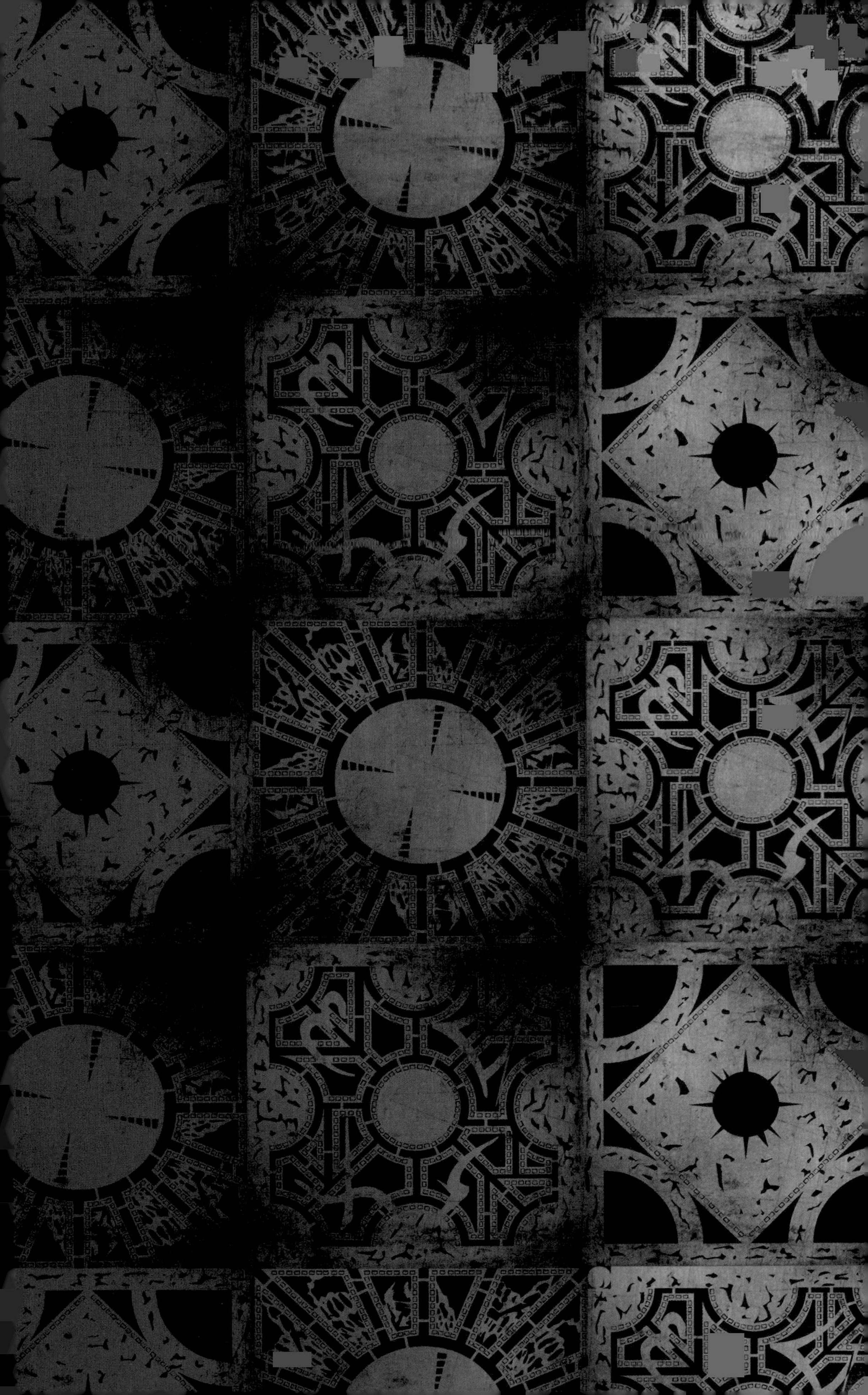

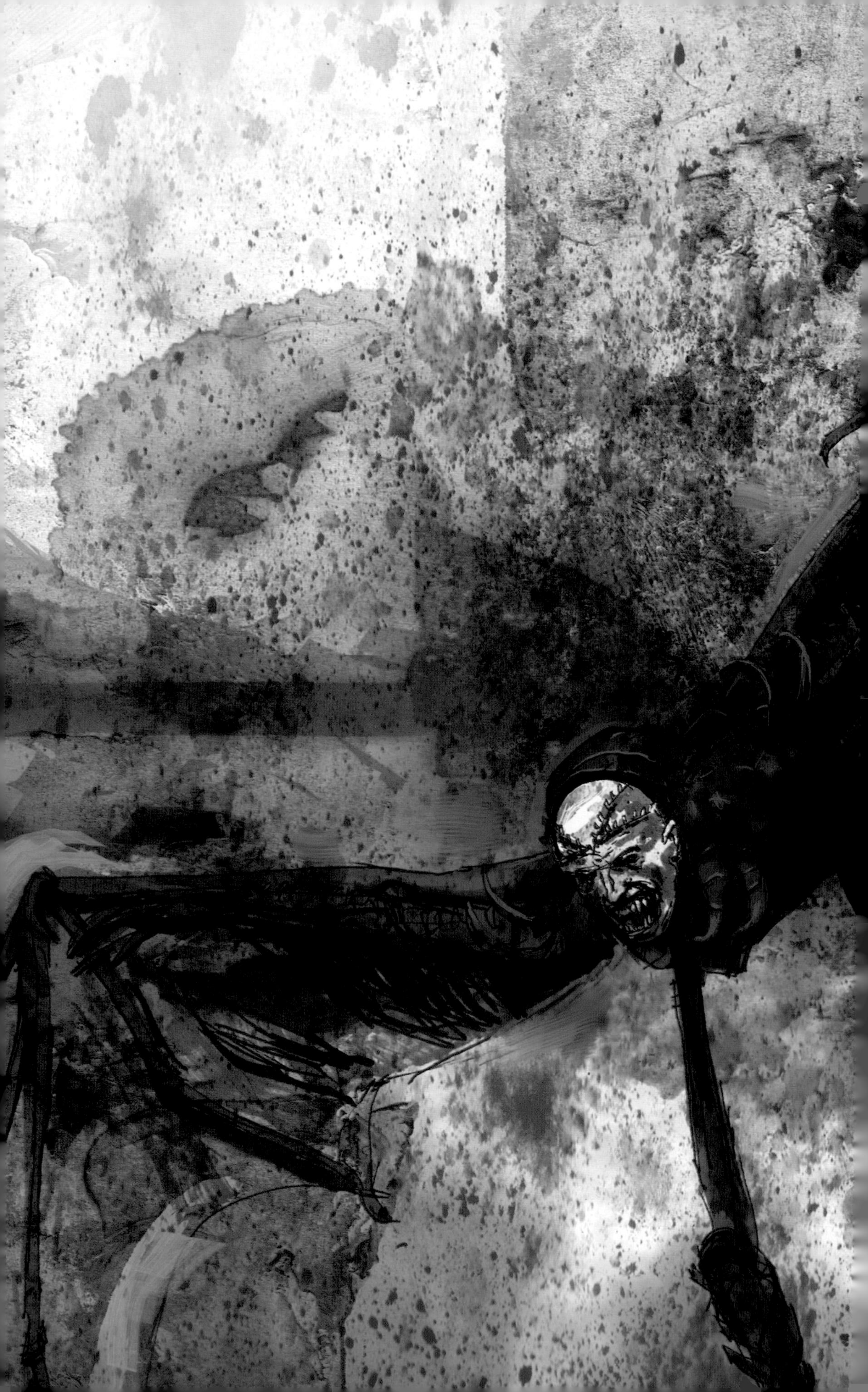

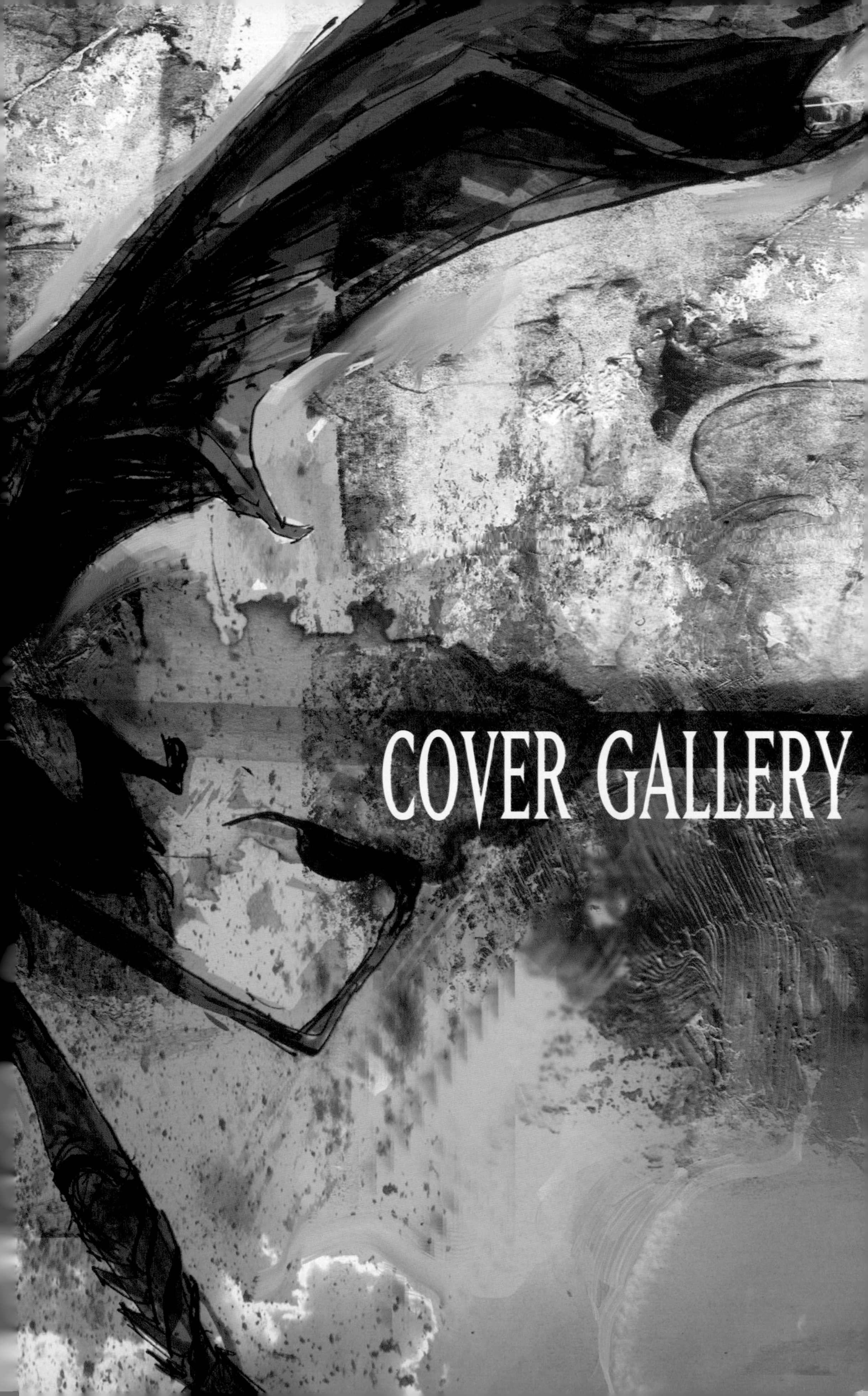
COVER GALLERY

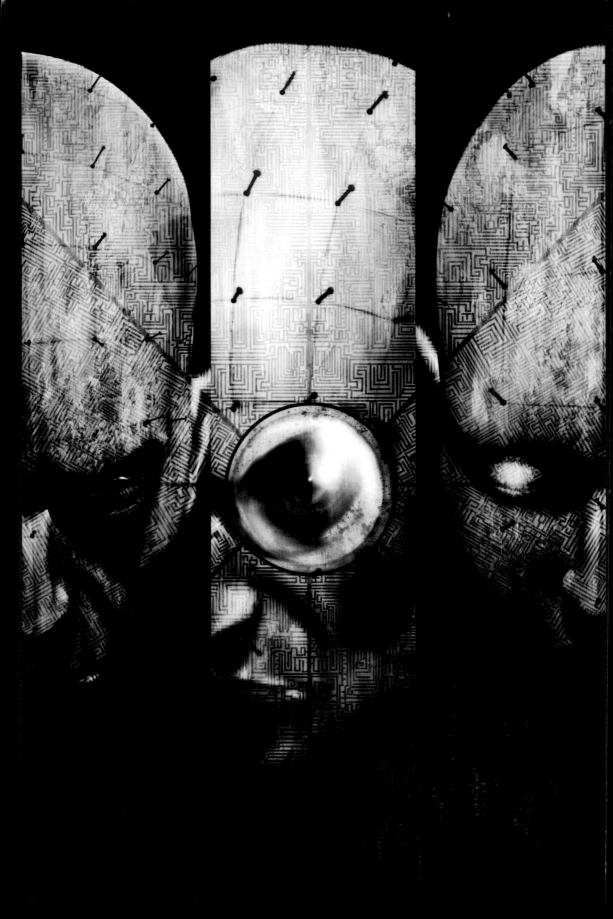

HELLRAISER 2013 ANNUAL: MENTON3

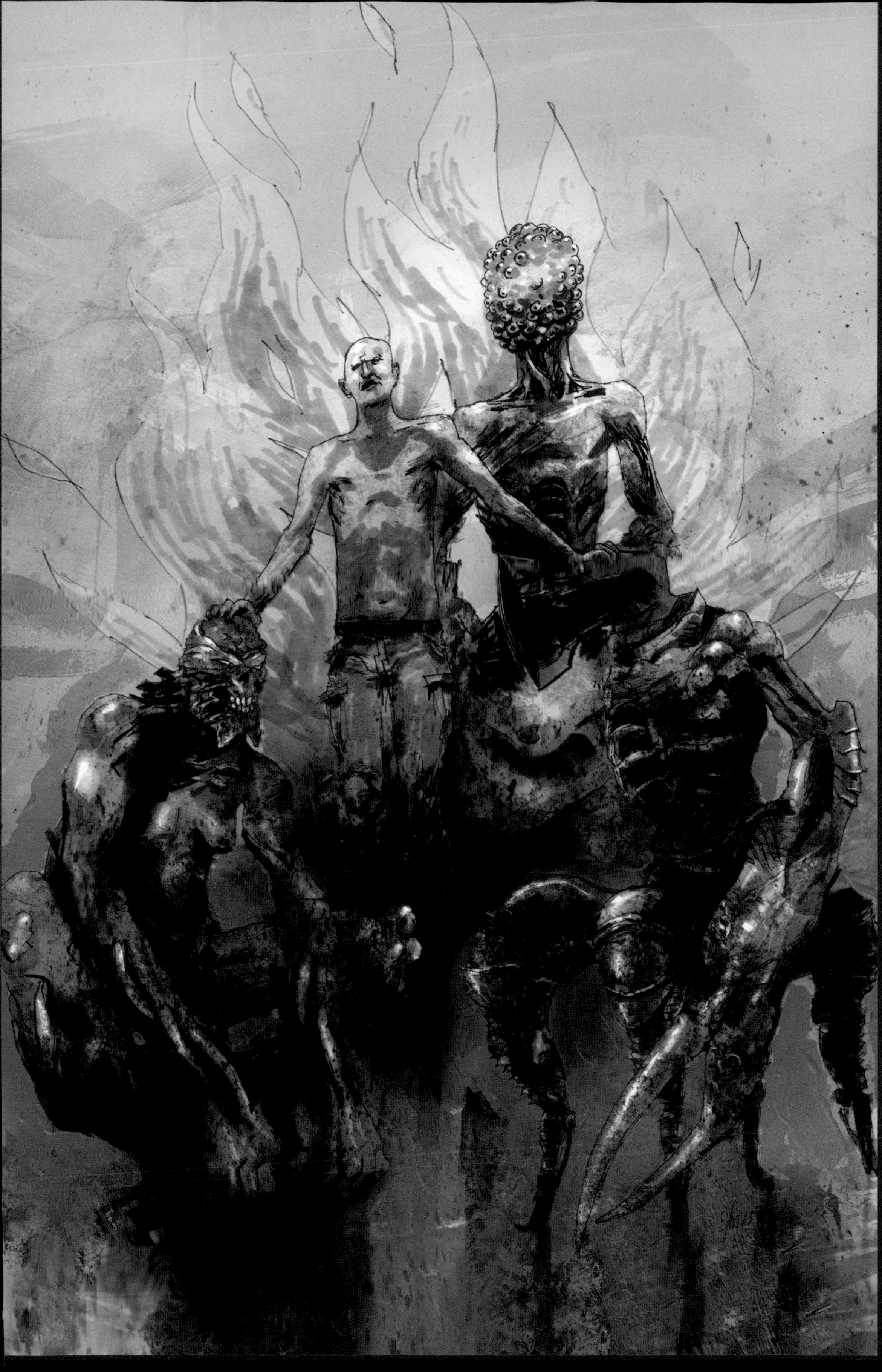

ISSUE NINE: SAMI MAKKONEN

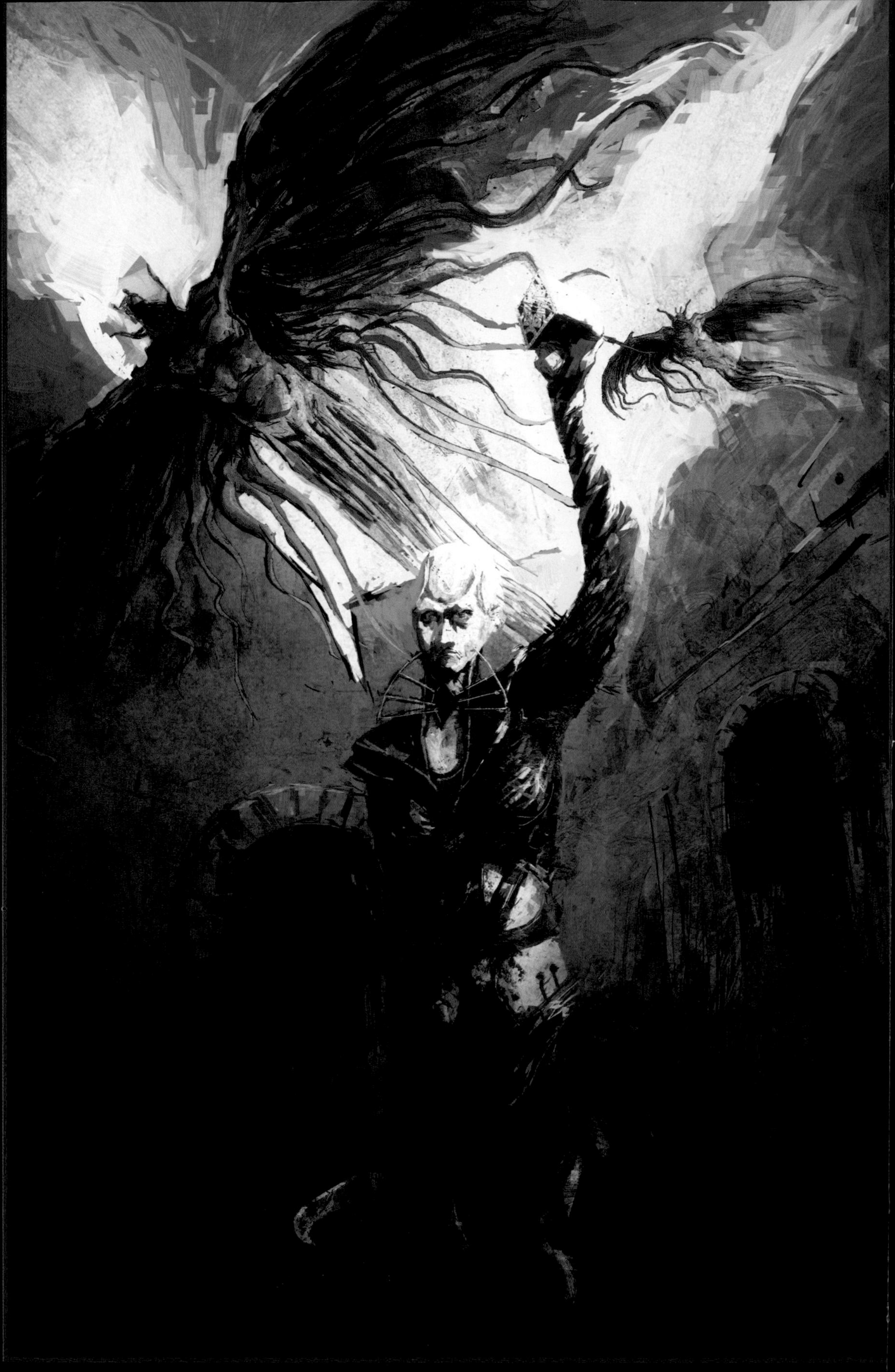

ISSUE TEN: SAMI MAKKONEN

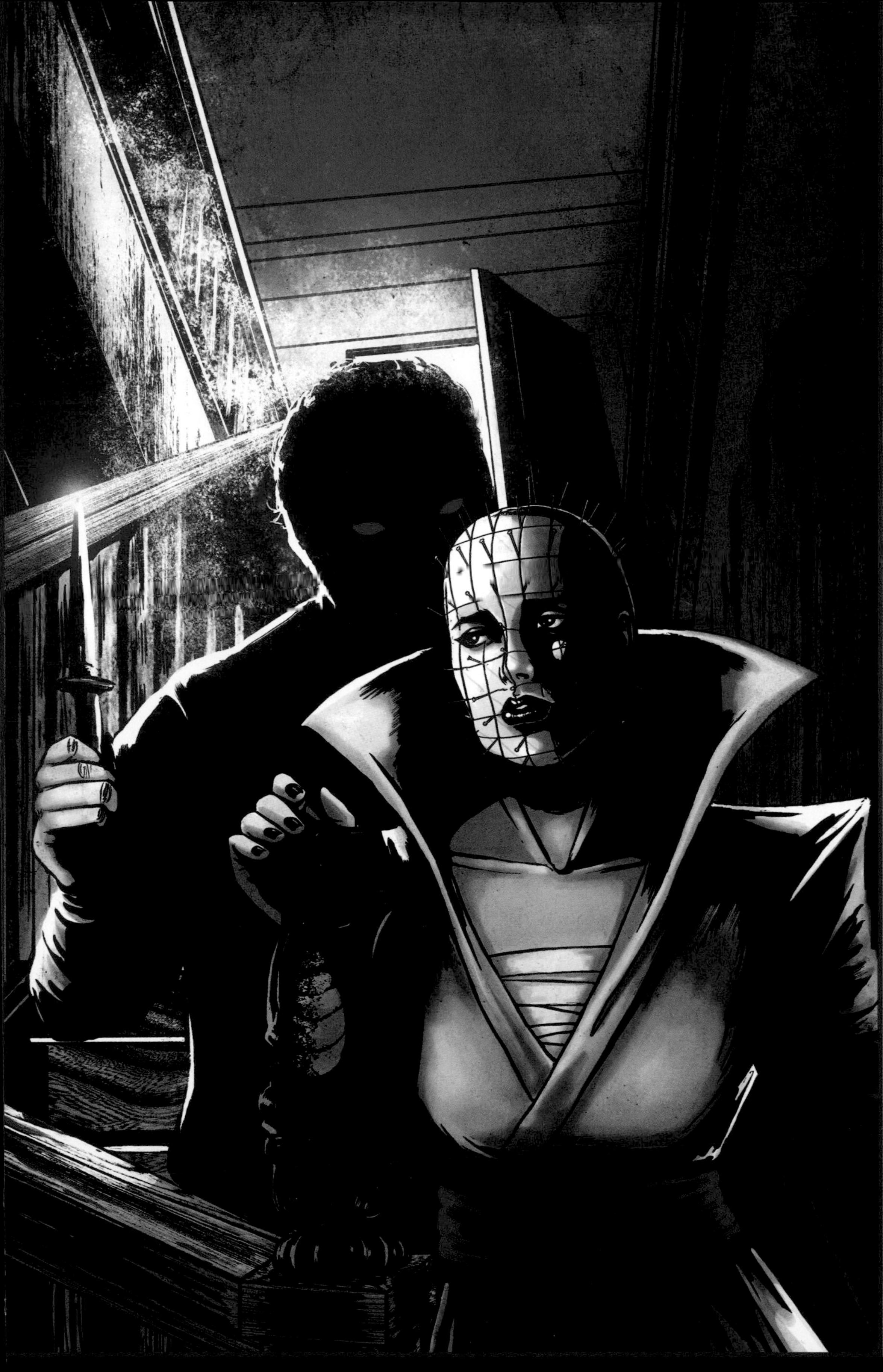

ISSUE ELEVEN: LORENA CARVALHO

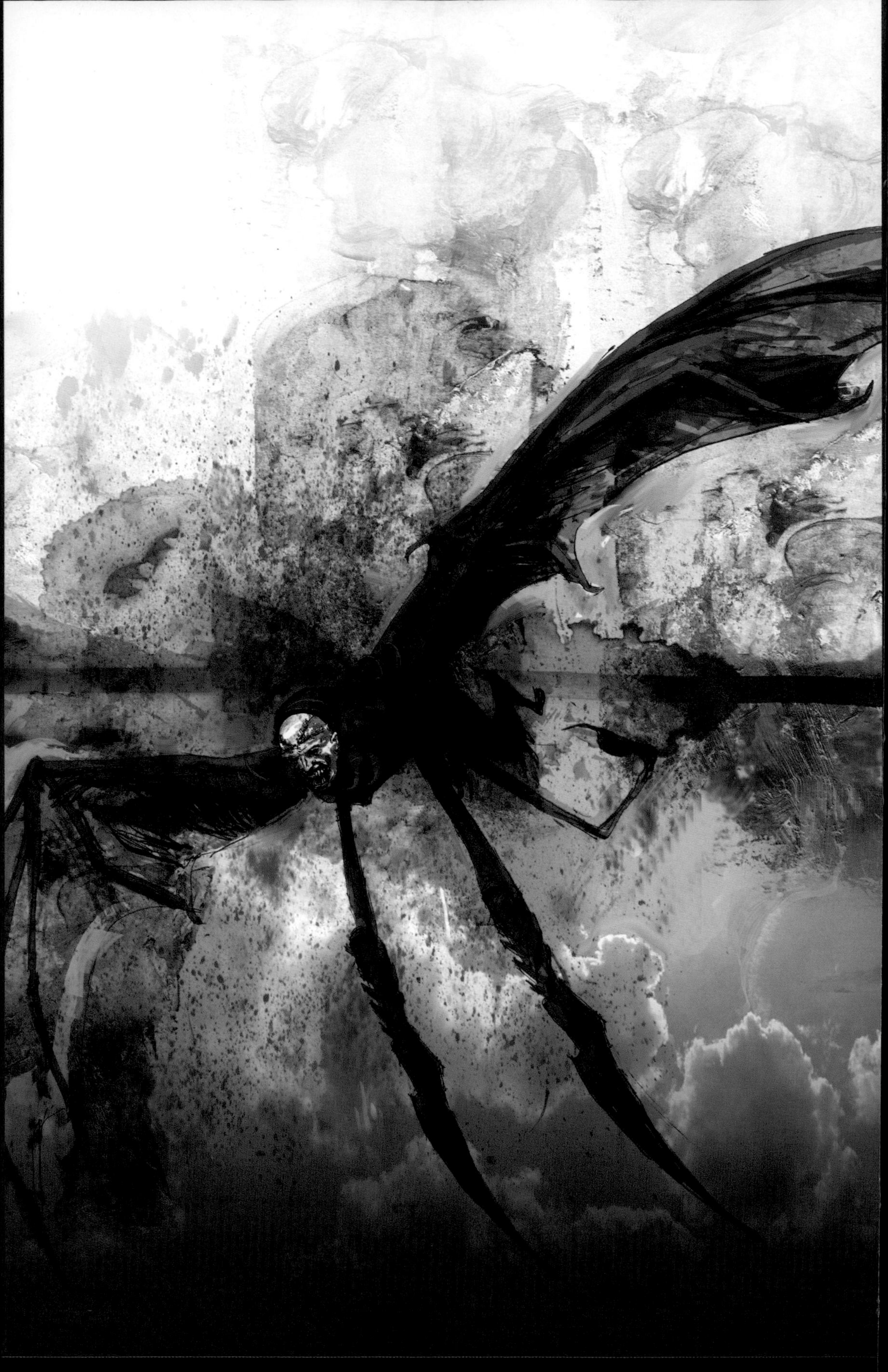

ISSUE TWELVE: SAMI MAKKONEN

THE DARK WATCH

COVER MOSAIC

TIM BRADSTREET   NICK PERCIVAL   FRAZER IRVING   SAMI MAKKONEN
CONZPIRACY DIGITAL ARTS   IBRAIM ROBERSON   LORENA CARVALHO   MENTON3

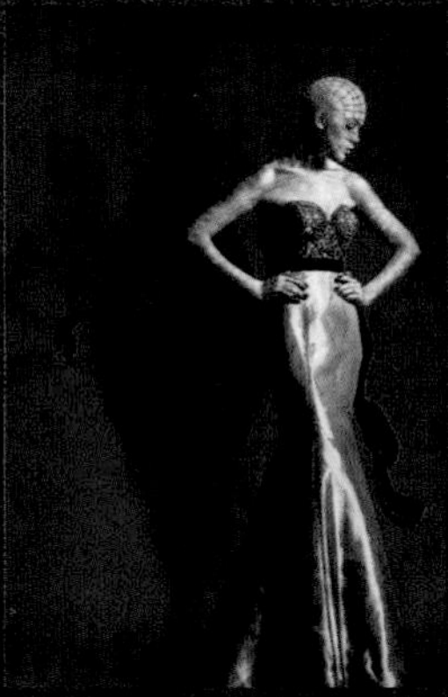
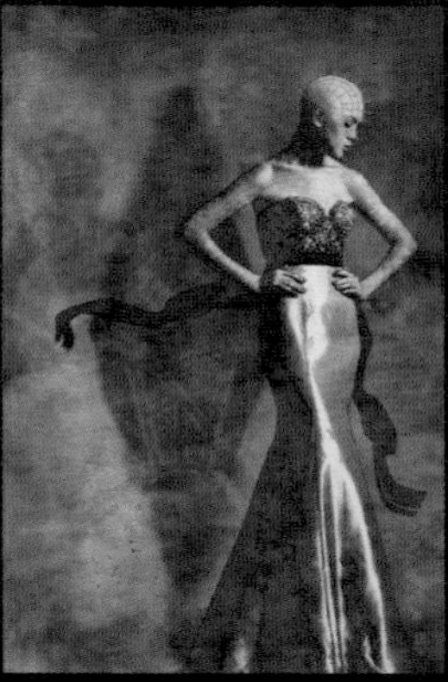
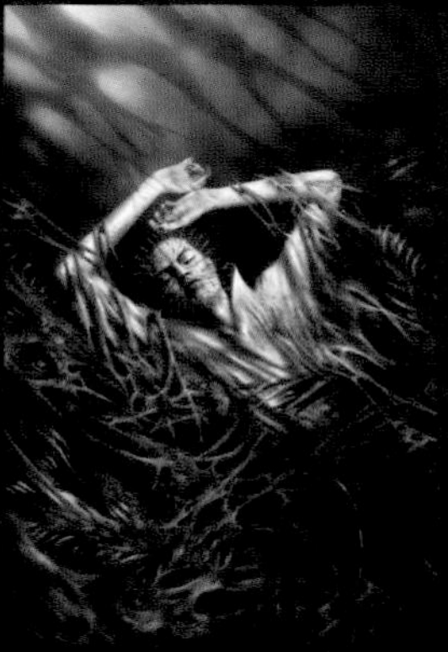
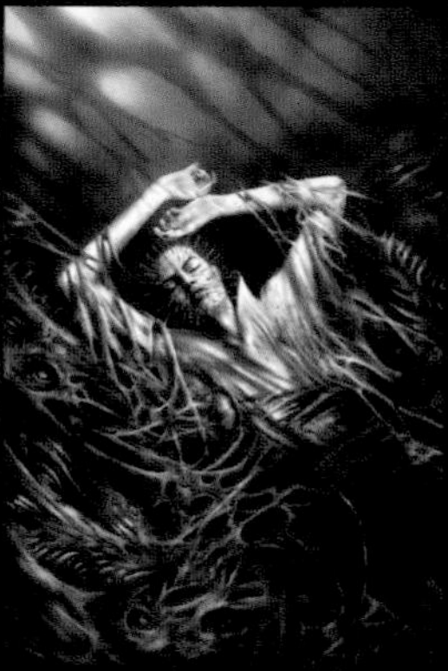
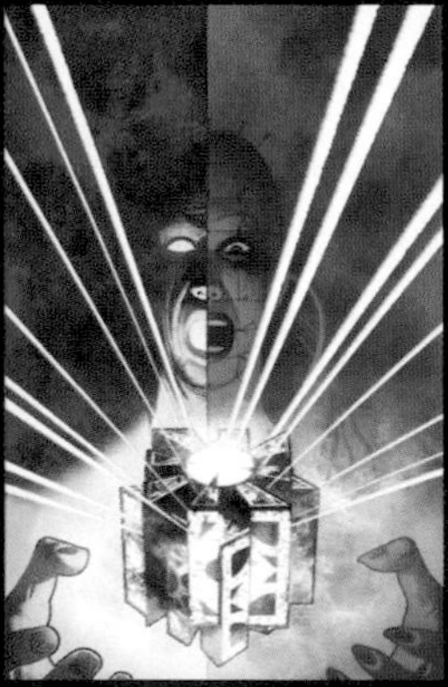
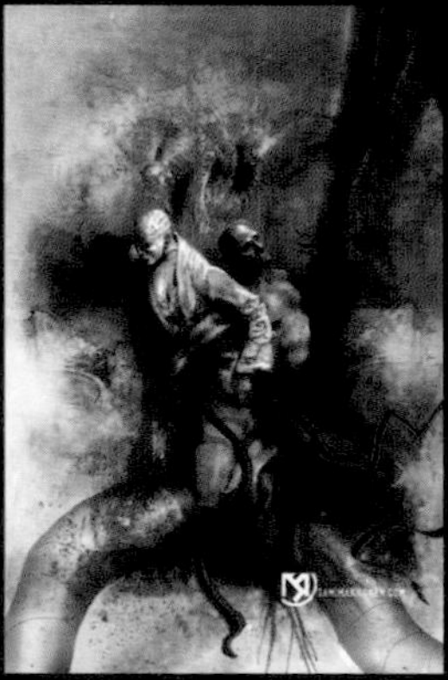
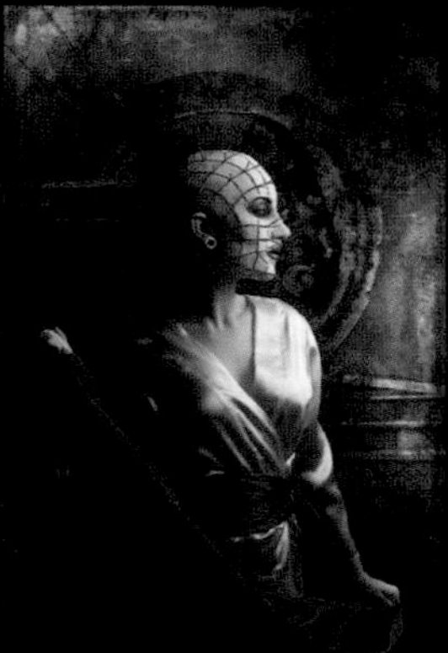
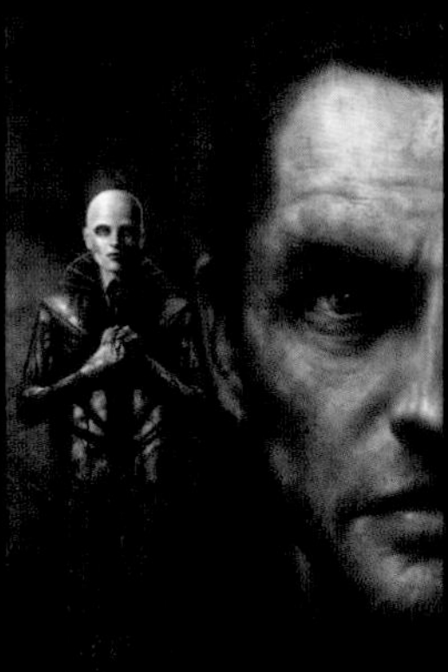
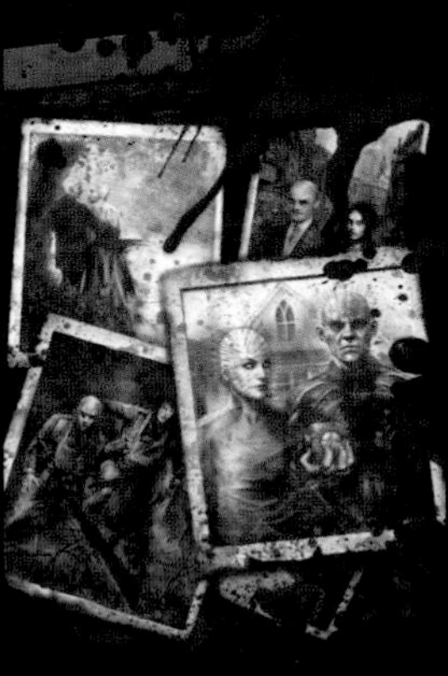
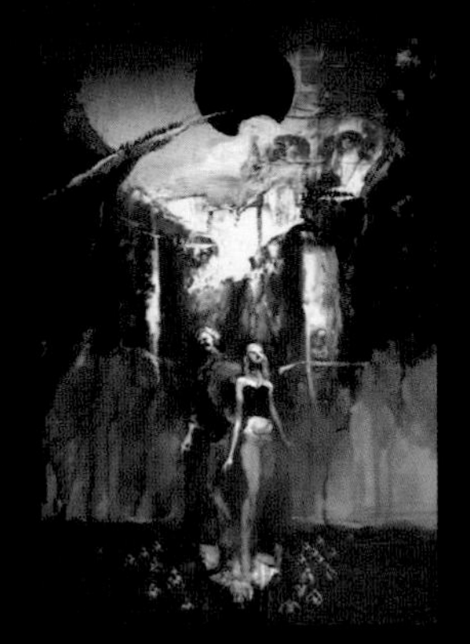
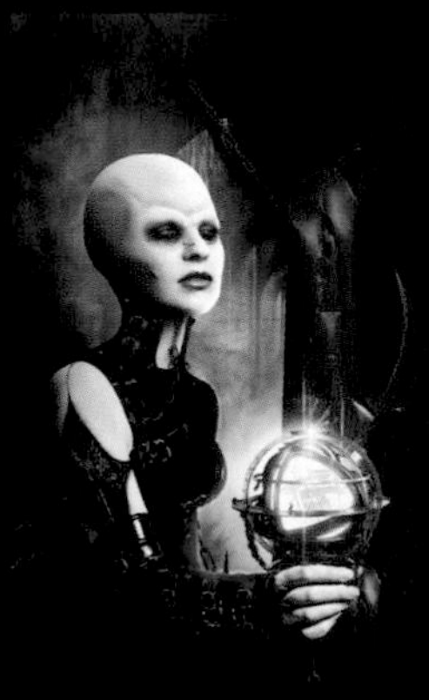

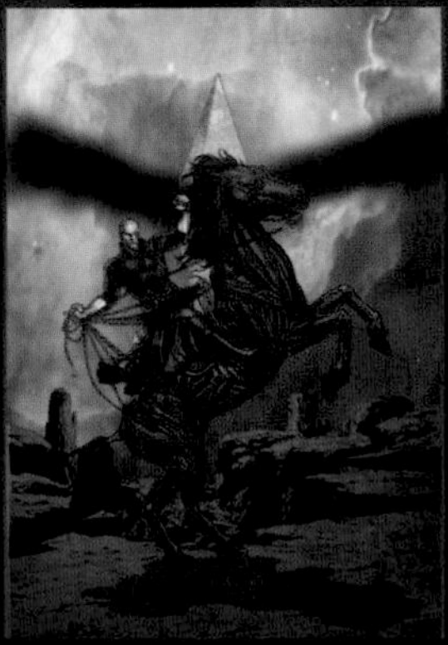
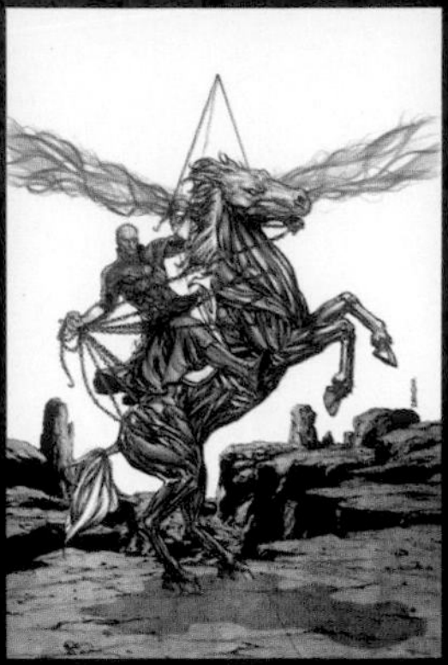
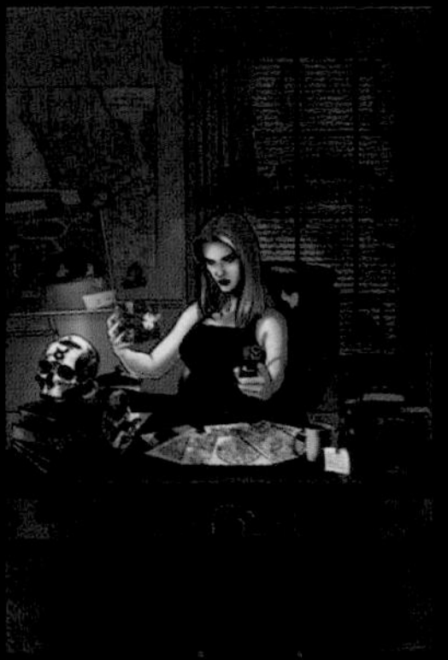
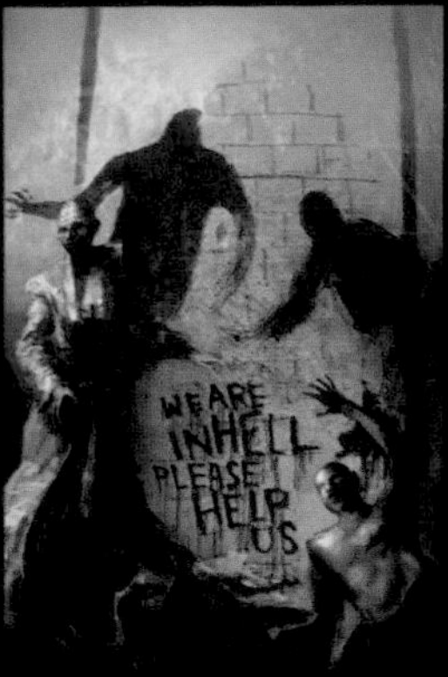
WE ARE
IN HELL
PLEASE
HELP
US
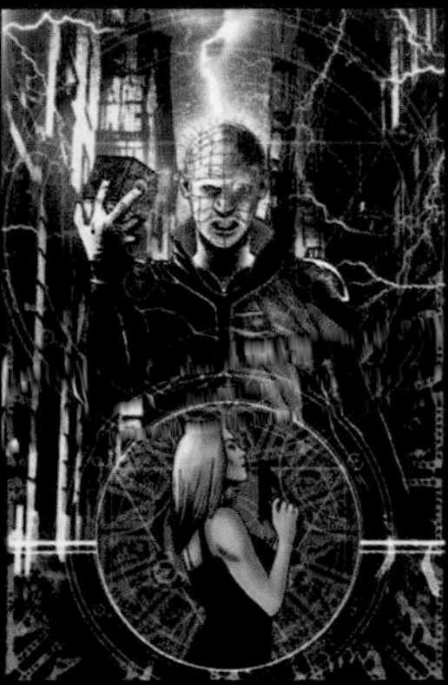
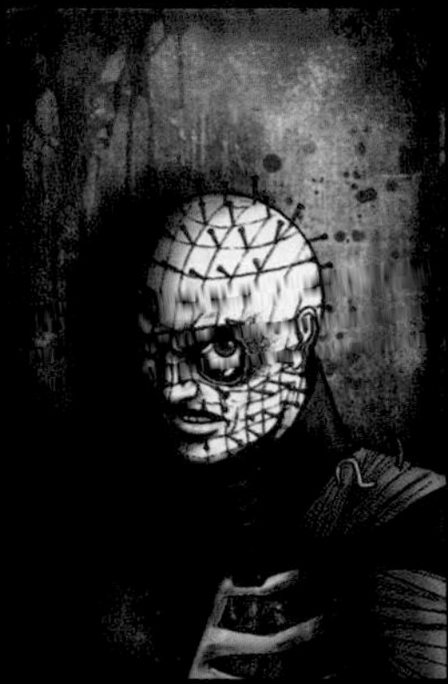
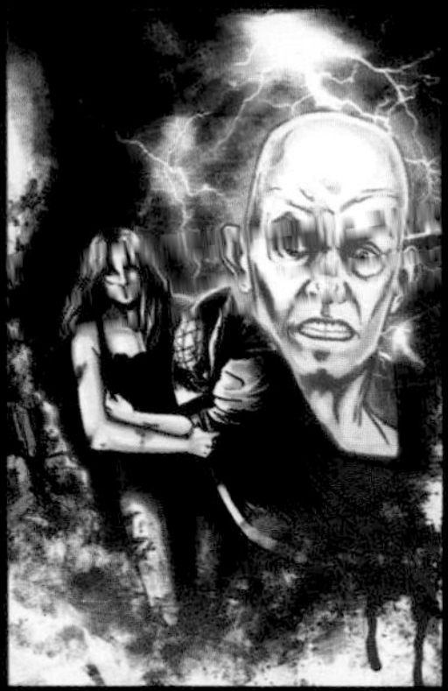
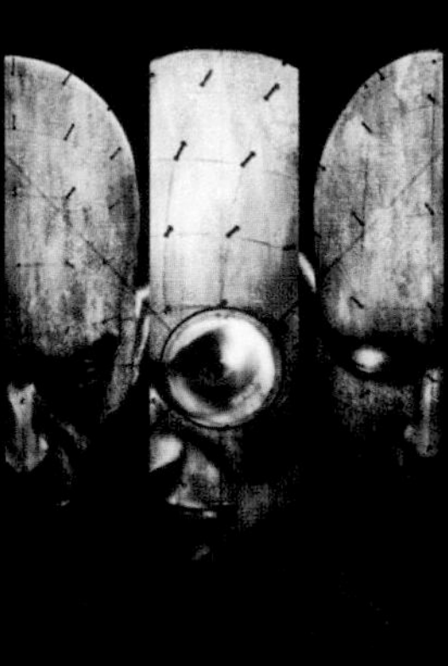
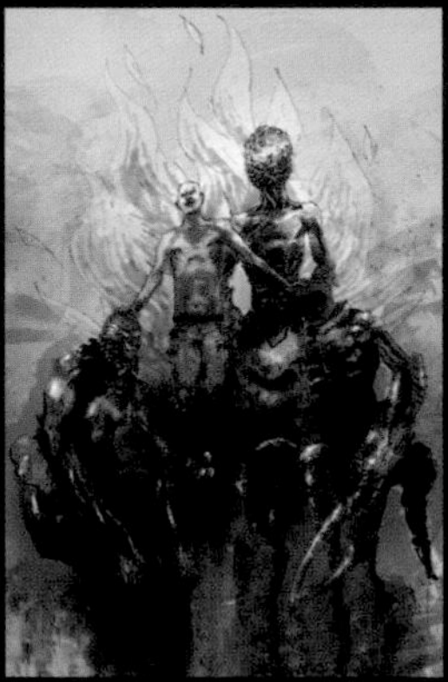
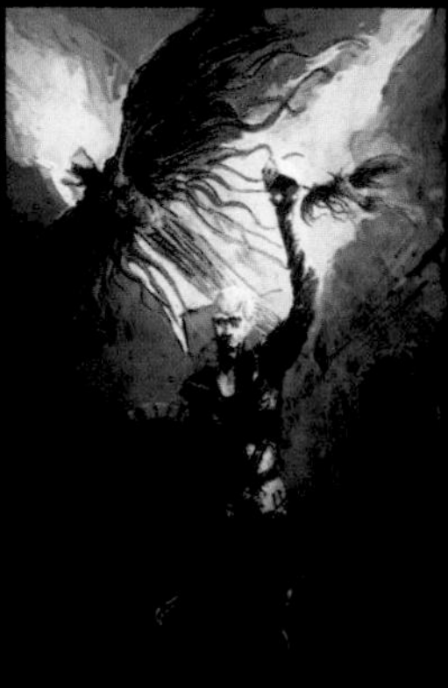
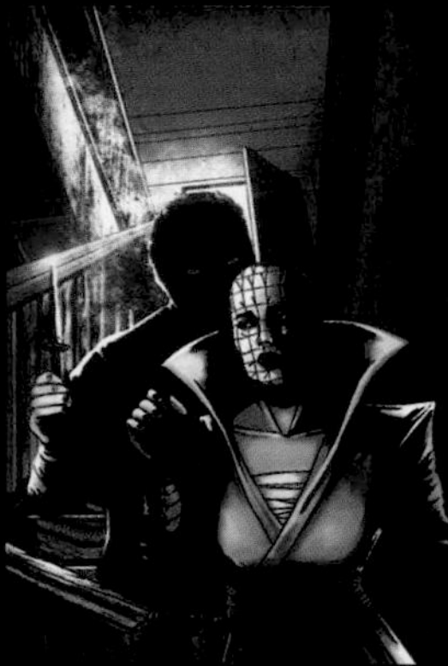
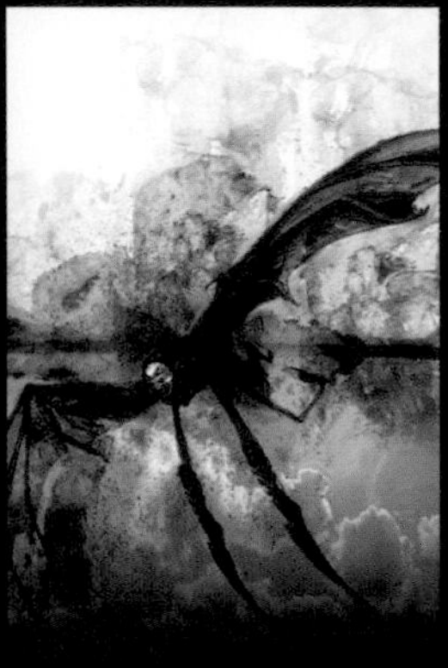

CLIVE BARKER'S

HELLRAISER

THE DARK WATCH